W9-AFG-859

CROSSING THE BAR

The Adventures of a

San Francisco Bay Bar Pilot

CROSSING THE BAR

The Adventures of a
San Francisco Bay Bar Pilot

CAPTAIN PAUL E. LOBO

San Francisco Bar Pilot 1977–2007

Seahorse Publishing

Dedication

To Captain Johan Sever, master mariner, longtime San Francisco Bar Pilot and a great friend, who took a huge gamble on a very young captain when he encouraged me to apply to become a San Francisco Bar Pilot. I am forever in his debt. His encouragement helped me to become not only one of the youngest San Francisco Bar Pilots ever appointed by California, but also one of the longest-serving ones.
I would also like to thank my wife, Carol, for encouraging me to write this book. Thanks to Klaus Lange for the beautiful pictures he took from the station boats.

Skyhorse Publishing books may be purchased in bulk at special discounts for sales promotion, corporate gifts, fund-raising, or educational purposes. Special editions can also be created to specifications. For details, contact the Special Sales Department, Skyhorse Publishing, 307 West 36th Street, 11th Floor, New York, NY 10018 or info@skyhorsepublishing.com.

Seahorse® and Skyhorse Publishing® are registered trademarks of Skyhorse Publishing, Inc.®, a Delaware corporation.

Visit our website at www.skyhorsepublishing.com.
10 9 8 7 6 5 4 3 2 1
Library of Congress Cataloging-in-Publication Data is available on file.

Cover design by Tom Lau
Cover photo credit QT Luong/terragalleria.com
Print ISBN: 978-1-944824-00-6
Ebook ISBN: 978-1-944824-01-3
Printed in the United States of America

CONTENTS

STAND BY ENGINES vii

1. STAND BY ENGINES 1

2. AGROUND WITH CAPTAIN SEVER 6

3. WHAT IS A MARITIME PILOT? 14

4. HISTORY OF SAN FRANCISCO BAR PILOTS 22

5. CALIFORNIA PILOTAGE 26

6. THE DIFFERENCE BETWEEN LIGHTNING AND
   A LIGHTNING BUG 33

7. MY LAST SHIPS 40

8. DON'T HAVE AN ACCIDENT ON A SLOW NEWS DAY 49

9. WHY DID THE *COSCO BUSAN* RAM THE SAN
   FRANCISCO-OAKLAND BAY BRIDGE? 53

10. SHIP HAPPENS 59

11. THE PORT OF OAKLAND 63

12. CHANGES 73

13. DAYDREAMS TO NIGHTMARES 81

14. OTHER TALES OF THE UNION PACIFIC BRIDGE
    AND SAM DAVIES 92

15. GREAT ESCAPES OF OTHERS 107

16. MY GREAT ESCAPES 115

17. MAN, IT'S DANGEROUS OUT THERE 142

18. A TOUGH WAY TO GET TO WORK 156

19. "THE SEA IS . . . FAST AT SINKING THE UNFIT". 173

20. THE CALM AFTER THE STORM? 194

21. CRAZY HORSE ON THE WAR PATH 201

22. ANCHORS AWEIGH: PILOTING FOR THE U.S. NAVY 205

23. SOME PILOTS OF NOTE 223

24. RIDE-ALONGS, OR WANT TO SEE SOMETHING
    REALLY DIFFERENT? 244

25. THE GOLDEN GATE BRIDGE 250

26. *ILLEGITIMI NON CARBORUNDUM*, OR WHY I'M
    GLAD I RETIRED 260

27. WOULD I DO IT OVER AGAIN? 267

STAND BY ENGINES

It was a dark and stormy night . . . so sea stories usually begin, but this is not that kind of book. While my book is filled with many hair-raising stories about several immense storms I lived through while piloting ships in San Francisco, it's more of a voyage through the many fascinating events that happened to me and the people who were part of my career when I worked as a First Class Ship Pilot on San Francisco Bay for almost a third of a century. I write about the history of piloting and the great variety of ships I piloted. I write about piloting errors that were my fault, the close calls I extricated myself from, and about many interesting events involving other pilots. Many of my partners, and pilots worldwide, were severely injured, and too many pilots died while I was a working pilot.

Many consider piloting to be the ultimate in a seagoing career, but it also has another side. The Coast Guard was always trying to run us, regulate us, or prosecute us; not all ship captains appreciated us, and the ships' agents and owners always thought we made too much money. The battle over pilots' wages goes back for centuries. Joseph Hanson wrote this about the Missouri River Pilots at the time of Custer's Last Stand in *The Conquest of the Missouri*: "His profession was a very difficult one to learn, requiring years of apprenticeship, and as the pilots themselves were the only ones who could train new men for places in their ranks, they took good care that their numbers were kept down to small and select proportions in order that neither their power nor the princely salaries which they commanded should be diminished . . . he could demand almost any wages he chose. . . ." Some things never change, except that Bar Pilots don't determine pilotage fees; the State of California does.

Over the years there have obviously been changes in the merchant marine. However, the pace of change over the last third of the twentieth century has increased by leaps and bounds. Three major changes were Huge diesel engines replacing steam plants; the total transformation of containerization; and the increase in the size of most ships, particularly containerships. As an example, since I retired, the MSC *Fabiola* (140,259 gross register tonnage, or GRT) became the largest container vessel to be turned around in the Port of Oakland. She was 150 feet longer than the longest ships I moved only a few years ago! I write about what it takes to turn massive ships in tight places. I try to explain the feeling of having a few ships almost get out of my control.

Changes for pilots occurred as well: regulations grew by the month, either from the California State Board of Pilot Commissioners for the Bays of San Francisco, San Pablo, and Suisun, called "the Commission"; or the Coast Guard. We went slower, didn't have maximum draft possible, had visibility restrictions, attended school after school, and had escort tugs moving loaded tankers. I write about the container ship *Cosco Busan's* tragic oil spill from its collision with the Oakland Bay Bridge in 2007. I didn't like the way the now infamous Captain John Cota was treated by the press, and by some of our partners and the NTSB. At the time of the accident, I was looking forward to retiring. Not John. He's still fighting like hell to get back his Coast Guard licenses.

I have included some history of piloting and San Francisco.

Even though I was fairly young to retire, or swallow the hook, at almost sixty-one, I was burnt out and tired of working 24/7. I was looking forward to no phone calls in the middle of the night, and I wanted to look at weather in terms of whether I could play golf instead of whether my ship would be rolling her guts out when I got off at the Pilot Station, or if I would get hurt. Also, the older I became, the harder it was to disembark off the new ships with higher and higher freeboards.

Everything in this book is true. Some events that happened to other pilots, or to me in particular, were downright frightening. This isn't to alarm anyone, but there are inherent risks, not only to ships in piloting waters, but also to pilots who handle them.

The nautical jargon here is meant to impart a feeling for real language aboard ships. For example, ships don't have left or right for good reason. These terms are what sets the Merchant Marine apart from the rest of the world, even from the Navy and Coast Guard, both of which I write about. Nothing made me crazier than hearing a Coastie say "boat" when he clearly meant ship.

"Smooth seas and fair winds."

—Captain Paul E. Lobo

CHAPTER 1

STAND BY ENGINES

Crossing the Bar
—Alfred, Lord Tennyson (1899)

Sunset and evening star,
And one clear call for me!
And may there be no moaning of the bar,
When I put out to sea,
But such a tide as moving seems asleep,
Too full for sound and foam,
When that which drew from out the boundless deep
Turns again home.
Twilight and evening bell,
And after that the dark!
And may there be no sadness of farewell,
When I embark;
For tho' from out our bourne of Time and Place
The flood may bear me far,
I hope to see my Pilot face to face
When I have crost the bar.

On the morning of April 26, 1981, the *California* got underway from Pier 7 ferrying my mentor, Captain John Sever, out to his final resting place. Like many other pilots and family members aboard, I wanted to wish John one last goodbye.

I realized John knew a lot of influential people, but judging by the attendance at his wake at New Saint Mary's Cathedral, he had many, many friends. I felt especially sad for John's wife, Louise, because he passed so young. Louise was always nice to me, like John was. It was comforting having such good friends because in the piloting business, not everyone does. Some pilots didn't appreciate John the way I did, but when I was twenty-six, he was like a God to me.

Bob Porteous, our senior boat captain, deftly maneuvered our Station Boat out toward the Golden Gate Bridge on a magnificent San Francisco day. Normally, she or her sister ship *San Francisco* would be on the high seas boarding pilots, but that morning she served a sadder function as John's bier. It was his last pilot boat ride. When we neared the Golden Gate, the engines stopped and the boat halted at mid-span. Captain Sever's last night orders stated this was where he wanted his ashes scattered.

Soon Port Agent Captain Arthur Thomas started reading from the Good Book as the boat sat motionless. As Art read a prayer, slowly the current changed from slack to ebb, as all the water in The Bay started going out to sea. Ever so slowly we started drifting west, out from under the massive rust-colored roadway directly overhead. You have no idea of the sheer mass of the Golden Gate unless you are underneath it, motionless, looking up at the crisscrossing gigantic girders. As I looked up, I wondered if bridge workers, high above us, doffed their hard hats when they saw us stop to honor someone who had sailed beneath them thousands of times piloting the world's ships.

The only humorous part of the service was when Captain Thomas glanced up, being a pilot like many there, and noticed that we were slowly drifting. He also knew if we moved too far, John's urn wouldn't be where he wanted it, so he quickened his reading. As "Amen" drifted away in a light breeze, the only sound heard was everyone quietly crying, including me. This was curious because Captain Sever could be a son-of-a-bitch when he wanted to be. I didn't know it when I met him, but John loved controversy and he usually got it. Once a crewman complained about our smoking on the Station Boat, which was still allowed then. Well, John, being John, waited until the smoke-free sailor went on watch, then lit up a big black Montecristo and blew blue smoke through the wheelhouse door crack to annoy the crewman.

Captain Sever's son-in-law Phil's job was to put John's ashes exactly where The Bay meets the edge of the Pacific. After the ceremony, he told me if John wasn't put in the precise spot, John would be pissed off for eternity, and I believed him! When he heard "Amen," like a shot putter, Phil arched his back, heaving John's brass urn as hard as he could, resulting in a big splash directly below the gigantic fog horns hanging under the bridge. Thank goodness the horns were silent or we would never have heard one word!

I took a moment to think of John's life. As I did, Captain Peter Crowell, one of my partners, threw in a bottle of Jack Daniels as I threw in one white rose.

"Why the booze?" I asked, thinking he had wasted a perfectly good bottle.

"So he can have one on the way up!" came the reply from a man who spent his entire career working on the sea like me. That brought another tear to my eye.

On the first day I became a pilot, Captain Sever advised me to start a log book. I'm glad I did. I wouldn't have been able to write this book without it. Religiously, I filled it with information about each ship I moved: her name, size, the time it took to complete the job, her tonnage, her master's name, and where I piloted the ship. Pasted inside was a list of the pilots working when I started. As they retired or went to see the Sky Pilot, I scratched a thin line through each name. That April I crossed out the one name I least wanted to, my mentor and friend. At twenty-nine, I couldn't conceive that Captain Sever, who was one strong guy, would become ill so young. The man who changed my life was gone at sixty-three. I was only thirty-four. Many pilots gave me a boost up the pilot ladder, but John was the reason I became a Bar Pilot so young.

Herb Caen, *San Francisco Chronicle*'s gossip columnist, wrote a nice article about John's funeral. I often wrote him about waterfront goings-on, and he published every one. On April 28, 1981, four years after I became a pilot, Herb wrote:

"'NICE DAY for a funeral,' commented Captain Paul Lobo, a bar pilot, as the pilot boat California *bobbed up and down beneath the Golden Gate Bridge on a sunny, windy Sunday of last week. Then as some 25 passengers fell silent, and only the scream of a gull could be heard, the ashes of 63-year old*

Captain John Sever, senior SF bar pilot, were thrown overboard. It was his wish. Put me there under the bridge, he said 'so I can keep tabs on you other pilots.' Once the ashes had gone, Captain Lobo tossed a decent bottle of booze over the side, 'so he'll have something to drink on the way up.' As California headed back toward the glorious skyline, Captain Lobo mused, 'Don't know why he wants to be down THERE, those three noisy foghorns'll keep him awake for sure.'"

Herb always could turn a phrase even if he confused me with Peter Crowell, who tossed in the booze.

John died a lingering death from stomach cancer at the Seamen's Hospital on Lake Street in San Francisco. I should have visited him more when he was suffering, but I just couldn't stand seeing my rock wither away. It was as if a part of me were disappearing.

John was a handsome devil with a full head of white hair, like the gent on Old Grand Dad whiskey bottles. He was always full of piss and vinegar and never afraid to tell you what he thought. I never questioned him because no one had ever been a better friend or went to bat for me as he did.

In October 1980, after I had piloted 1,000 ships, I wrote John a "Thank You." Just six months later, eight bells rang for him, which didn't seem possible.

In 1975, John told me he would get me into the pilots in one year, but as much as I appreciated his faith, I didn't believe anyone had that kind of influence. I found out later he had friends in high places such as Morris Weisberger, the President of the Commission, who he dined with every Tuesday at Scoma's on Fisherman's Wharf. In the end, I waited two years, but to be considered so quickly was unheard of, especially at my age. When I was sworn in, Captain Sever informed me I was the youngest commissioned pilot since 1850. I was one month younger than Captain Francis Diggs, whose slot I took when he retired.

Before I was commissioned, in addition to working on The Bay, I started The Captain's Scribe, a small stationery business, on San Francisco's famous Union Street. One day the phone rang while I was there. John's deep bass was on the other end.

"Have you opened your mail?" he tersely asked.

"No. I've been here all morning. What's up?" His question took me by surprise.

"Go home and open it!" With that, he hung up, leaving me shaking my head.

I never questioned John, so I closed my shop and raced up Octavia Street to my apartment on Vallejo Street. How he knew my mail was already delivered just added to his mystique. Sure enough, amongst the junk was a letter with the Commission's return address. I was nervous and stood for a long time, then I let out a deep breath and ripped open the letter as if I'd won the lottery. To my delight, it said I was the next candidate to be sworn in as a San Francisco Bar Pilot! I had indeed won the lottery. Thanks to John, I had achieved my dream.

I never wanted to disappoint John and I don't think I did, because I only made a few trips to San Francisco's famous Ferry Building, where the Commission was. His photo sits proudly on my desk next to my Ship Master and Pilot Licenses to remind me of where I came from and who helped me. Without him, I might never have become a San Francisco Bar Pilot, something I was extremely proud to be for thirty-one years.

CHAPTER 2

AGROUND WITH CAPTAIN SEVER

When I moved to the Bay Area, there were three groups of ship pilots: Bar Pilots brought the ships in from sea, while two other groups did most of the ship dockings and river piloting. One was California Inland Pilots' Association (CIPA), while the other consisted of Crowley Maritime employees, called Red Stack pilots.

I worked for the Army Corps of Engineers (the Corps), where the deck officers did all of their own piloting. The Corps is responsible for maintaining all Federal channels so there is adequate under-keel clearance for ships. We dredged channels all over The Bay, which is how I obtained enough round trips to qualify for my Coast Guard Unlimited First Class Pilot's License. By doing my own piloting, I believed I had what it took to be a ship pilot. The only place I considered being a pilot, besides Chesapeake Bay, was San Francisco, so I started my quest by meeting Captain Don Fuller, president of the International Organization of Masters, Mates and Pilots (MM&P) local in San Francisco. He liked my idea and encouraged me to get my pilot's licenses. As soon as I was back aboard my ship, I started studying the Coast Guard requirements for pilot, which included reproducing exact copies of the charts of San Francisco from memory. I studied the charts until I knew the entire Bay in my sleep.

After two and a half years with the Corps, I still had no piloting prospects, so I quit to attend the University of California, Berkeley, to get an MBA. While I was there, the CIPA asked me to be their dispatcher. I didn't really want an MBA anyway, so I gladly quit Cal thinking I could get my foot in the piloting door. By working for the CIPA, I got to know all the docking pilots, which was a good and a bad thing. On my time off I rode on hundreds of ships day and night, watching them dock ships all the way to Sacramento and Stockton. Working for the Corps was good experience, but watching other pilots was how I really learned how to handle large vessels.

In the fall of 1973, I first met Captain John Sever when he came through the dispatch office to hang out with the docking pilots. Occasionally I also saw him at nautical functions such as Propeller Club meetings. I thought if I attended these "rubber chicken" lunches and pressed the flesh enough, maybe I'd meet someone who might assist me in my quest. My idea worked because I met a lot of interesting people, but for some reason John took a shining to me. At one luncheon, he invited me to sit at the Bar Pilots' table. That day, he encouraged me to be one of them and not a docking pilot. I didn't think it was possible to be a Bar Pilot until he asked me.

One of the Pilot Commission's main functions is to appoint pilots. When Captain Francis Diggs retired at seventy in 1977, it created a vacancy in the pilot roster, which I filled. Regrettably, six months after I took Captain Diggs's place, I attended his funeral at the National Cemetery for WWII veterans. I've been retired far longer than he lived after I took his place on the pilot roster.

In February 1977, the Commission issued me a state Bar Pilot license, allowing me to pilot any ship of any size into and out of San Francisco and her tributaries. The next step was to be voted in by the San Francisco Bay Bar Pilot Benevolent & Protective Association, the pilot corporation. New pilots buy out the retiring pilot's share of the corporation. When I bought Francis's share, I became an equal partner of California's oldest continuously operated business.

Being commissioned at twenty-nine caused unrest among several pilots, and they petitioned the Commission to rescind my appointment even though I was already sworn in. They cited my age and supposed lack of experience for such a demanding and dangerous job. Maybe they didn't like that I was Captain Sever's choice. The Commission appoints new pilots. It isn't in the hands of the Bar Pilots. President Morris Weisberger told the doubting pilots I was qualified and to vote me in. The Commission wouldn't budge, so my doubters tried to blackball me, hoping to keep me out of the Benevolent & Protective Association. When Captain Sever heard what was happening, he wouldn't hear of it. He hired John Henning, his attorney, to represent me. With his help I was voted in. My controversy just added to the debates John liked to create.

Well, thirty-one years and thousands of ships safely moved later, I proved my antagonists dead wrong. Not only did I go on to have a long and successful career, but almost everyone who voted against me had terrible luck: One pilot glanced off the Bay Bridge with a loaded tanker and later drowned; one was seriously injured in a ship explosion; one did hundreds of thousands of dollars of damage to Pier 94 when he lost control of a ship; one who was commissioned one month before me quit for no reason; and one was seriously injured falling off a pilot ladder.

Governor Jerry Brown signed my commission in 1977. Just before then, I had been captain of the *Komoku,* the last commercial freighter sailing on San Francisco Bay. Not only was I captain, I also did my own piloting. I was also captain of a very large railroad ferry, *Las Plumas,* doing my own piloting on her, as well. This is important because ship captains almost never handle their own ships. Pilots do. So, given my experience and expertise, I didn't think I was too young. Neither did twenty-five professionals who wrote letters on my behalf to the Commission. Among those were two Coast Guard captains, State Senator Milton Marks, Al Chiantelli (Assistant San Francisco DA), ship captains, ship pilots, ship agents, and all of my former employers.

At last my goal came true. I was officially put "on the board." This "board," as opposed to the Commission, refers to the way pilots are dispatched. Each pilot's name and call sign are etched on a 2 × 12 inch piece of plastic that the dispatchers insert into a vertically slotted "board" next to their desk. All pilots in rotation have their names inserted there. When a pilot finishes a job, his board is pulled out and the others slide down. When I returned from a pilot assignment, I went to "the bottom of the board." It's simple, but it's still used today even with modern computer dispatch programs. Before computers, the dispatchers used yellow legal pads, writing the ships' names in pencil and where they were going. A pilot's name was written next to a ship. After a lot of erasures, this turned into a pilot roster that was Xeroxed and handed out. Because ship times change so frequently, that list was immediately out of date!

Before I was commissioned, I was told to take trips across the Bar for familiarization. That's when I got to ride with John. I was also with him on my first piloting job, which turned out to be one of my most *unforgettable* experiences with him. It seems funny now, but it wasn't amusing when it happened.

Port Agent Captain D.S. Grant informed me that Captain Sever, who was the senior pilot, would go along with me as a check ride. I didn't mind. You never knew what you might learn from the senior pilots.

All pilots must do these check rides if they've been "off the board" for any time, such as working in the office. This made sense because I hadn't been on a ship for a while. I wasn't the least bit worried because I had worked all over The Bay for years, but I was glad to have John along.

My first assignment was to move the tanker *Keystoner* from Shell Oil out to San Francisco Sea Buoy (SB), where ships take their pilots. San Francisco Bay has a huge horseshoe-shaped sandbar six miles west of the Golden Gate. Because ships "cross the bar," our pilots are called Bar Pilots, similar to other pilot districts such as the Columbia River and the St. Johns River.

The SB is where three shipping lanes—ones from the north, south, and west—converge eleven miles west of the Golden Gate. It marks the entrance to San Francisco and where one of our 85-foot heavy-weather Station Boats remains within a three mile circle around it. Twenty-four hours a day, every day, no matter how awful the weather, one of our boats is always "On Station." New York and San Francisco are the only ports left with station boats. Our boats don't leave the pilot boarding area unless it's Change-day, when one boat is relieved by her sister or there is an emergency.

A cab drove us to Martinez, then into Shell Oil's enormous oil refinery. The tanker *Keystoner* traded petroleum products between the East and West Coasts. She was waiting to sail.

After 9/11, all maritime facilities beefed up security so private cars are forbidden on all wharfs. Refineries were particularly security-conscious. All cars were searched, even if they were just dropping off pilots, as if they were entering an embassy. Pilots have state-issued IDs, and our bags were searched even though the guards knew all of us.

That was the first of hundreds of times I entered, as a pilot, one of the Bay Area's seven refineries that sit along the waterways going up to Stockton and Sacramento. The cab left us at the gangway, and John and I hiked up to the main deck, where the mate-on-watch escorted us to the navigation bridge, then introduced us to Captain Shellenburg, the ship's master.

After introductions, I had the tugs put up the tow lines on the bow and quarter. Then the crew dropped the mooring lines. Once clear of the dock, my first ship was officially "underway." I had both tugs back up slowly pulling the *Keystoner* off the berth and out into the stream. After I dismissed the tugs, I ordered "Half Ahead" and we started down the Carquinez Strait toward the sea.

It felt fantastic standing on that bridge and being in control, something I had dreamed about for years. When I was riding observer, I wasn't quite sure I'd be a pilot until I ordered that first "Half Ahead" and the mate answered my bell order with "Half Ahead, sir!" as he moved the Engine Order Telegraph's (EOT) brass lever to the Half. The EOT made a loud jingle as the engineers far below answered and the ship started making way. (When EOT's handles are moved, a chain system going down to the engine room causes bells to ring. When the engineers answer, the bell stops ringing so the bridge knows the order is being carried out. This why engine orders are called Bells.)

I had worked long and hard to be on that bridge. I have to say I was very proud of myself. I had piloted my own ships for years, but being a pilot on a large commercial vessel was different because I wasn't the captain. I was the local expert and counsel to captains. For the next twenty years or so, most ship captains I piloted for were far older than I, and I always wondered what they thought of my age.

I didn't realize it at that glorious moment, but Captain Sever and I had committed a cardinal sin of piloting. We didn't take into account low water in Pinole Shoal, about eight miles downstream. Even though the *Keystoner* was relatively small (501 feet long; 69 feet wide) and only 11,000 GRT, she was drawing 35 feet, which was also the charted depth of Pinole Shoal Channel. This would lead to a big problem. I wasn't concerned about anything because I was with the "senior" pilot, but I wrongly assumed John thought of everything. Obviously he hadn't. It was also my error and I should have known better. Maybe I was just nervous, because I didn't think about the ship's draft. A pilot's number-one job is keeping ships off the bottom, so what I did was dumb, to say the least.

I was the pilot assigned. I had the "Conn," which is a nautical term for who has navigational control of the ship. I gave the orders, and unless the master objected to the way I handled his ship, the crew would do as I told them. If anything went wrong, it was my neck, not John's.

About an hour into our passage, the ship was moving nicely down the first mile of Pinole Shoal Channel exactly in the center of a series of buoys marking San Pablo Bay's deeper part. Every year I worked for the Corps, we dredged this channel because of the constant shoaling caused by silt drifting down the Napa River and from hundreds of rivers up in the Sierra Nevadas far to the east. This channel must be maintained to 35 feet so ship traffic can safely cross over the shoal en route to Sacramento and Stockton. Many channels around The Bay require routine dredging.

Pinole Shoal has nine buoys spread over six miles, marking its edges. If the ship went outside with our draft, she would run hard aground almost immediately. As the *Keystoner* passed two buoys marking the midway point of the shoal, I needed to alter my course about 20 degrees to port to head down the last several miles of the channel. On this leg, looking west, you see Mount Tamalpais on the Marin County coast straight ahead. If you look closely, it resembles a sleeping woman, her hair flowing down the mountainside to the left, with her torso to the right, lying on her back gazing up at sky.

When the ship was exactly where I wanted her, I ordered port rudder. Immediately the helmsman moved the huge wooden steering wheel hand over hand to the left as I waited for the ship to react. As the ship started swinging, just as suddenly she stopped—along with my heart—as the ship ran aground. I was confused because the ship was in the center of the channel judging by two buoys equally distant from the ship's sides. I'd never been aground before, so having the ship lurch to a halt was a sickening feeling. Well, you can't put two pounds of crap into a one-pound sack. In my case, I was in crap up to my neck. It dawned on me that we had failed to take into account low water! My first trip as pilot and I was aground. I wondered what the pilots who had opposed me would have to say if they found out.

I took Captain Diggs's call sign, Foxtrot. For the next thirty-one years, I used that to identify myself on my radio. Some ports just use the ship's name. John's sign was "Tango." I thought Tango and Foxtrot, the two dancers, better think of some new steps quickly to get us out of the jam. John immediately took the Conn from me and started issuing orders. I didn't say a word. I just prayed that he could extricate the ship from the chaos I had just gotten us into.

John barked "Half Astern, now Half Ahead" over and over as he "backed and filled," meaning going ahead and astern to wiggle the ship free. Eventually it paid off because the ship slipped off the low spot. Once afloat, we resumed our trip as if nothing had happened. It probably took ten minutes, but it seemed like an eternity until John passed the Conn back to me. I acted as if nothing had happened, but I was too green then to have carried off that refloating by myself. As I mentioned before, those old-timers knew a lot of tricks, and I was learning fast.

John took the old man aside, whispering that he didn't think reporting the grounding was warranted because it was "only mud" and there was no damage and almost no delay. San Francisco's channels are mud, so a grounding doesn't usually harm a ship. It's embarrassing, but, as I learned, it need not be the end of the world.

Captain Shellenburg went along with John, and no one ever knew I ran aground. Captain Sever and I never even talked about it afterward. "Ship happens," and this is the first time I am telling this story. That mistake taught me a valuable lesson, helping me to stay out of trouble for the next thirty-one years. From then on, I always *double* and *triple* checked *all* my calculations in regards to ship's depth, drafts, and the height of the mast above the water called "air draft," for passing under bridges. Piloting is an ongoing learning experience. I learned something new almost every day trying never to repeat any mistakes I'd made.

Captain Alan Clarke was another counsellor and friend from whom I learned as much as anyone because he was the slickest pilot I ever saw move a ship. I never once heard him raise his voice moving a ship, something I can't say about myself.

He advised me: "Good pilots get out of trouble, because *all* of us get into it!" I couldn't imagine Al ever making a mistake, but all of my career I tried living by his advice.

So started thirty-one years of piloting. I went on to handle over 6,100 ships of all kinds and sizes, in every condition and weather, 24/7. This is that story.

CHAPTER 3

WHAT IS A MARITIME PILOT?

"He who commands the sea has command of everything."
–Themistocles (524–459 B.C.)

When I first met my wife, Carol, on a passenger ship no less, she asked me what I did. Instead of saying, "I'm a Bar Pilot," I said, "I'm a valet parker for ships." Normally if I mentioned I was a pilot in the Merchant Marine, someone might ask, "What airline do you fly for?" Carol understood right away.

English Law Article 742 of the Merchant Shipping Act of 1894 defined a pilot as "any person not belonging to a ship who has the conduct thereof," or in nautical parlance, someone other than a crew member who has the "Conn," or control over the speed, direction, and movement of the ship. The pilot speaks through the ship's master, who is ultimately responsible. If he's not content, he may assume it himself, which is rare and never happened to me.

Maritime pilots have years of seagoing experience, are specifically trained to maneuver ships, and are local experts. To get to work, he or she (for brevity I will only use 'he' from now on) climbs aboard vessels using a "Jacob's ladder."

Pilots are mandatory in most ports, and all U.S. states with sea ports have a state pilot authority that selects and disciplines pilots, and sets pilotage rates. This has worked well for hundreds of years because state

14

pilots are not obliged to the ship, but to the state. Therefore, pilots are more likely to make decisions based on safety considerations rather than monetary ones. A state pilot relieves the master of economic pressure that can compromise safety. Because pilots aren't employees, they can make independent decisions without fear of losing their job.

Pilots have captains' licenses but only act as pilot, not captain. To differentiate the two, sometimes we are called "Mr. Pilot." Captain Nancy Wagner, America's first female ship pilot, said crews often call her Mr. Pilot.

The origins of the term "pilot" probably comes from the Dutch, where he is a *piloot*. Only Spanish-speaking countries call us "El Practico." Everywhere else in the world we are pilots.

"The Commandant has cited the following cautionary language: 'Piloting requires the greatest experience and nicest judgment of any form of navigation. Constant vigilance, unfailing mental alertness and thorough knowledge of the principals involved are essential. Mistakes in navigation on the open sea can generally be discovered and corrected before the next landfall. In piloting there is little or no opportunity to correct errors. Even a slight blunder may result in serious disaster involving perhaps loss of life. . . . It's the proximity of danger which makes piloting so important. The question of avoiding collision in the heavy traffic of harbors . . . is essentially a problem of keeping his ship in navigable waters.'"

Archeologists have found evidence of maritime activity from over 7,000 years ago, so pilots have been around in one form or another since biblical times. When ships in ancient times first ventured offshore in the Mediterranean, they no longer hugged familiar shores, so they didn't know the particulars of strange ports, depths of water, or the currents. Professional mariners entering a foreign port even with the proper charts were tested without a pilot. Experts were needed to guide vessels into port, so resident fishermen with "local knowledge" sold this information to visiting ships, thus acting as the first pilots. This system evolved over centuries until today there are highly trained, extremely regulated local specialists handling ships worldwide. Most ports have pilots standing by 24/7 to board vessels whether required by port authorities or states.

There are no pilot holidays. I piloted every holiday, including many New Year's Eves. Once, not only was it blowing like hell, but it was also foggy. No party hats that night.

Even the Bible mentions pilots, so we like to say we are the world's second oldest profession, right after prostitutes. The Jacob's ladder, the rope ladder used to board ships, is almost the same as in ancient times. The Bible references it in Genesis 28:10-12: "*Jacob left Beersheba and set out for Haran. When he reached a certain place, he stopped for the night because the sun had set. Taking one of the stones there, he put it under his head and lay down to sleep. He had a dream in which he saw a stairway (ladder) resting on the earth, with its top reaching to heaven and the angels of God were ascending and descending on it.*"

"Pilot" is also mentioned four times in Ezekiel 2. This makes perfect sense because some pilots think they are gods on the water.

I first learned about pilots from my dad, who worked thirty-five years for the American Can Company in Brooklyn. One reason I went to sea was that I didn't want to commute like he did. Every day, no matter what the weather, it took him over an hour to get to his plant by public transit. When I went to sea, I only walked up a few decks to the bridge to go to work.

Sometimes my family visited his big factory located near the Bushwick docks. It was exciting seeing all those monstrous machines mass-producing hundreds of items out of metal that are now made with plastic, which is probably the reason American Can, once a Fortune 500 company, was swallowed up by Dart Industries and is no longer. American Can's distinctive logo CANCO affixed on a landmark water tower is long gone, just like my dad.

I remember one day driving into New York from Long Island on the Belt Parkway passing Fort Hamilton, which once guarded the Narrows. My alma mater in Fort Schuyler is just up the East River from Manhattan in the Bronx. It guarded the east entrance to NY Harbor. New York Maritime College is the nation's oldest nautical school. In 1964, the Verrazano-Narrows Bridge was opened right over the top of Fort Hamilton, just as the Throgs Neck Bridge spans Fort Schuyler.

As we passed by, a massive black-hulled freighter was slipping out of Lower New York Bay with a white bone in her teeth. My old man mentioned that the men who moved those ships were called pilots. They were members of a guild that was impossible to join unless you were the son of a pilot. I'm not sure why he knew anything about them other than that his plant was near the docks. I didn't give his words much thought because I couldn't imagine going to sea, much less becoming a sea pilot. When I was young, I wanted to attend the Air Force Academy and be an airplane pilot. I didn't do either, and I'm glad I didn't.

Piloting was briefly discussed at the school where I studied to be a Third Mate, just as being a judge might be discussed at law school. At Fort Schuyler, being a captain was only a dream, we were just trying to graduate. Eventually I beat the odds by becoming one of only about one thousand American pilots that are both state and federally licensed.

In 1992, my friend, Captain Bob Dean, President of the New York-New Jersey Sandy Hook Pilots Association (est. 1694), invited me to celebrate Columbus's 500th anniversary with his pilots. Many Sandy Hook pilots are New York graduates, but I was the first alumnus to become a San Francisco pilot. Two other alumni later joined me. The Pilot Boat *New York* led a spectacular parade of tall ships up the Hudson River. Cadets from around the world stood in the rigging of their square riggers in a long line. As they came under the Verrazano Bridge, foghorns blew in greeting. The parade ended at the George Washington Bridge. We passed Fort Hamilton, where my dad first mentioned our pilot hosts so long ago. I had come full circle.

As the *New York* passed Manhattan's West Side passenger ship berths, I laughed, thinking back to the memory of my old Aunt Lillian. She invited our family to a bon voyage party on the *Queen of Bermuda* when sailing to Bermuda was a big deal. In 1955, farewell parties were a tradition, but after 9/11, these lavish parties were forbidden and only passengers are allowed on board. Well-wishers must wait on the dock for the ship to sail.

My parents, grandparents, Aunt Betty, Uncle Gene, my brother Peter, and my cousin Susan were stuffed into my aunt's stateroom drinking, smoking, and having a fine time celebrating her one-week cruise. The thing

I remember most, other than being confined to that small room, wasn't the massive white ship; rather, it was a black porter. I can still see him wearing a white cutaway jacket that contrasted with his face. After a few hours, he came through the passageway, hitting a big brass gong and crying out, "All visitors ashore! All visitors ashore!" He returned several times and each time his pleas grew louder and more urgent. The adults ignored him as they grew happier drinking Manhattans and whiskey sours and smoking up the room like they didn't have a care in the world. They also didn't seem the least bit concerned about the continuous announcements on the ship's PA system: "Now hear this, now hear this. The *Queen of Bermuda* is about to sail for Bermuda. ALL visitors kindly disembark!" Everyone acted like they were going to Bermuda along with my aunt and her traveling companion, Leddy. Thinking we were going to be trapped, I started to sweat and fidget. In my mind's eye I saw the crew lowering the gangway onto the dock, stranding us. I didn't want to go to Bermuda on that giant ship, even if my parents went with me. I panicked and starting bawling, begging my folks to save us from a week of luxury at sea. Eventually, I happily made my escape down the Furness Lines gangway, which by some miracle was still attached to the ship. We joined thousands of New Yorkers waiting to send off my aunt's enormous white ship.

As I looked at the ship's three big red-and-black-striped funnels, I noticed an old man in a business suit leaning over the bridge's dodger holding a walkie-talkie and pointing at something. Next to him stood the captain, magnificently dressed in a stiff white dress uniform and wearing a high pressure hat ablaze in gold embroidery. I didn't know it, but the man in the suit was the pilot.

As the crowd waited impatiently for something to happen, the ship's big steam whistle blew a thunderous notice that all of Manhattan and probably half of New Jersey could hear. The pilot was warning everyone that the ship was about to back out of her slip into the mighty muddy Hudson. As the cloud of white whistle steam swiftly drifted away, the liner's crew started loosening the ship's mooring lines. One by one, the line handlers muscled them off their rusty bollards and dropped them into the water. When the last line was aboard, the ship was free of her grip on New York and underway. Two smoke-puffing McAllister tugs with their distinctive red and white stripes on their stacks pushed on the ship's bow.

I watched in awe as the pilot slowly backed the biggest thing I had ever seen in my entire life into the middle of the river, and the *Queen* and my Aunt disappeared behind the pier and were gone.

Little could that small upset boy ever have imagined that someday he would be standing on the bridges of passenger ships looking down as people waved goodbye to their friends and loved ones.

I would later pilot over 119 passenger liners from the tiny *Enna G* to the 92,627-ton *Coral Princess*.

Captains want to be pilots for numerous reasons. Some for the money and some to be with their families. For me, it was all about handling ships. I knew from own piloting experience I had the feel. I had one of my classmates quit our pilot apprentice program because he never felt comfortable handling ships, so no matter how much he might have earned, he returned to something he was comfortable being, an APL master.

We had at least one pilot (if not several) who was often seasick but toughed it out to be with his family. If you have ever been seasick, you know how hard that must be.

One of the nice things about piloting is there is no paperwork other than filling out a simple form about the ship for billing purposes. All the paperwork I needed was already in my head. I spent hundreds of hours riding on ships for experience, and then an equal amount of time studying for my pilot exams. The most difficult part was convincing the state you were qualified.

In general, we were left alone to execute ship moves, which meant putting all the pieces together to successfully move something as large as 1,200 feet long and 180 feet wide with 50 feet of draft. Every time I moved a ship I had do it perfectly; there was no room for error. I didn't need to be told I did a great job, the ship in the right spot with no damage was immediate proof. There aren't many professionals who get job satisfaction like that. Handling all the different varieties of ships from around the world always made me feel great. Mark Twain thought few people had more power than a ship pilot. In *Life on the Mississippi*, he wrote, "Your true pilot cares nothing about anything on earth but the river, and his pride in his occupation surpasses that of kings."

If a vessel floated, I probably piloted it. I moved car and crude oil carriers, wheat and petcoke bulkers, and ships carrying live animals, like pigs and cattle, that smelled to high heaven. I piloted cable layers such as SS *Long Lines*, paper carriers, passenger ships of all sorts and sizes, ships filled to the gunwales with munitions, ones with 100 percent liquefied ammonia, and one Polish fishing boat. The largest ship I ever moved was the *Alaska Frontier* (110,693 GRT), while the smallest was the 160-foot Mexican yacht *New Century*. I also handled every class of naval ship, from submarines to supply vessels to research ships to aircraft carriers. Every job was interesting, some much more than others for many reasons, including the danger of certain jobs.

One of the most exciting jobs I ever did was piloting the semi-submersible *Sedco 708*, an oil rig constructed at Mare Island Naval Shipyard. She just fit under our highway bridges and was one of the most massive vessels I ever piloted, towering hundreds of feet above the water.

On May 7, 1977, she was sitting in Anchorage #5 near Richmond Long Wharf. There I climbed aboard an ocean-going tug from the *Drake*. The large tug was going to tow the rig to Santa Barbara once I got her out to sea. I had to direct not only the sea tug, but six other tugs assigned to work with me. After the rig's crew heaved up her anchors, I got the rig moving, being careful to have all my tugs pull with just the right amount of tension. If they didn't, the rig could have drifted off course or gotten out of my control as I maneuvered her around Angel Island. After we safely passed under the Golden Gate and I no longer needed a tug for stability, I radioed that particular one to cast off their tow line. Everything was going along smoothly until I dismissed the *Sea Robin*. When I did, her towing hawser jammed on her winch, almost putting her into "Irons." Lucky for all of us, her tow line was under such strain that as the oil rig moved past her, the *Robin*'s line parted, setting her free, much to my relief. If not, she might have rolled over and sunk because there was no way for me to stop the rig with all her momentum. After I disembarked, the sea tug towed the rig south, where she was sunk and drilled for oil.

I never wanted anyone injured on my jobs, and thankfully none ever were. Sailors on ships and deck hands on tugs get injured or killed far too often. I saw tug tow lines and ship mooring lines part. Seeing a mooring wire part and whiplash is a frightening experience.

Pilots are often mentioned in literature. The mariner was met by a pilot boat near the end of his voyage in *The Rime of the Ancient Mariner*. In James Clavell's *Shogun,* John Blackthorne is the *Erasmus's* pilot, although he is more like a navigator than a present-day pilot. Like a modern pilot, he has more local knowledge than his captain. Rodrigues, another pilot, said this about Blackthorne: "He is a pilot before everything else!"

In Gilbert and Sullivan's comic opera *The Pirates of Penzance,* Frederic's father directs nursemaid Ruth to apprentice his son to be a pilot, but she mishears indenturing him to be a pirate until his twenty-first birthday. Sometimes I think steamship companies also get the two confused.

Ever since reading Mark Twain's *Life on the Mississippi*, I knew I wanted to be a steamboat pilot like him. He wrote about his apprenticeship and how demanding and exciting piloting was and how much respect pilots commanded on the river. Twain earned the same salary as the Vice President of the United States. On my travels across America, I have visited his boyhood home in Hannibal, Missouri; his stately home in Hartford, which looks like the wheelhouse of an old steamboat; and his final resting place in Elmira, NY. I know when he quit piloting he missed being up in the wheelhouse, as I do. There is nothing like it.

CHAPTER 4

HISTORY OF SAN FRANCISCO BAR PILOTS

One of the colossal near misses in history occurred in 1579 during Sir Francis Drake's round-the-world voyage, when the *Golden Hind* landed for repairs just north of San Francisco, missing its now-famous entrance by only a few miles. His landing spot in New Albion, what Drake called California, is located at Drakes Bay. It's officially recognized by the U.S. Department of the Interior.

The history of California has always revolved around ships, especially San Francisco, which has one of the greatest natural harbors in the world. Oddly enough, it wasn't discovered by mariners, but by Spanish missionaries. This could be because San Francisco's winds are predominantly northwestern and strong. These winds blow toward the coast, creating what seamen call a "Lee Shore." These onshore winds made it difficult for square-rigged ships to maneuver away from shore, a dangerous situation for ships that preferred to sail downwind. The inability to sail close to the wind along with tremendous amounts of coastal fog may have accounted for sailors not "discovering" San Francisco Bay. Low-hanging clouds often give San Francisco's entrance a uniform gray appearance, so without binoculars or radar, it's hard to distinguish the entrance from the surrounding hills.

It wasn't from the sea, but from land, that explorer Spaniard Gaspar de Portolá discovered The Bay on November 4, 1769. From atop Sweeney Ridge in present day Pacifica, Portolá looked down on an immense harbor protected from the sea with plenty of fresh water in what was to become San Francisco. He was first to see one of the finest harbors in the world. He was 119 miles off course and wrongly assumed he was looking at Drakes Bay, now called the Gulf of the Farallones. Portolá was wrong about his location, but what a discovery! Great harbors are cherished by navies worldwide, and until the 1990s, San Francisco had a huge U.S. naval presence, which unfortunately it no longer has.

On August 5, 1775, the *San Carlos,* captained by Juan de Ayala, is believed to be the first ship to sail to enter The Bay and anchor near present day Angel Island.

California was originally part of New Spain, becoming part of Mexico when Mexico was emancipated in 1822. It became a U.S. territory with the Treaty of Guadalupe Hidalgo, which ended the Mexican War of 1845-1848, the same year James Marshall discovered gold at Sutter's Mill. Talk about timing.

San Francisco, or Yerba Buena, was a very quiet place until 1848 with no civilian homes; there was only the Mexican Army garrison at what is today The Presidio. In 1835, only twenty-five ships entered the sleepy little port of San Francisco. Today, although not the world's biggest commercial harbor complex, the Bay Area handles over 8,000 ships a year.

One might think the entrance to San Francisco is named for the Gold Rush or for its rusty-colored bridge (which is not a gold color at all; in fact, it's called "Red Lead"). No, it was Army Captain John C. Fremont who named the entrance in 1846, saying it reminded him of the Golden Horn in Istanbul. Fremont is renowned for fighting in the Mexican-American and Civil Wars and was the first U.S. Senator when California became a state in 1850. Mount Fremont and the City of Fremont are named for this hero.

Until the Gold Rush, California was sparsely populated, with the occasional vessel dropping anchor in Monterey Bay to buy hides, fresh produce, and tallow from the big coastal rancheros. The Gold Rush changed all that. Soon untold numbers of ships began arriving carrying argonauts from around the world. Even before it was named Golden Gate, Chinese immigrants called California "Gumshan" *(Gold Mountain)*. They came by the thousands from Toisan, in Guangdong.

Only a few years after the Gold Rush, a settler named Hinton Helper said this about San Francisco: "I may not be a competent judge, but this much I will say, I have never seen purer liquors, better cigars, finer tobacco, truer guns and pistols, larger dirks and bowie knives, and prettier courtesans here in San Francisco than in any other place I have ever visited, and it's my unbiased opinion that California can and does furnish the best bad things that are obtainable in America."

Sir Francis Drake is sometimes called the "First Pilot of the Farallones" because of landing in Marin County. However, British merchant officer William Richardson was aboard *Orion* in 1822 when she came to take on provisions. Richardson, who spoke Spanish, went ashore to palaver with the local authorities but never returned to his ship, or to England. He thought the small settlement of Yerba Buena was indeed *bueno* especially after meeting Señorita Maria Antonia Martinez, the Commandante of the Presidio's daughter at a fiesta. He fell in love and like millions of others never left. Martinez is a town on the Carquinez Strait named for her and is a major oil refinery hub. Directly across the straits is Benicia, one of the first of seven cities that were capitals of California. Valero has a huge refinery there.

Richardson was the first of many sailors who jumped ship in San Francisco, but it became epidemic during the Gold Rush. It's illegal under ship's articles, but that didn't stop sailors from deserting and heading to the Sierras. To solve this crew shortage for ships heading back around the Horn, San Francisco, not China, invented a solution called "Shanghaiing." "Crimps," or thugs hired by shorthanded ships, "Shanghaied" unsuspecting drunken sailors, forcing them to sail against their will.

Empty ships sailing south needed weight to counterbalance the wind's force on the sails, so they loaded stones in place of cargo. Many East Coast streets are still paved with California granite.

Richardson taught the Mexicans navigation in exchange for letting him stay. He was the first person to sound and chart The Bay and became

San Francisco's first harbor master. Due to his ship handling ability, he became the first pilot; thus, he should be considered the grandfather of the Bar Pilots.

Considering the great role Captain Richardson played, it's strange that there is so little to remind us of him in San Francisco. Only one short street is named for him, and a plaque in present-day Chinatown denotes the location where he built San Francisco's first wooden house he called *Casa Grande,* which started out as a tent made out of sail canvas. I'd wager few people living above Richardson Bay in multi-million dollar homes know for whom it's named.

CHAPTER 5

CALIFORNIA PILOTAGE

When California became the thirty-second state, regulated pilotage was thought to be so important to commerce that California's Third Article of Incorporation created a Board of Pilot Commissioners, making it the state's oldest board. The Governor nominated, and the Senate approved, twelve pilots, who became the original Bar Pilots. This act eliminated competition between pilots, allowing a pilot monopoly in exchange for control over them. When pilotage isn't mandatory, ship captains might handle their own ships to save pilotage fees with the inevitable groundings and collisions soon following. For instance, when Argentina voided mandatory pilotage to lower costs to shippers, within one week two ships piloted by competing groups collided. So in the end it didn't save the shippers much.

Over the years San Francisco's pilotage was extended to include San Pablo and Suisun Bays and the Port of Redwood City. For environmental protection, in 1984 California mandated that the Bar Pilots amalgamate with the docking and river pilots. Our pilotage district now encompasses an area from the Pilot Station into San Francisco Bay, including all tributaries and the ports of Stockton, Sacramento, and Redwood City. This is over 200 miles of waterways with 100 separate docks, facilities, and dry docks. In 2001, cruise lines were granted permission to call at eco-sensitive Monterey Bay, eighty miles south of the Sea Buoy, if they hired Bar Pilots to guide them. Prior to 1849, all ships had to anchor at Monterey to pay Mexico customs duties, no matter where they were going in California. Cruise ships now drop anchor where Richard Henry Dana did in *Two Years Before the Mast*.

San Francisco pilots use the term "hooked on," meaning to get maximum ship speed. In port, maneuvering speeds are used: "Dead slow ahead, Slow ahead...," and so on. When I wanted more than maneuvering speed, I'd ask for "sea speed" or I'd say "Hook'er on!" Sea speed can take some time to achieve, especially on steamships when more steam has to be created in the boilers, but it saves a lot of time for a ship, especially if it's pushing against a strong current.

Before the Commission's creation, rival pilot groups hailed arriving ships at sea in open boats. These hearty mariners threw grappling hooks onto them and pulled their makeshift pilot boats alongside, claiming the right to pilot them. Thus, they were "hook'd on." Anyone with a boat and a hook could pilot, since there were no standards of who was a seasoned pilot. The 1850 law abolished this practice, ensuring that all ships would be treated equally. Pilots no longer piloted ships offering the most money, or that were the fastest. The confusion of competing boats hailing ships in the fog, especially before radar, must have been something to observe.

In the years prior to becoming a pilot, in addition to riding along with pilots, I often chauffeured them to their jobs as a favor for helping me. One was Captain Swede Anderson, who taught me a lot. Swede was a salty old pilot who earned his licenses the hard way, working his way up from deckhand to pilot. Swede, like Captain Grant, was like another gruff character from Jack London's *The Sea Wolf*. He was as tough as nails, but I liked the way he didn't take crap from anyone, especially helmsmen. One day I went with him to Port Chicago Naval Weapons Station to move a ship. He couldn't determine the ship's draft because it was so poorly marked. Rightfully, he refused to sail a ship fully loaded with bombs knowing it could lead to problems. He would rather not get paid than take a chance. This taught me a big lesson: pilots don't have to sail if they are in doubt.

Prior to the pilot merger, the docking pilots were under pressure to get jobs. Unlike Swede, some pilots would make the ship agents happy by doing something borderline, such as using one tug to dock a ship, which I never saw anywhere in the world but in San Francisco. Allowing the ship owner to get that extra ton on board might be good for the company, but cutting corners in piloting has led to dire consequences. After the merger, ship agents no longer had any say in who piloted their clients' ships. Whoever was next in rotation took the job, which didn't make some agents happy.

Because ship masters visit so many different ports, it's impossible for them to be as proficient at ship handling as pilots working in a port day after day. Gaining local knowledge and honing ship handling skills by piloting more and more ships is something that no ship captain, no matter how gifted he is, will ever obtain just by going to sea. Watching a pilot move a ship is one thing actually doing it's another. Even with Coast Guard pilot endorsements, a captain might never have the knowledge essential to pilot safely in San Francisco.

After a rough voyage or being in heavy fog, a captain might be fatigued just when he needs to be at his sharpest. The last thing he needs is to add piloting to his already-weighty responsibilities. Piloting can be a challenge even on fair days and much more so in fog.

In the last forty years no Bar Pilots have ever been responsible for two ships colliding. A perfect example of why ships hire Bar Pilots was in 1971, when the *Oregon Standard* and *Arizona Standard*, 17,350 GRT each, collided in dense fog near the Golden Gate Bridge. This was San Francisco's most infamous and largest oil spills. Oil drifted as far north as Duxbury Reef fifteen miles away. Both masters assumed the role of pilot, both worked for Standard Oil of California (now Chevron), and both misjudged The Bay's swift currents. Each captain possessed a Coast Guard pilot endorsement, but that does not necessarily make a captain a qualified pilot. I passed my exams long before I started piloting. If these small tankers had been today's size ships, this spill would have been beyond catastrophic.

"A lawyer who has himself for a client is a fool" could be applied to this travesty, because if Bar Pilots had been aboard, this collision wouldn't have happened.

Chevron, one of the world's largest companies, still bypasses the California Harbors and Navigation Code's mandatory pilotage laws through an exemption that allows "Enrolled" U.S. vessels, not in foreign trade, to be piloted by the ship's master if he has a Federal pilot's license.

Despite spilling 121,400 gallons of oil, the immense cost to Standard Oil, and the environmental impact, their Chevron captains continued to pilot their ships right up to the end of my career. Once those ships were inside The Bay, they used a Chevron company pilot or us to dock their ships.

We didn't like having non-Bar Pilots move ships for several reasons. The obvious one was we didn't get paid, but second, we didn't know the skill level of the captains piloting. Meeting another ship in fog with someone with little training driving could give pause for thought. For example, U.S. naval vessels, also exempt from the piloting regulations, on rare occasions didn't take a pilot. Sometimes Navy ships would bypass the Pilot Station and proceed into San Francisco without a Bar Pilot, even in fog. Sometimes, without telling Traffic, a Navy ship would slow down right in the middle of the channel and wait for us to pass them, which is a bone-ass thing to do. After we overtook them, they would increase speed and fall in astern of us following us into port. Obviously, this isn't a safe way to transit into a port, especially a big one like San Francisco. This illustrates why all ships should hire pilots, even exempt vessels. I always avoided getting anywhere near ships without Bar Pilots on them.

Our pilots know the local conditions like the backs of their hands. For example, in the spring, when there is heavy snowmelt in the Sierra Nevadas, the Water Department lets excess water run out of the huge reservoirs upstream. This extra water can result in little or no flood current upriver, which, while rare, changes the whole docking scenario. Extreme water conditions also reduces bridges' vertical clearances, restricting the passage of some ships, especially empty ones. These spring runoffs also created extra-large ebb currents all the way out to sea, and this is something a ship captain wouldn't know about. There were times when the amount of water going under the Golden Gate Bridge far exceeded NOAA's tide tables, which were usually very accurate, so extreme caution had to be taken. I had many ships shoved sideways during these extreme ebbs approaching the Golden Gate. Because I knew the local conditions, I anticipated what would happen and turned my ship into The Bay much earlier than normal.

This was especially critical in fog, when you can't see what the currents are doing. If I didn't turn early, the ship could have turned around in a circle, going into opposing traffic. This was particularly so with underpowered ships and what happened to the two Chevron ships.

Captain Keon Dan was a Mate on the *Oregon Standard* and was asleep when the two ships hit. Dan comes from a long line of seafarers; he and his father were ship masters, and his brother was a mooring master in Southern California. Dan joined the Bar Pilots in 1985 when we became friends and watch partners. We rotated on the Board, two weeks on, two weeks off year-round for the next twenty-two years. He was the perfect partner because he and I changed our days off all the time. We also attended Port Revel Shiphandling School together three times and retired on the same day.

An applicant for Bar Pilot must hold a valid Coast Guard Merchant Marine Master's License and have sailed on it for at least two years. Getting the required sea time takes many years. The applicant must also pass all tests for a Coast Guard First Class Unlimited Pilot's License from the Sea Buoy into San Francisco and all her tributaries. This includes reproducing, from memory, exact copies of all charts. They start with big blank pieces of paper and fill them in. I spent hours upon hours memorizing the characteristics of every navigation light, whistle, foghorn, buoy, the height and width of every bridge, where all the cable crossings areas are, and what the current and water depth was at any given time or place anywhere in our pilot district.

The Coast Guard is not involved in the selection of pilots; they just issue these endorsements.

The next step is taking a difficult written exam developed with the help of academics hired by the Commission at California Maritime Academy. To make a fair exam, all questions were formulated by pilots. All answers were referenced by a text book, e.g., Chapman's *Piloting . . .*" I helped this process twice.

Unless an applicant had prior experience, such as working in another port, he began one to three years observing senior pilots, eventually handling thousands of ships of all types under supervision. I always insisted my apprentices handle my ships if they were comfortable, even if they had just started. At some point they had to do the complete job no matter how difficult it was, especially at night. This training can be hair-raising, not only for the apprentice, but also for the training pilot whose license is always on the line. Allowing apprentices to get into trouble was nerve-racking, but apprentices had to see their mistakes and correct them quickly because things go wrong when moving ships all the time.

Some things about being an apprentice haven't changed. For example, Captain Horace Bixby taught Samuel Clemens his craft in the 1850s. He advised young Clemens, "I learned steamboating by wholly devoting myself... I quickly learned, as you must..., that the science of piloting is a jealous master. You must concentrate all your attention, interest and efforts on getting it down. You must be able to steer by day by the picture in front of you and by night by the picture inside your head. And then know that you know it, otherwise you will have no courage and you'll not only be useless, you'll be dangerous. A steamboat floats on a pilot's memory, not on the river's water. It would soon come aground if it was otherwise." This is as true today as it was before the Civil War.

Besides all the hands-on training, all pilots and apprentices are required to attend the world-famous Port Revel Shiphandling School located in the petite farming village of Viriville, near Grenoble, France, chosen because of its mild climate and because there is little wind at the training facilities. The school was created to teach Esso Oil Company's captains the basics of ship handling, but over 60,000 pilots have attended their eight-day course. Sogreah, an engineering company, runs the school. The French countryside may sound like a strange place to learn ship handling, but I learned a ton about piloting there I thought I already knew. Fourteen years after I became a pilot, I attended Port Revel for the first time. I wish I had done so earlier in my career, because it helped me to be a better pilot. Pilots stayed at the Hotel Bonnoit. It was rated by Michelin, so we didn't mind the cuisine, either.

Upon arriving in France, we'd overnight in Lyon, the "Gastronomic Capital" of France. The last time there, Morgan Hoburg and I dined at the internationally famous Paul Bocuse Restaurant for a one-of-a-kind experience. No other pilots wanted to spend the money, but pilots being frugal is another story.

Port Revel sums up its philosophy: *because this is still the best way to acquire certain reflexes which, when the time comes, will make all the difference between being good and being the best. Training on the scale models provides experience that could never be gained on real ships for the simple reason that neither ship-owners nor local authorities would allow such risks to be taken. Scale models allow the ship handler to make mistakes.*

Port Revel's models look, feel, and act like the real thing. Along with honing our docking techniques, we did anchor and emergency drills. Ship scenarios, specific to San Francisco Bay, were created. We also learned about shallow water effect and passing another ship head-to-head in a very narrow channel, which the Houston Pilots call the "Texas Chicken." We also learned overtaking another ship in a narrow channel is a terrible idea, because all the pilots who attempted it crashed the models together, even old-timers like Nick Ernser and Al Carlier. Every move was electronically recorded so we could see where we made mistakes or where we needed improvement. We could crash 200,000-ton model tankers without doing millions of dollars in damages or going to jail.

When I started my career, I never thought I would attend so many schools or spend so much time and money doing it. We had no choice, we had to up our game all the time.

We also attended Marine Safety International's simulator located inside the San Diego Naval Base. My turn was a few days after 9/11, when the based was locked down like a prison. There we learned how to use modern tractor tugs for tanker escort work and emergencies.

We also attended MM&P's Maritime Institute in Baltimore. They have two state-of-the-art full-scale ship bridge simulators. We also studied pilotage law.

Becoming a pilot is a long and laborious journey, but it was definitely worth it. I received great satisfaction in doing a demanding, yet incredibly dangerous job.

CHAPTER 6

THE DIFFERENCE BETWEEN LIGHTNING AND A LIGHTNING BUG

When someone asked me what I did for a living, most often they thought I flew an airplane. It's true that airline pilots and ship pilots share the same title of captain, and almost all aeronautical terms such as bulkheads, port and starboard, and red and green running lights are derived from ship parts; but to misquote Mark Twain, the difference between these two types of pilots is like the difference between lightning and a lightning bug! Airplane pilots have only been around since December 17, 1903, when the Wright Brothers perfected controllable flight, but sixty-six years later we landed on the moon. Ship pilots have been around since biblical times, but most ships today still have only one rudder and one propeller, so ships haven't evolved at the same pace as flight.

As I flew across the country recently, I listened to the plane's pilots talking to Air Traffic Control (ATC), and it seemed everything that the pilots did, except fly the plane, came from their controllers. They were told air speed, altitude, what runway to land on, and what the wind speed and direction were at the airport. To get the real scoop about how planes interact with ATC, I asked retired Delta Air Lines Captain Al Leland to explain how their system worked because it seemed so different from our traffic control, called Vessel Traffic Service (VTS), which mainly gives us ship movements. Al said ATC was needed because of congestion. He wrote, "The company picks the route, altitude, etc. Dispatchers using computers get the most fuel efficient route. The FAA approves or makes changes, but the pilot can request changes once airborne. These changes are usually predicated on traffic, etc."

Modern jets can land themselves, steer on a runway, and automatically apply the brakes. The pilot doesn't have to do anything until the airplane is stopped. Airplanes use autopilot for cruising but are manually landed. Pilots like to land manually because it's fun, but the worse the weather, the more the pilots are required to use automation. Visibility requirements are only to ensure pilots can see taxiways to pull off the runway. Ship pilots still sail by the seat of our pants because there is very little automation.

The FAA encourages autopilot because it allows pilots to look for other aircraft. Ships only use an "autopilot" called "Iron Mike" on the ocean. Hand steering must be used entering port, and many times I wished the ships had used Iron Mike because of all the poor helmsmanship I dealt with. The only ship in the world that docks herself is the *River Queen* in Frontierland.

Virtually all airlines require their pilots to use instrument flight plans, something we didn't have. We orchestrated the whole docking evolution in our heads.

I'm not taking anything away from airline pilots' skills, but there is no comparison in the way commercial airplanes and ships are controlled.

Captain Leland told me ATC is primarily used for aircraft avoidance, but useful for other things, including weather, landing delays, and runway closures. Maritime pilots get little help from VTS.

Airline pilots could fly without any help from ATC if there were only one plane flying, which obviously isn't the case. Bar Pilots could easily move ships without VTS simply by using checkpoints, as is done in some ports like Los Angeles and Chesapeake Bay.

San Francisco was the first big U.S. port to have VTS, but if it's so important, why isn't it required in every port? Controlling traffic in

San Francisco Bay is nowhere near as complicated as air traffic. Ships basically move slowly, so there is less mental strain on VTS operators than on ATC centers that are handling many planes at once. On a busy day there might be ten ships moving at the same time on San Francisco Bay, but this could be spread over 200 miles, so most of the ships wouldn't be near one another. Captain Al showed me a very complicated map of O'Hare Airport. Seven active runways allow up to eighty-four planes per hour to land. Try doing that with ships that can take thirty minutes to turn around. VTS didn't tell me how to move, position, or handle my ships, which is as it should be because their personnel don't have the nautical experience to advise a master mariner. Other than a few odds and ends, like seagoing tugs or yachts, we never piloted anything as small as Coast Guard vessels.

The Captain of the Port's (COTP) duties involve enforcing port safety and security, environmental protection, regulating the protection and security of vessels, harbors, and waterfront facilities, anchorages, security zones, safety zones, regulated navigation areas, and water pollution. He can order ships to go to an anchorage, deny entry to the port, or forbid them to move in less than one-half-mile visibility. I always thought the Coast Guard should stick to things like rescues and security and leave the way ships are moved to the professionals who have been doing it long before there was a Coast Guard, which was started as the Revenue Marine in 1790.

I thought VTS was good for one thing: giving information. Regardless of what they told me, I'd always double-check because more than once they didn't warn me about other vessels I met in transit. Not knowing what's around a bend in a river can be dangerous. Captain Al said he had the same problem with ATC.

As required, I always checked in to get traffic reports, and sometimes I asked for weather along my route. If an anchorage was crowded, I'd ask for anchored ships' exact positions because we were forbidden to anchor ships closer than a half a mile to each other so ships had enough swinging room during tide changes.

In my opinion, VTS never prevented any accidents. For example, Prince William Sound had VTS when the *Exxon Valdez* ran over Bligh Reef.

When a jet taxis to a gate, a man with a set of lighted orange wands helps guide the plane. Captain Leland's comment: "Only required if other aircraft or ground equipment is in close proximity. Most places now have a taxi line to follow and a traffic light to tell you when to stop. . . . I bet a ship pulling in has somebody talking to whoever is driving telling him how many feet to contacting the dock." I told Al we never had anyone talking to us from the dock, and there aren't any lights to guide us. All we ever had was a simple sign on a sawhorse. Lining up the ship's bridge wing with that sign is about how technical we were.

Here is what it's like docking a large ship in a rain storm: Imagine it's the dead of night; it's raining and the wind is howling. You are standing on the tenth floor of a building that is 1,100 feet long. You are wearing foul weather gear with its hood pulled over your head, peering through the driving rain trying to locate a white Toyota pickup truck on the dock a city block away. Because modern ships' bridges are 100 feet above the water, everything looks small from that height. The Toyota has its flashers blinking, and its headlights are pointed at a three-foot-wide sign on a sawhorse that reads BRIDGE in red letters. That's what it's like conning a ship into a berth in Oakland.

Sometimes, as the ship settles perfectly next to the sign, the guard would move it. The last thing I wanted to do after wiggling 1,100 feet of ship between two other ships was to reposition her, but we tried to make the dock man happy.

There are no yellow lines to keep a ship on track, no lights indicating that you are approaching too fast, and there are no voices telling you to avoid traffic or that your engine has stopped. And there is no co-pilot helping you dock the ship. A ship pilot eases a ship into the dock until it rests flat against the wharf all by himself, all by feel.

Every time I approached a channel or dock, I had to know exactly which way the current was flowing and how strong it was and how it would affect my ship. No computer gave me this information. I could determine the current or height of the tide anywhere in the entire Bay Area by extrapolating NOAA's tidal data at the Golden Gate Bridge. As Captain Bixby said, "A ship floats on a pilot's memory."

Moving a ship today is done much the same way it has been done since 1829, when Josef Ressel, a Czech-Austrian, invented the screw propeller.

With a few exceptions, like naval and passenger liners, ships only have one propeller and one rudder. Imagine moving something as large as the Empire State Building like that!

In the last fifty years, the greatest advancements in shipboard operations have been the widespread use and size increase of diesel engines and the introduction of electronics like collision avoidance radars and computers, GPS, and Electronic Chart Display (ECDIS), which didn't exist in 1969 when I began going to sea.

Of course electronic aids are helpful, but there is an inherent risk in using them. The best way to determine what a ship is doing is to look out the windows; everything else is just an aid. Captain Bill Burnett, another golfing-pilot friend of mine from the Fraser River, B.C., once stood at a pilot convention discussing laptops (Personal Pilot Units or PPUs): "Look out the bloody windows, mate! That's where it's happening." Maybe I'm old school, but I like to think I had a "feel" for what was going on all the time. Pilots are becoming more and more reliant on PPUs, but there have been plenty of mistakes made using them, and PPUs can make navigating seem like a game.

Ship pilots don't have one-way traffic or the option of berthing facing the wind like airplanes; ships berth for cargo reasons, not weather. The only time I docked ships facing the current was at river berths.

Airplane pilots are rated by types and how many engines a plane has. When a maritime pilot goes aboard a ship, he expects the layout and electronics to be different, as well as the crew.

We are expected to handle every ship, no matter their size, how many engines, or what equipment is aboard. And there is no standardization on ships as on airplanes. Pilots have to know how to use every instrument no matter who manufactured it or how old it is. Airlines usually own the same type of planes with the same layout on each one.

According to Bernoulli's equation in fluid dynamics, ships in shallow water "squat"—as the ships moves faster, it drops lower in the water. The increase in draft has led to groundings, as happened once in under-keel Channel. After that accident, the COTP mandated that we maintain at least a two feet under keel clearance. At Port Revel we were told "shallow water" was anything less than twice the ship's draft, which made us laugh.

They didn't believe us when we told them how we moved loaded tankers with 50 feet of draft within 2 feet of the bottom. I timed my moves to be at any shallow spots along my route exactly at high water. Considering how different each ship handles, positioning them at exactly high water is not a science; it's an art.

Commercial aircraft are separated by at least 1,000 feet, are evenly spaced out, and land from the same direction. We couldn't maintain any kind of separation because in San Francisco ships are often within a few feet of other vessels, such as when passing dredges working in the channel, tugs moving tows, and sometimes thousands of small vessels.

It's not unusual for an inbound ship to enter the Oakland turning basin, then back up 1,000 feet. In this way, I made turning room for the second ship to turn around. Once she was turned, we both proceeded west to our berths together. Meanwhile, a third ship departed ahead of us. I took pride in doing these well-choreographed maneuvers that were risky in a sense, but if we didn't do them ship traffic would become congested, causing our customers time and money.

When the Bay Bridge celebrated its fiftieth anniversary, The Bay was almost solid with yachts anchored watching the fireworks. It reminded me of what Admiral Ernest King said after the Normandy Invasion: "There were so many craft involved . . . that one could almost walk dry-shod from one side of the channel to the other." Except in this case it would have been from Treasure Island to San Francisco. Several ships sailed that night having to thread their way through this phalanx of yachts without any assistance from the Coast Guard cutters patrolling for safety reasons! Yachts were impeding the ships' safe passage, a clear violation of Rule Nine of the Rules of the Road, but that didn't matter to the Coast Guard. I venture to say, if private planes crossed in front of 747s at San Francisco International Airport without permission, there would be hell to pay. Small boat owners, in general, don't seem to know the Rules of the Road. There are no Coast Guard license requirements to own motor-or sailboats unless you are taking passengers-for-hire.

In contrast, all plane pilots must have a license, know the rules, and obey them.

As you can see, there is a huge difference between airline and ship pilots.

CHAPTER 7

MY LAST SHIPS

On November 7, 2007, the Pilot Boat *Golden Gate* gently nosed her thick black rub rail against Pier Nine as I stepped onto her deck saying "Morning" to the deckhand who was waiting to see if I fell into cold San Francisco Bay six feet below. Actually, his main function is to prevent this because docking pilot Captain John Torres had a heart attack on a ladder and fell into The Bay. The *Inland Pilot*'s operator was alone and couldn't save Torres, who died helplessly in the water. His widow sued the pilots for negligence but didn't win. Now all our run boats used to ferry pilots out to the Pilot Station, to ships at anchor, or to Oakland have deck hands trained in first aid and lifesaving.

I stepped through the aft watertight door, taking a seat to BS with the boat captain, Steve Messenger, as he drove me across The Bay. When I arrived at the pilot office at 0330, I noticed several more ship departures scheduled after mine. I knew the boat would be busy in the next few hours shuttling pilots. My day had just gotten underway, but Steve's crew was looking forward to the end of their twelve-hour shift at 0600.

As we skipped across The Bay at 22 knots, the cold mist had reduced the visibility, so Steve blew the foghorn as a precaution even though The Bay was empty save for us. As the mist turned into fog, I remember thinking, *Thick fog in November, all the way into Oakland Outer Harbor? Weird.* San Francisco is famous for sea fog, but the majority of it drifts through the Golden Gate in summer, and it usually dissipates around Alcatraz Island. For thick fog to be all the way into Oakland was unusual, so my instincts told me it probably wouldn't clear anytime soon.

Off to starboard we couldn't even see Matson's Dock only a few hundred feet away as we passed it. In a short time as we approached my dock, Steve backed off the throttles slowing the boat, but it wasn't until we almost landed that we saw my ship directly ahead of us. I walked up to the foredeck as Steve deftly landed our bow against a wooden stringer piece directly aft of the ship's stern mooring lines. After hopping off, I waved goodbye and looked up at the 41,985– ton American container-ship *Sea Land Meteor*. Whenever I stepped onto a dock, I always looked at the ship's draft marks. These are white six–inch numbers painted on both sides of the hull with six inches between them. If the water is at the top of 30 or "XXX" on some ships, then the draft of the ship is 30 feet, 6 inches. I always wanted the correct draft because I had run the *Keystoner* aground, and I never wanted that to happen again.

As I made my way along the eerily quiet pier toward the gangway, I looked at Maersk's trademark: the ship's aqua blue hull. American-owned Sea Land, founded in 1956, was recently bought by Maersk, a huge Danish conglomerate.

Because the fog was particularly cold, I stuffed my hands deep inside my coat's felt-lined pockets to warm them as I walked to the gangway, just as I had countless times before. I was retiring soon, so I moved a little slower than usual, savoring what turned out to be the last time I would ever stand on a container pier. As I did, I looked up at the humongous black container cranes with Sea Land painted on them in large white letters. All their booms were vertical, which gave me the feeling they were saluting me goodbye as I walked under them. Often times when I arrived, the cranes would be out horizontally, slinging boxes over the ship's side as the longshoremen rushed to finish up cargo operations by sailing time. Whenever the stevedores were working cargo, I was careful not to get run over by all the semi-trucks swirling around the docks. I was also vigilant while walking under working cranes because longshoremen have been crushed flat by falling boxes! Nothing to worry about today, not a thing was moving on the dock.

I was alone except for the linemen who were sitting at the bow and stern in old battered Toyota pickup trucks waiting like sentinels. After they finished throwing off the mooring lines, they were free to go home, unlike me, who was assigned to move two ships. As the saying goes, "The ship doesn't sail without the pilot," so everyone was waiting for one last guy, me. The *Meteor* was ready to go to sea and so was I.

Little could I have imagined as I made that solo walk that life for professional ship pilots would change forever, and maybe not for the better. In a few hours, the *Cosco Busan* would fishtail into the San Francisco-Oakland Bay Bridge, spilling 53,569 gallons of nasty bunker oil (ship fuel) and sending many sea birds to an oily grave. The career of her pilot, Captain John Cota, was virtually over when the first drop of bunker oil gushed into The Bay.

The *Meteor* was 847 feet long from stem to stern. This might sound like a lot of ship and she is, but by today's standards she is only medium sized. By comparison, she was only 35 feet shorter than the most famous ship that ever floated, the *Titanic*. I told many apprentices not to think about how large a ship is. They must be convinced that they are bigger than any ship, so ego is an integral part of moving massive ships. If you lack conviction, you'll never be a good pilot.

More than forty-five years ago, I went with an old-time docking pilot named "Hambone" Bossingham, who was sailing the *Santa Paula*, an American tanker, out of Shell Oil Martinez. Hambone's trademark maroon beret covered his bald head, and under its floppy brim was a face full of deep crevices, from his relentless smoking.

On that cold misty night, I had no idea if I would ever fulfill my dream of being a river pilot. No one ever promised all the "wannabe" pilots, like me, that they would make it into the docking pilots' association, but maybe old Hambone thought I would because while exhaling blue smoke in my direction, he said bluntly, "If the butterflies in your stomach don't go away after six months, get another career!" I had worked on ships for years, but I had butterflies just watching him move the very first ship I ever rode on as a pilot observer.

The ship being so large and getting underway, in what I considered fog, made what Hambone was doing seem like magic. As I observed him maneuver the ship off the dock and then down Carquinez Strait, I thought, *One day that could be me.* And that made me a little nervous, but it would be years before I issued my first commands on the *Keystoner* in 1977.

There is no question about it, in the beginning I had butterflies. Whether it took six months for them to go away I don't recall, but they did because I learned to control my doubts. As a pilot, I could never second-guess myself, although a certain amount of tension is actually a good thing because it keeps you on your toes.

After thirty-one years of moving thousands of ships, I had the confidence to climb aboard any size ship, under any conditions, and do a good job. I knew what I had to do as I bounced up the two-story gangway. Several scruffy crewmen wearing paint-spattered coveralls were waiting for me so they could heave up the gangway once I got aboard.

Holding steaming mugs of coffee, they greeted me, "Mornin' Mr. Pilot." I touched my cap in return as the Second Mate escorted me to the waiting elevator. No matter how crappy a ship was, if it had an elevator I was happy because far too many ships, even new ones, didn't. Stingy ship owners think it's okay for their crews to walk up as many as ten decks, not to mention shore visitors and aging pilots like myself. If you just climbed up the Jacob's ladder from sea level and have to walk up ten decks, believe me, it's very tiring. A few ships without elevators put a little pilot flag on a chair halfway up to the bridge. Maybe they thought resting there might prevent heart attacks. It was a joke, but what wasn't funny was when Captain Mauldin had a heart attack climbing up a long ARCO tanker ladder and had to be medevaced off by Coast Guard helicopter.

The largest tanker I ever boarded was the 110,693 ton *Alaska Frontier.* She easily cost over $500 million to build, but her owners, one of whom was an ex-roommate of mine, omitted putting in an elevator to save money! These gigantic tankers have very high sides even when fully loaded, so after I climbed up 40 feet of pilot ladder, I was winded. When the Chief Mate started walking up the inside ladder to the wheelhouse, I asked him where their elevator was. I wasn't in the mood to walk up five more decks to the wheelhouse and thought he was kidding when he said they didn't have one.

I was scheduled to have shoulder surgery in a few days, and then swallow the hook on January 1st, so I was hoping for a routine departure. I wasn't superstitious as some captains are on their last voyage because they don't want anything to spoil a good career, but I have to admit I didn't want any problems in my last days.

Whenever I entered a navigation bridge, I looked for three things: the captain, a hook to hang my jacket, and the coffee pot. If the old man wasn't there, I'd ask the Mate who he was. I say "he" because I only piloted for one female captain, Karen Devine, the *Arco Prudhoe Bay*'s master. Many ships are on a "liner service," so they return regularly so I might see the same captain over and over. For example, I piloted the *Coastal California* nineteen times and the *Exxon Baytown* forty-one times. I knew the *Meteor*'s captain because I had docked her the day before.

As I sat in the wheelhouse drinking coffee and reading my paper, I was sure we wouldn't sail anytime soon as I looked at the thick fog wafting across the foredeck, which reminded me of snow. Every so often I'd walk out onto the port bridge wing into the cold breeze. The cold helped wake me up, but I was also checking the visibility to the west, where I had to move the ship. Occasionally I saw the green can buoy abeam of the ship marking shoal water a few hundred feet away. I could also just barely make out the silhouette of another ship sitting astern of us. I knew we couldn't move unless I could see all the way past the other ship, which was hundreds of feet behind us, and the buoy off to port. Once clear of them, my tugs would muscle the ship over toward the middle of a little turning area we called a turning basin. That basin wasn't round, it was more of a triangular shape so it could make for some interesting turns.

If I couldn't see, I would just be guessing. Even with radar I wouldn't be too comfortable turning a long ship 180 degrees in fog, being so close to another ship and shoal water nearby.

I never started a job in fog, I always waited. If I was underway and fog set in, I had no choice, I kept going. This happened once when I was aboard the *Exxon Baytown* heading to Martinez Terminal, which is one mile east of the Union Pacific Rail Road Bridge. As I moved her toward the lift bridge, what had been poor visibility changed in an instant. Just as the bow entered between the lift bridge's two towers, the bridge and the foredeck vanished as fog enveloped us. It was as if we had disappeared. I couldn't even see the sides of the bridge we were passing only 145 feet away! The only thing I saw was the railroad bridge's center lights directly above the ship's range lights as we silently slid under them. I had no choice, I proceeded. Once off the dock, I stemmed the current using the ship's engine as my tugs gently pushed the ship sideways until I saw the loom of the pier's yellow fog lights. As long as the ship was parallel to the pier face, I was okay. That docking worked out well, but I didn't want to start out one of my last piloting jobs in heavy fog.

The *Meteor*'s captain came up to the bridge just before 0500 and we chatted a bit, but we didn't bother with the "master-pilot" exchange where he and I went over the ship's particulars, because it was obvious we weren't sailing anytime soon. We decided to wait one hour, then check the visibility. I was glad *Meteor*'s captain didn't pressure me to sail, as some masters might have. After our talk I asked for the Pilot Cabin so I could lie down.

Just prior to 0600 I returned to the bridge, but nothing had changed except it was getting to be first light. We decided to have the tugs standby until 0800, so I radioed them: "standby to standby." At 0800 I came back up again, and Sea Land had decided it would be cheaper to re-schedule than to keep everyone on overtime indefinitely. With that, the captain told me I was free to go back to the City, so I dismissed the tugs, which got underway to their base almost immediately. Then I used my cellphone, hoping to hear Peter, the dispatcher, say I was relieved of duty and could go home. Instead, I learned I couldn't get a ride for a while because Captain John Cota was sitting in Anchorage #7, his ship was leaking toxic bunker oil after glancing off of the Bay Bridge. One of my partners, and friends, was regretting sailing and was in for a lot of heartache.

Several times I scared myself when I almost lost control of a ship and it nearly made me physically ill. I couldn't fathom how terrible John felt sitting alone on the ship's bridge after slicing a hole in her hull.

As it turned out, the *Sea Land Meteor* was my last containership, or have been on since, because I docked her the day before.

Despite having been on duty since 0400, I was surprised when I arrived at the pilot office, I was re-assigned to another ship. This meant riding out on *Golden Gate* to the Pilot Station. At least I would get lunch, and with all the mess going on, I was glad to take a ship to anchor, a much easier job, no matter her size, than to pilot a containership and turn it around and dock it.

At 1215, I boarded the Greek tanker *Cap Guillaume* (81,244 GRT). An hour later as I took the ship around Alcatraz Island, I noticed there were only a few oil skimmers working the big oil slick. Unfortunately, the current had turned and the oil was literally everywhere and the oil recovery boats looked tiny in comparison.

Two days later I boarded my last ship, another Greek tanker, the 40,038–ton *Cabo Hellas*. I realized I was wrapping up a very remarkable career and was stunned how quickly thirty-one years and thousands of ship moves had passed. It was a proud, but very somber moment for me as I looked out over the ship's tank-tops as I conned her in toward San Francisco on a glorious California day.

Of a more immediate concern than my retirement was the ongoing oil spill still drifting around two days post-accident. As I came under the Golden Gate for one last time, there were still rainbow–colored streaks of oil all over the central Bay. More oil recovery boats than on the day of the spill were trying to clean up the mess, but it looked useless. It was like trying to mop up water from a burst pipe with a tissue.

One thing that struck me as very peculiar was that The Bay's largest spill recovery vessel, *Spill Spoiler II,* passed me as I entered The Bay. I was surprised when she radioed Traffic she was going to check for oil offshore. I thought cleaning The Bay would be her primary mission. Thousands of birds live around The Bay and thousands of boats sail on it and as cold as it is, some people swim in it. I thought the authorities would be doing everything they could to remove the oil from The Bay's surface because once the oil drifted offshore it would dissipate. Stopping the source of the oil should have been the primary objective.

As I guided my last ship past San Francisco's North Point for one final lap around The City waterfront, I gazed a little longer than usual at Lilly Coit's magnificent tower honoring the firefighters of the great quake of 1906. Too soon the ship passed in front of the Ferry Building's famous clock tower seen in so many movies and TV shows, especially *The Streets of San Francisco*. Our clock tower is almost an exact copy of the Cathedral of Seville's bell tower *La Giralda* I saw in Spain. Columbus is supposedly interned there. I also got a kick out of standing on Calle de Admiral Lobo nearby.

Quietly the ship passed under the A-B span of the Bay Bridge, the opening closest to The City coasting by the AT&T Park off to starboard, where I attended many Giants games with my friend Bernie Stoler. It's a much better ballpark than a former tug base. As the ship neared the north end of the anchorage, I took some of the way off as we passed AAA Ship-way. I moved many ships in and out of their dry docks.

When the ship was just north of Pier 80, I ordered, "Hard aport. Stop engines," to a young Mate standing near the EOT. The helmsman threw the wheel over to port and the Mate rang up STOP. The engineers far below in the engine room answered STOP, and the RPM counter on the bulkhead above me dropped to zero. Soon the bow started swinging slowly to port, eventually pointing directly into the incoming current. The tired sea-weary old tanker lost all of her momentum during the lazy left hand turn, so I didn't need to give her an astern bell. STOP was the last bell order of my career.

"Okay Captain, you can let go your port anchor. Please pay out five shackles and hold on." I looked forward as the crew released the wind-lass brake, which sent red rust flying as the chain rumbled through the hawespipe down into the water. As the current pushed the ship backward, the chain slowly paid out until it took a bite and fetched up. Soon enough the tension on the chain slacked off, leaving it hanging in a big loop in the water. The ship was safely anchored exactly a half mile from two other ships also lying at anchor directly in line with them. The ship was calmly at rest after crossing the entire Pacific Ocean.

Smiling at the weary-looking Greek skipper, I said, "Captain, this is my last job. I'm retiring today!" He looked at me in disbelief. I was only sixty.

Shaking the hand of the last ship captain I ever piloted, I said, "Geia sou" (goodbye).

He grinned at me through a salt and pepper five o'clock shadow hand-ing me a bottle of Johnny Walker Red saying "Geiá sou." I received more booze from Greek captains than any others, and I always appreciated a jug, as we called them. As I let go of his hand, I said, "Efharistó," (thank you) for the last bottle of Johnny Walker I ever received. I called Traffic, telling them I was anchored, and gave them an ETD of when the ship might leave the anchorage. My voice choked a little saying, "Foxtrot, out," for the very last time, ending my long career.

It was a very bittersweet moment, but I was glad to be able to retire, more so as I live it. When everything went as it did, I knew I would miss such a big part of my life. It was a perfect way to end my career. A daylight job, on a calm day moving a tanker into anchorage—it didn't get any better than that.

As I waited at the top of the pilot ladder, I looked at the *Cosco Busan*. She had been repositioned and was anchored across from where we were. She was surrounded by yellow oil booms dripping with oily smudges. Where had they been in the first, critical stages of the spill? I looked at her sad state thinking, *I could have been the one to put that big hole in her while trying to expedite a ship move for a customer.* When I went to bed the night before, I'm sure I wished I had John's 0800 job so I could get a little more shut-eye. Now I am eternally grateful I didn't because it turned into a career-ending assignment. I might have wound up in Pilot Hell instead of Captain Cota. Being in the media spotlight would have been bad enough, but going to prison for making an error would have been intolerable. I often thought back to what might have been, and it gave me the creeps for a long time.

Spanning thirty years and 11 months, I piloted more than 6,100 ships, if my log book is correct. I ended my career without getting seriously hurt and with only a few incidents. I was no virgin, but I think I did a good job. I was one lucky son-of-a-bitch and I knew it, thanks to Captain Johan Sever, who took a huge gamble on a young man back in 1975. Rest in peace, my friend.

CHAPTER 8

DON'T HAVE AN ACCIDENT ON A SLOW NEWS DAY

On November 7, 2007, the container ship *Cosco Busan* sailed from Oakland into history. Pilots soon learned they could go to jail for giving ship masters navigational advice, something we have been doing without fear for centuries. It must have been a slow news day when oil marred San Francisco Bay's magnificent 400 miles of shoreline. In San Francisco, the epicenter of environmentalists, the spill made world-class headlines. Because pilots pride themselves on keeping the sea free of oil, this mess affected us deeply.

For so minor an accident, this had broad implications. I say "minor" in terms of costs and damages compared to some horrific maritime accidents, such as the *Amoco Cadiz* or the *Torrey Canyon*. They broke apart, spilling hundreds of thousands of barrels resulting in environmental catastrophes. America's worst oil spill, *Deepwater Horizon,* in April, 2010, spilled 206 million gallons into the Gulf of Mexico. Eleven people died and BP paid over $42.2 billion, so monetarily the *Cosco* spill, which cost $80 to $100 million, was minor.

The Coast Guard's *Incident Specific Preparedness Review of 11 January 2008* stated, "While this not a *particularly* large spill, the event received extensive media coverage . . .," meaning the press had a field day. They made it out to be a record, which it wasn't, but it definitely was an ecological mess. Three other Bay Area spills far exceeded the *Busan*'s: The 1977 Standard Oil tankers' collision spilled 1,121,400 gallons; SS *Cape Mohican,* a *federally* owned tanker, spilled 81,900 gallons (1995); and Shell Oil's refinery in Martinez leaked 432,000 gallons into Suisun Bay's wetlands. Those events didn't get nearly as much media attention. This doesn't dismiss this accident. No oil spill is forgivable, but I believe if the cleanup had started immediately, the spill might not have been as bad.

Mariners already knew the severity of spilling oil. It had been drilled (no pun intended) into my head for years from the time I was a cadet. Failure to notify the Coast Guard can result in five years in prison and up to $250,000 in fines!

Within seven minutes of notifying VTS about the collision , Captain Cota phoned the Port Agent to get help. By 0837 he phoned the COTP while pilots, delayed by fog, started calling every government agency having anything to do with pollution to get started as soon as possible.

Golden Gate finally picked me up, returning me to Pier 9, when I got my first look at *Cosco Busan* lying in Anchorage #7. We passed a huge multicolor slick moving into the South Bay because it was still flooding. I had never seen an oil spill so I didn't know what to expect, but there were no oil recovery boats and it had been almost two hours since the accident. It was shocking seeing oil flowing unabated. Oil booms should have surrounded the ship, and it doesn't take a rocket scientist to deploy one. I think the cleanup cost millions extra because no one arrived until the oil had dispersed. When the current changed, it just got worse.

California's standard for *"on-water containment"* must start within six hours, which is insane with San Francisco's strong currents. Six hours is a lifetime. Twenty years earlier, after *Valdez,* the government supposedly became serious about oil pollution. They should have learned time is of the essence. Despite running aground in good weather, it took days for that cleanup to start. After *Valdez,* specially designed skimmer boats were positioned around The Bay, supposedly manned 24/7 for instant deployment. *Spill Spoiler II,* in Richmond, was only six miles away. If she had gotten underway immediately, it should have taken less than one hour to arrive at Anchorage #7, so the oil companies didn't get much for their oil prevention investment of five cents per barrel imported into The Bay. It wasn't as if we piloted the occasional tanker like some ports. We move tankers 24/7 to seven different refineries and twenty-seven different liquid cargo berths. I piloted 1,751 tankers, not counting oil barges, integrated tugs, or Navy oilers.

The Coast Guard didn't even know much oil was spilled, reporting, "The *Busan's* chief engineer wasn't helpful to the initial pollution investigation."

Instead of learning how to combat spills, the government learned how to create more committees. The Bay Area has eight: The Coast Guard, NOAA, California Office of Spill Prevention (OSPR), a representative from Southern California OSPR, Pacific States/British Columbia Oil Spill Task Force, California Coastkeeper Alliance, Baykeeper, and S.F. Department of Emergency Management. After the 1995 *Mohican* spill, these agencies were supposedly ramped up for the next spill. Because the *Busan's* oil spread around the entire Bay. I don't see how they were any more prepared than before.

Marine accidents rarely happen but have high consequences when they do. The damages are enormous, and everyone looks to vilify someone. John Cota picked up that role, but in my opinion both he and the crew share the blame. Charging seamen for errors in judgment is costly and devastating to those who unfortunately err. This rush to judgment is symptomatic, not only of U.S. Federal prosecutors, but worldwide. Prosecutors want to make names for themselves by making human error grounds for serious prison time, so mariners are being criminalized as a result. Seafarers' Rights International wrote that 25 percent of 3,480 ship masters interviewed, from sixty-eight countries, said they faced criminal charges relating to marine casualties. Seafarers' Rights raises awareness of mistreated seamen providing assistance to them.

Here is an example: In March 2006, Captain Wolfgang Schroeder was incarcerated for six months in Mobile, Alabama, because his ship, *Zim Mexico II*, touched a container crane, killing an unfortunate electrician working on the crane. Schroeder was charged under the *Seaman's*

Manslaughter Act, despite the fact the electrician wasn't a seaman. The accident was caused by bow thruster failure, but Schroeder was charged with negligence anyway. Prosecutors demanded the maximum penalty even though as master he had an excellent safety record. He was considered a hero during the 1987 *Herald of Free Enterprise* disaster near Zeebrugge, Belgium, when one hundred and ninety-three people lost their lives. His efforts earned him citations for his heroism, but this wasn't taken into consideration.

CHAPTER 9

WHY DID THE *COSCO BUSAN* RAM THE SAN FRANCISCO-OAKLAND BAY BRIDGE?

How does a 905-foot ship wind up hitting a huge bridge in fog? Was it equipment failure, drugs, incompetence, a poorly trained crew, or bad luck? I will try to explain what happened and why Captain Cota got a bum rap.

At 0748 on November 7, 2007, twenty-seven-year pilot veteran Captain John Cota piloted the People's Republic of China-crewed 65,131-ton *Cosco Busan* out of the Port of Oakland. After traveling less than two miles, the ship's port side glanced off the wooden fendering of the San Francisco-Oakland Bay Bridge, ripping a 212-foot gash in the ship and resulting in a bunker fuel spill. In the end, Captain Cota lost his mariner's licenses, his career, and his marriage. Just his criminal defense cost $2.8 million, and he still went to Federal prison for ten months for making a piloting error. This was something I never heard of before this accident.

Between Oakland Bridge's "D" and "E" towers there is 2,310 feet, plenty of space to easily fit a 105-foot-wide ship. I didn't think a ship would ever hit it or cause that the kind of damage. I did think one of narrower upriver bridges, such as the Union Pacific Railroad Bridge in Martinez or the 270-foot-wide Rio Vista Bridge spanning the Sacramento River, might get nailed because of a helmsman's actions, equipment failure, or a piloting mistake. Compared to them, the Bay Bridge was comparatively easy to pilot through. Oil spills were always on my mind whenever I moved monster-sized tankers, sometimes only two feet above the sea bottom, or whenever I piloted through bridges in fog. I never thought about oil spills in relation to containerships. I thought any containership damages would occur when one of them smacked a dock, or worse, touched a crane, or worse, knock one over.

No matter which of the Bay Area's seven highway or railroad bridges I piloted through, I was always on my toes, to stay as close to the center of the spans as possible. I always put the ships' masts directly under the white lights marking a bridge's center. I especially liked seeing them in fog!

Moving ships in fog can be disorientating, so it's imperative that you trust your instruments and your judgment. Foghorns are fair as navigational aids, but they can be deceptive, and you can never really be sure exactly where they are in relation to the vessel. Sometimes, as in Cota's case, they aren't functioning at all.

San Francisco Bay is renowned for its incessant fog and wicked currents. When a ship is pointing into a current (*stemming the tide*), the current has very little influence except to slow it. However, when current works against a ship's hull, she immediately reacts, no matter how large. If there is five knots, like the day of the accident, the force is tremendous. Water doesn't compress, so piloting into Oakland can be a challenge with any ship because at some point, the ship will be perpendicular to the current, meaning the ship will be affected by it.

Many classmates were masters: Tommy Thoens and Dick Beza (Maritime Overseas), Gerry Hasselbach and Lloyd Rath (APL), Wes Winters and Bob Groh (U.S. Lines), and John Piatrowski (ARCO), to name a few. When they visited San Francisco, I liked piloting their ships. One captain I especially liked piloting for was Mike Bozzone, skipper of Matson's SS *Maui*. She sailed from the West Coast to Hawaii and I moved her over twenty times. Mike had his share of hair-raising experiences entering

Oakland Outer Harbor. He was so concerned, sometimes he called me to get the latest tidal information on what to expect on arrival. I asked Mike for a captain's perspective of what it was like entering Oakland during a big ebb current. He wrote, "Basically, those experiences were like a five star Disneyland ride in real time. I was a very happy camper when Matson abandoned the Oakland Outer Harbor Terminal."

Approaches into Oakland could be very nerve-wracking, not only for captains, but also for pilots. It's not our fault ships sometimes get squirrelly, it's just a result of the Bay's swift currents imparting so much energy it easily moves ships sideways or can cause them to get out of control. Ships often fishtailed, which can be very uncomfortable unless the pilot reacts quickly.

We entered Oakland 24/7, so anticipating how currents would affect ships is what we got paid for. I'm still amazed at how few accidents our pilots had as ships grew longer and wider with ever-increasing drafts.

Pilots routinely move ships in fog and foul weather because if we didn't, ships would soon stack up on the ocean or wait at anchor. With ships' high costs, plus unionized longshore or oil refinery workers costing thousands of dollars per hour waiting to unload them, any delay must be avoided. Shippers won't tell you this, but they want pilots to move in fog. During a recent West Coast longshoreman strike, it took over a month for the Port of Oakland to get back into sync.

In their lawsuits, ironically, Regal Stone Ltd., *Busan's* owners, demanded that the Port Agent should close *The Bay,* or the *Bar* as they called it, whenever visibility was limited. If this were the case, I wouldn't have moved half as many ships as I did because I was always moving in fog. Also, the Port Agent wouldn't have gotten much sleep if the dispatcher called him every time the fog rolled in.

I never maneuvered near a dock in fog unless I was already underway and couldn't safely anchor, which happened to me many times. If I stopped in fog, I took the risk it might drift into something or run aground even if it wasn't making way. Leaving the dock in fog is different. To me, departing in fog would depend on if I thought the fog would lift, which way my ship was pointing (did I have to turn the ship around?), the current's direction and velocity, and other traffic to deal with. Remember, ships want to move.

I was often pressured to move in fog. On December 10, 1979, *Enna G*'s captain begged me to dock his small passenger ship in zero visibility. I refused, instead anchoring her off Pier 80. Moaning his arrival was delayed at sea, he kept asking me to dock his ship. He said how much money it cost and his passengers were anxious to disembark. He said that on a previous visit, another pilot docked his ship in fog. I should have done what Captain Lee Fosse, a retired Puget Sound Pilot and golfing buddy of mine, did. Lee asked captains like this for pilot names willing to dock in fog so he could call them and have them come and do the job! In my case, I told the captain I didn't care what other pilots did. We both had to agree. His ship might be late, but as far as I was concerned, I wasn't. For me, sitting waiting for the fog to lift made for a longer day. My concern was the safety of his ship, the port, and protecting the environment. Captain Sever's business card read, "*The schedule is flexible, safety is not!*" This was something I lived by my whole career. Besides trying to make things run smoothly, the ship's schedule wasn't my concern. The beauty of being a state pilot was I wasn't under any economic pressure to do anything, unlike the captain, who thinks about schedules and costs.

I'm certain if there was damage to Pier 80, he would have pointed to me. Whenever I was aboard a ship I was the only one who wasn't an employee of the ship, so if anything went wrong, would the crew stand up for me? The next section answers that.

Once a captain lied after an accident, and it wasn't the pilot's fault. *Ferncroft*, a small freighter, regularly unloaded newsprint imported from Canada at Pier 27. She never hired assist tugs, instead relying on a weak bow thruster to dock. Ships don't have to hire tugs, but their owners are responsible for any damage. In the *Ferncroft's* case, whenever she was almost alongside, her captain always took back the conn. While rare, it happens. This same captain whacked Pier 27 twice. The second time, he blamed pilot Captain Herb Rosen even though every pilot knew the *Ferncroft's* captain caused the accident. A lie detector test proved Rosen's innocence, illustrating how pilots can get blamed even when they aren't at fault.

The *Thorssegan,* another paper carrier, hit the same pier when her pilot lost control during a big ebb tide. Dropping an anchor still didn't prevent damage. The Commission ruled "pilot error," stating the underpowered bow thruster and 800 HP tug *Polaris* were not sufficient. That made no sense because San Francisco agents order the tugs, never us. A captain who has never visited San Francisco doesn't know what size tugs to order. So why should a pilot's career be on the line because an agent might receive a better price from one tug company? It's always about the money; it should be about safety. This is economic pressure on captains put pilots in the position of convincing them that the tugs ordered are wrong. This was a pain, especially at sailing time, when expensive linemen were standing around. After the *Thorssegan* accident, I often insisted on more powerful tugs and used her as an example.

In May of 1994, I piloted the *City of Nanaimo* into Oakland Inner Harbor with the same *Polaris*, which in my professional opinion was insufficient for a 24,470-ton ship drawing 31 feet. I told her master she wasn't sufficient, having less than 1000 HP. Unfazed, he said his agent was dating the *Polaris's* owner and couldn't do anything! I told him he was crazy risking his ship's safety and my career to save a few dollars. He just shrugged his shoulders.

It helped to have thick skin because one of the toughest things about piloting was to stand firm when a job was set up incorrectly. It was better to delay a ship than get into a jam that could cost millions of dollars and end your career.

I think that Captain Cota's twenty-seven years of experience, the direction the ship was facing, the favorable current, and the fact that the captain agreed to sail all added up to why the *Busan* left the dock. Our pilots went under the Bay's bridges in fog countless times, so it's a reasonable maneuver with the right equipment. Captain Cota can be heard on the Voice Data Recorder (VDR) saying to Captain Sun, "You can single up, captain, *if you want.*" Cota also asked, "Is it safe to leave?" prior to the ship letting go. No one will ever know how much visibility there was, but I don't think this was the be-all-end-all as to why the ship hit the bridge. Tug *Solana* said she could see a quarter of a mile entering the estuary and other traffic, like ferries carrying hundreds of passengers, were active, so traffic was moving.

Twenty-twenty hindsight has shown getting underway was a cardinal mistake. Both the NTSB and the Coast Guard pointed the finger at Captain Cota, but by law, the master is in charge of his ship. He alone has the final say in whether to sail or not. Captain Sun testified he thought he might lose his job if he delayed the ship. This shows that he didn't know his own power as master. Also, masters can stop sailings simply by not letting the mooring lines go, so it's preposterous to think that only Cota made the decision to sail.

The *Cosco Busan* was facing west, was starboard-to pointing into flood current. She was in the next-to-the-last berth in the Inner Harbor with no ships blocking her, and no other large vessels were moving. Hypothetically, if Captain Cota had been underway and was passing Pier 56 and fog enveloped his ship, he would have proceeded out to sea as he did, just as we did whenever we sailed out of the anchorages in fog.

All the ships that didn't sail because of fog, mine included, had to turn around, had contrary currents, or had to maneuver around other vessels. Captain Cota had the easiest job and the one that would have sailed soonest.

CHAPTER 10

SHIP HAPPENS

Every day, pilots worldwide deal with things beyond their control. Some of them may have influenced events on the day of the *Busan* crash. Not to give Captain Cota a pass on the collision, but things go wrong on ships all the time, and a lot has to do with poorly trained crews, substandard ships, and equipment.

Ninety percent of the world's trade moves by ship, as well as 60 percent of all oil. In 2014, trade was valued at $20 *trillion* with more than 1.5 million seamen employed worldwide. In 2014, U.S. port revenue to businesses, incomes, and economic output was $4.6 trillion, or about 26 percent of the nation's total economy. Pilots control this commerce, moving the world's largest moveable objects at all hours of the day and night in any weather. They also deal with international crews, often from different countries on the same ship. Many of these crews barely speak English, as required by SOLAS Regulation 14-4, or have a common language among themselves. This can, and does, lead to misunderstood orders. Pilots also never know if the ship's equipment is in working order or if the crew understands how to use it properly. Pilots have even become ill drinking contaminated water aboard ships.

Every docking scenario is different and something pilots have to be comfortable with. The current might be fair or foul, but in San Francisco, ships move constantly unless there are unusual circumstances. During my career, the Golden Gate Bridge closed several times due to high winds, but ship traffic seldom stopped.

Working as a *team* is imperative. The bridge team must check on one another, including the pilot. The bridge team must help the pilot by ensuring his orders are carried out. This is why all orders are required to be repeated in English. The mate's job is to relay orders, ensure the helmsman turns the rudder in the correct direction and steers a proper course. Time and again, mates didn't pay attention and too often they stood around gawking at the radar screens as if they were TVs, failing to maintain a good lookout or the helmsman. The more eyes looking around the ship, the better.

This, however, doesn't mean that the captain interferes with the pilot. He may voice his concerns, but must have faith in his pilot or the whole system doesn't work. For example, a pilot might be anticipating a big current change up ahead of the ship, but a captain might think the ship is pointed in the wrong direction. By telling the old man my plans ahead of time, I made him more at ease so he wouldn't interfere with what I was doing.

The *Cosco Busan*'s crew testified that they had never heard of Bridge Resource Management, so they probably weren't paying attention to what the pilot was doing as the ship approached the Bay Bridge. If true, they were not backing up Captain Cota, as required. The officers admitted they hadn't read the *Coast Pilot, The Sailing Directions,* or the *Light List* prior to arriving at the SF Sea Buoy. Therefore, the crew didn't know much about the port they were visiting. They also didn't read the ship's safety manuals required by fleet policy.

In 1991, I piloted the empty bulker *Golden Farmer* from the Sea Buoy fifty-five miles upriver to Pittsburg to load petroleum coke. Petcoke is a bi-product of cracking crude oil. It's considered too dirty to use in the U.S., but okay for the Third World. This gritty, black, granular powder was the dirtiest cargo we ever moved. When the holds were sealed tight, the black, sandlike substance still drifted into all parts of the ship, even into my hair.

After a ship passed the U.P. Railroad Bridge at Martinez, I didn't have any wiggle room for poor steering, especially in the dark. The helmsman couldn't steer worth a lick, so I demanded he be replaced with someone who wouldn't steer us off the chart or, worse, hit a bridge. With all the tight turns ahead in Suisun Bay and the severe cross currents I had to negotiate, I didn't want to babysit a helmsman who obviously had little experience.

About an hour and a half later, the ship was eighteen miles farther up river at Riverview, where there is just enough room and deep water near Antioch Point to swing a large ship around. After my turn I'd retrace my steps back down through three-mile-long, zigzagging New York Slough to Diablo Service's to berth port-side. Just when I was about to order Half Ahead, I saw in the blackness the same helmsman I dismissed earlier standing at the steering station, ready to steer as if nothing had happened earlier. I refused to move the ship until the captain removed him for a second time. The captain didn't seem to understand how important steering was, not just for me, but also for his ship's safety. This constant disregard by some ships for their own safety always puzzled me. An American ship would have removed the helmsman, but I venture to say an American sailor would know how to steer, because in thirty-one years, I never replaced an American.

Most people wouldn't believe that during my career hundreds of helmsmen turned the rudder the wrong way! How can something as simple as "Go left" (port) or "Go right" (starboard) get mixed up so often? So often in fact that there are signs on the bulkhead directly in front of the helmsman with big arrows pointing "RIGHT" and "LEFT"(Port and Starboard on non-U.S. vessels), but they still got mixed up. To protect myself, I always looked at the Rudder Angle Indicator after each order I gave because I didn't trust any helmsman. I ran aground three times: when a pilot crowded me out of a channel; when I stopped on a shoal spot in the San Joaquin River; and with Captain Sever, but I never let any ship get out of my control over a rudder command.

If the captains understood English, I kept them informed of everything I was going to do. Unfortunately, with language barriers this quickly goes out the porthole! The Coast Guard requires all ships entering San Francisco Bay to have their anchors manned and ready to be let go before Mile Rocks, the first lighthouse on the starboard side coming from sea.

If I told a captain to do this and he told his crew in his native tongue, I was at a big disadvantage because I never knew if he relayed my order properly. This is why English is required, just as it is for air traffic control.

Time and time again I had problems communicating with captains who spoke limited English, just as happened on the *Cosco Busan*. It's not important to have a conversation with these captains, but it's vital to be able to convey what needs to be done with the ship. Not understanding the crew made a difficult job more so. The *Busan's* crew spoke some English, but did they understand what was really happening? Most of the conversation on the VDR was in Mandarin, so I believe Captain Cota's last job was an unenviable one. He was working the ship by himself with little aid from the Chinese crew.

CHAPTER 11

THE PORT OF OAKLAND

Needless to say, the Port of Oakland and the Bar Pilots are joined at the hip. If the Port hiccuped, we got a fever. For example, the Pacific Merchants Steamship Association, the ships' representative that hires the longshoremen, once fired a crane operator who insisted that there should be three operators per shift instead of two. Few jobs have two highly paid men for every position, but that's how they work: one man working, one man resting. The two-man rule is a holdover from when stevedores hand-stowed the cargo, which was a very labor-intensive, tough, and dirty job, unlike loading containers, where the cranes do most of the work. Not the I'd want that job, but it's a lot easier than shlepping cargo in a dank, dimly lit cargo hold.

Containers stacked on deck, believe it or not, are only attached to the ship's deck using a few steel tie rods and turn buckles. When one container is set down on another, the lock twists, marrying them together, allowing containers to be stacked without each individual one having to be lashed directly to the deck. They work well but are not foolproof. According to the June, 2014, issue of *Maritime Executive,* over 1,500 boxes are lost annually, and those that don't sink become hazards to navigation.

Because one of their union brothers was fired, the International Longshore and Warehouse Union struck the port for a week in protest, causing millions of dollars in lost revenue. This included us because we didn't move any ships into Oakland during the strike.

The Port grew significantly since I became a pilot, especially after container traffic grew exponentially with the People's Republic of China. We pilot tankers, passenger liners, bulkers, and others such as cable layers, but our livelihood depends on the success of Oakland because such a large percentage of our tonnage goes there. With containerships approaching the size of large crude carriers, this is a sizeable.

What once was a small backwater port has turned into the nation's fifth-largest port by volume, after Los Angeles, Long Beach, New York, and Savannah. Oakland once had a tanker berth with oil storage facilities in the middle of what is now Berth 24. In the '70s, that area was leveled to make room for the ever-increasing container trade. Containerization's biggest requirement, aside from container cranes, are acres of flat real estate to sort and store containers.

San Francisco had been *The Port* on the West Coast since the 1850s, but it lost the race to be a big container port as the dry-cargo merchant fleet converted to containerization and most of it moved to Oakland, leaving San Francisco's once-thriving finger piers idle. The old piers were turned into offices, parks, and other venues. Our pilot office at the end of Pier 9 was a working pier just before I became a pilot. In fact, I watched Captain Lee Brown dock an old steamship into the south berth, where we now tie up our Station Boats. He had a hell of a time getting her in due to the strong current. Lee was the first pilot I ever followed up a pilot ladder.

Except for Pier 35, our passenger terminal, only Piers 27, 80, and 94-96 are still used for cargo loading. The City front, once filled with steamships from around the world during the Port's heyday, is no longer. Oakland stole most of the cargo fair and square because San Francisco didn't have big container sorting yards or a direct rail link to the east.

Oakland always had a railroad spur going right into the port. San Francisco had rail tracks, but trains coming from the East had to travel all the way around the south end of The Bay to get there or go by ferry. San Jose-San Francisco commuter trains also use the same rails, which slows down the freight trains.

A few years before I became a pilot, I was captain and pilot of the Western Pacific Railroad's ferry *Las Plumas,* named for the Feather River Canyon in the Sierra Nevadas, where their trains pass through on the way to Salt Lake. She was 350 feet long and carried twenty-eight railcars, and was the last railroad ferry serving Oakland and San Francisco.

We moved railcars from the Oakland Mole at the end of the Oakland Estuary to Pier 80 in San Francisco or to Fisherman's Wharf. San Francisco was a busy port in the 1970s, when ships were still loaded by long-shoremen muscling the cargo into the ships' holds and securing it for sea. When the Port of Oakland expanded, the same rail spur we used became part of the Port's new integration plan to move containers east by rail. The Estuary, once a mile of riprap, was widened, and five new berths were built to handle the new megaships with lengths up to 1,250 feet.

When I piloted *Las Plumas* in the mid-70s, it was faster to move rail cars across The Bay by ferry than around it, so WP had a terminal near Pier 45 right in the middle of Fisherman's Wharf, where we landed every morning around 0600. After I docked the ferry, my crew lined up our deck's railroad tracks with ones that went up and down the Embarcadero. You can still see the old railroad ramp near Pier 45, long abandoned. When a locomotive showed up, it backed the rail cars off the ferry, moving them down The City front to different ship piers.

After the cars were off, my crew, and occasionally myself, would walk across the Embarcadero to a funky old joint called the Eagle Café to get breakfast. A few times, I caught them sitting at the bar drinking their "breakfast." When they saw me come in, they'd surreptitiously pour their shots into their coffee. I should have reported them, but I never did.

Pier 39, which was close to our ferry terminal, was developed into a world-class tourist attraction filled with shops and restaurants. The builders wanted to knock down the Eagle to build a parking structure, but there was so much public outcry, the builders had to change their plans. Instead, a very big crane physically lifted the "Eagle," plates, grease and all, placing it on the second story of Pier 39, which opened on October 4, 1978. My kid sister, Carol, worked there one summer.

After they moved the Eagle, it was as if nothing had changed, it was still 1975 inside. The décor and food were the same. The Eagle was different from the other chic restaurants there. Years later, I still went there to get breakfast. Out of habit, I looked at the well-worn counter for my old crew, but I never found them. By then, *Las Plumas* was scrapped and the once-busy piers were dormant. The Eagle is now a fish joint. What a shame, it was a great greasy spoon.

Crossing the Bay Bridge, you have to pay a toll heading to San Francisco, but it's free going east to Oakland, which should tell you something about Oakland. Gertrude Stein infamously said, "There is no there there," referring to Oakland, which was construed to mean that Oakland wasn't worth going to. Stein grew up in Oakland, and her famous quote haunted Oakland for decades. What she was referring to was that after thirty years of living in Paris, she found her house, her school, her park, and her synagogue were no longer there. So for her, there was no longer a "there" there. There is definitely some there now because The Port is huge.

In 1852, when the Oakland Estuary, which divides Oakland from Alameda Island, was only 500 feet wide with two feet of depth at low tide, California granted Oakland corporation status. In 1874, the Estuary was deepened and larger wharfs were built, creating a viable port.

In recent years, The Port expanded again, but this time they spent over $1.4 billion, most of which was invested in the new intermodal facility including dredging six million cubic yards of mud to get the channel down to 50 feet and allowing the world's largest cargo ships to enter. The dredging spoils were used to create Middle Harbor Shoreline Park.

The new park was once home to the Oakland Army Base, where I once sailed from on one of the first full containerships, the *Seatrain Georgia*. There were few shore side container cranes in 1974. She was constructed with a big "whirly" crane instead of traditional booms and winches. Our crane swung the containers aboard, dropping them into the hold, where the longshoremen using fork lifts slid them back deep into the hull. This wasn't very efficient, but it worked. She also didn't have cell guides that secure containers in neat stacks like modern ships.

Georgia supplied all the cargo for the U.S. Army's Kwajalein Missile Range in the Marshall Islands. Kwajalein Atoll, owned by a king and leased to the Army, once was the scene of a great WWII battle. It covers

750,000 square miles. The first time I sailed there, the pilot, who knew I also wanted to be a pilot, asked me if I would like to work on one of his tugs. When I realized that the main island was only three miles long by a quarter of a mile wide, I passed. Living on a tiny island didn't appeal to me.

Because the Atoll is west of the International Date Line, it should be a day ahead of the U.S. The Army didn't want any confusion about what day missiles would hit the lagoon after flying from Vandenberg Air Force Base in California, so they kept West Coast time. The Army told me every missile fired hit the center of the lagoon, but they wouldn't tell me how long it took for them arrive. I think it took less time than the ten days my ship took to steam there.

Oakland was the first West Coast port to have a container crane, but it was eventually outpaced by LA-Long Beach. 1900 ships a year call at Oakland with more than 2.24 million containers handled and growing, partly because of LA-LB port congestion and because shippers want to transship containers to Sacramento and Salt Lake City almost directly east of Oakland. Oakland is also the closest container port to California's vast farms.

Because of the huge increase in container traffic, double-stack railcars were developed, allowing one railcar to carry two containers versus one. Twice as much cargo passes through the same railroad tunnels that were blasted through the Sierras in the 1860s.

The Oakland Estuary is a dead end, so ships obviously have to be turned around. APL once owned the longest cargo ships we moved at 860 feet, which we turned off their dock, where there is 1,100 feet of swinging room, but it's not a turning basin.

When container companies calculated it was more efficient to have wider and longer ships and live with the fact that their ships would stay either in the Pacific or the Atlantic, they created ships that are too large for the Panama Canal's 110-foot-wide locks, which only accommodate ships that are 965 feet long and 105 feet wide. These ships are call Post-Panamax. As of this writing, the Panama Canal Authority is undertaking their largest project since Teddy Roosevelt opened the canal on August 15, 1914, by building locks big enough to handle "Post-Panamax" ships.

I stood next to the new locks and they are mind-numbing, even for a pilot.

Compare these new Post-Panamax ships to the ships that won World War II, the Liberty ships, many of which were built in the Bay Area. The S.S. *Jeramiah O'Brien*, one of two surviving Liberties, is only 441 feet long and 56 feet wide and weighs 10,900 GRT. She is homeported in San Francisco, and six of her could easily fit on the foredeck of a modern ship.

I was a transportation major at New York Maritime College, so I did an internship with American President Lines, located at the foot of Manhattan at One Broadway. All the big steamship companies, had offices on Broadway then, even White Star Line, *Titanic's* owners. At APL, I learned to run the shore side of a steamship company as opposed to operating the ship itself, which I was studying at college. Several classmates wound up running steamship companies, something I had no interest in.

In the 1850s, the forerunner of American President Lines was American Mail Line, which transported U.S. mail via the Isthmus of Panama north to California. Mail Line later merged with Dollar Line, becoming American President Lines, which was shortened to APL. Eventually, APL was bought by Neptune Orient Lines (NOL), of Singapore. This premier U.S. shipping company was bought by a foreign one, then they moved their U.S. operations to Arizona! An 1850s steamship line was now headquartered in a landlocked state. Companies will do anything to get out of California's anti-business climate.

Malcom McLean, a trucking executive, thought it would be more efficient to move cargo in units, not in break bulk as previously done, so he is credited with being the father of containerization when he started Sea Land Services in 1956. This, however, was predated by Sea Train Lines, which converted a ship in 1928 to carry rail cars to Havana. The *Ideal X* was the first full containership but she only carried fifty-eight containers. Compare that to today's containerships, that carry 19,000! It's all about integration: moving a box from a truck to a ship to a railroad to a truck. In essence, steamship companies became extensions of trucking companies.

After my internship, APL presented me with a framed photo of the S.S. *President Adams* passing Point Bonita Lighthouse at the entrance to San Francisco. In 1968, I'd never been to the West Coast, and little did I know that someday I'd pass that lighthouse almost every day of my piloting career and California would become my home. Point Bonita is right across the harbor entrance from Point Lobos (no relation to me) on, San Francisco side. Maybe it was ordained that Paul Lobo would be a pilot there.

On December 1, 1989, I handled my first mega-containership, the 905 foot × 135 foot C-10 *President Adams*. When I moved her, I never thought ships would get longer or wider, but I was wrong by hundreds of feet! This length or beam wasn't extreme, as we already piloted immense VLCC's (Very Large Crude Carriers) and aircraft carriers, but they didn't go into Oakland. I was the first pilot to learn how to handle these immense containerships at Marine Safety International's ship simulator in Newport, R.I. The new ships were not only longer, but also had hundreds of containers stacked five-high on deck, which older ships didn't have. When you look over the longer deck loaded with containers, there is an optical illusion that the ship is much closer to objects in front of the ship. When approaching something dead ahead, like a pier, it disappears far sooner than it did on the shorter ships. In other words, the "blind spot" in front of the ship increased dramatically. Soon these large ships became common-place—except we *really* had to pay a lot more attention.

Because there isn't enough swing room at APL, we came up with a plan to turn around the longer ships by going a few miles past the APL terminal farther up the Estuary to Grove Street Pier, a steel importing dock where there was more room to turn around. The commercial docks ended there because it's too shallow after Government Island. Ironically, the first container crane on the West Coast was installed in 1959 on Alameda Island at Encinal Terminal, when containerization was a novelty. Huge ships turned in front of the little-used container dock, which burned down in 2010.

A ship going to Grove Street would pass no-longer-used graving docks where liberty ships were launched during WWII. They are now used as yacht harbors, houseboats, and restaurants lining the Estuary. I piloted ships so close to houseboats I could see people waving at me from their bedroom windows. Mega-ships' bridges are one hundred feet off the water, so you can see a lot more, including Jack London Square, home of the *First and Last Chance Saloon* made famous by the author.

A limitation for the larger ships were two car tunnels named the Posey and Webster Street Tubes, buried 35 feet under the Estuary. They run from downtown Oakland to Alameda Island and limit ships' drafts to 35 feet. When Oakland dredged the Estuary down to 50 feet and created *Schnitzer Turning Basin,* we no longer used Grove Street. We called the new one Schnitzer because their steel scrap dock abuts the basin. Schnitzers, Steel loads old cars and scrap metal into bulkers that haul it to the Far East.

An area 1,500 feet across was created, allowing 1,100-foot ships to turn around. 1,500 feet seemed like a stretch to me because it always felt like a big ship took up the whole space, plus you could knock down two navigational markers at the North and South ends if you got close. Two hundred feet of clearance on each end of a ship sounds like a lot—except when you are on the bridge looking forward across 850 feet of containers. There is also no "bail out" room if anything goes wrong, and if the ship is not in the center, it could hit Schnitzer, Matson Dock, the old reefer dock, or the dry dock on the Alameda side. Few pilots in the world turn ships in such a tight place as we do.

Modern ships have gigantic diesel engines, some as large as 90,000 horsepower, which is nice at sea, but a concern for pilots in tight places. "Dead Slow" can create up to knots in an instant, which quickly eats up room in the basin, so you had to be very frugal in how the engines are used. And if you used too many "bells," you could also run out of *starting air* because ships only have so much compressed air used to start the diesels. I never wanted to hear "Mr. Pilot, we're getting low on air!" when I was in a tight spot.

When we first used Schnitzer, ships loading at their dock were required to move out of our way to give the longer ships more swing room, so we only maneuvered during daylight with little current and had extra tugs. These parameters were dropped and we started turning ships 24/7 with only two tugs, and ships at Schnitzer didn't have to move out of the way, which I thought a mistake. I was always waiting for a ship to touch one a scrap ship, but hasn't happened—yet.

The challenge of turning large ships around at Schnitzer wasn't to touch any of the "hard" parts like the Schnitzer dock or a ship sitting at it. I always made clockwise turns, trying to skim by their dock to get as much room ahead of the ship as I could get. I was careful not to move the ship too far into the basin or it could contact the old Coast Guard dock, which is now Starlight Tug's base. When the ship is 90 degrees into the turn, it's pointing at the two beacons north and south. This is okay except when there is any amount of current, because when 1,100 feet of steel is perpendicular to it, the ship acts like a gigantic cork in a bottle and moves bodily sideways so you can easily run of room. The trick to turning safely was to let the current pass by the ship as quickly as possible so the ship would not get set one way or the other. If you didn't have a strong enough tug or had a weak bow thruster, this could make for some tense moments. Trust me, it was no fun if the ship got too close out to anything, so I always tried to use my tugs to their best advantage. For example, if it was ebbing hard, I had my after tug pull the ship up into the current as hard as she could, allowing the bow to fall down with the current. Then I would go astern on the ship's pulling it bodily backwards up the Estuary. This allowed the bow to swing clear of Bay Ship and Yacht's dry-dock with plenty of room. This was the part I always worried about the most.

Last, the stern had to clear the corner of Matson dock, where there were usually one or two ships loading cargo for Hawaii.

Oftentimes, officers standing on the bow and stern gave me clearances that didn't add up to 1,500 feet, so I did a lot of extrapolation. I talked to my tow boat captains constantly, getting updates as the swing progressed. The tugs were right at the ship's water line so they could see better than the mates who were higher up. They kept me informed if I was getting too close at either end and were invaluable to me.

For example, one night a tractor tug was trying to lift the *Mokihana*'s stern up against a very strong ebb into the turning basin. Jan, one of The Bay's few female tug captains, radioed me in a voice tenser than normal, "Cap, you're getting too damn close to Schnitzer. You'd better do something! *Fast!*" She saw my predicament before I did, because the bridge on that ship was located on the bow. Just as the stern was about to hit the dock, I threw the rudder hard over and gave the engines a kick ahead, blasting a wall of water toward Schnitzer and lifting the stern safely away from the dock. Then I backed down hard on the ship's engine, which pulled the ship back up into the turning basin where she was supposed to be. Jan's warning helped me because from 650 feet away on the bow, I wasn't aware I was so close back aft. I liked working with Jan, she always had my back, but ship does happen.

CHAPTER 12

CHANGES

I d' like to make several points about changes that took place over the years I worked: changes in the merchant marine have been taking place forever, but in my forty-year career, as you can see by what happened at the Port of Oakland, the pace certainly quickened.

Steamships once employed about forty-three crewmen, but the increase of diesel engines and modern computers put the death knell on many seagoing jobs. Modern ships don't man the engine room at night because diesel engines don't have to be constantly tended to like a steam plant; therefore, the black gang is smaller. Also, diesel ships' engines can be directly controlled from the bridge, thus bypassing the engineers. Modern ships only have one Third Mate where there used to be two. The Chief Mate, in charge of the deck gang, now stands a watch; previously he didn't. Pursers, carpenters, day-men, and finally the radio operator, called "Sparks," were all given the deep-six. I never thought Sparks, who was responsible for all communications with shore, would become obsolescent, but today radio transmissions are automated. Sailors can now make phone calls in the middle of the ocean and even watch satellite TV.

When I first went to sea, I sailed on break-bulk ships with booms and winches used for loading cargo. On my last deep-sea voyage, I sailed on one of the first full containerships, the *Seatrain Georgia*. Containerization changed the shipping forever, so ships are no longer stowed by hand. Old break-bulk ships could load about 1.5 tons per hour, while containerships load up to 10,000 tons per hour. Everything that's not bulk, like rice, is stuffed into aluminum truck bodies and lifted aboard. Roughly 20 million containers are at sea and some 50,000 are abandoned every year. Some are even turned into homes. From an officer's perspective, it was a lot more interesting watching different cargos come aboard then stowed deep in the holds, as opposed to watching aluminum boxes come over the side one after another. With containerships also came the exponential increase in their size. During my first full year, I piloted about 5 million tons of ships, but during my last, I moved over 6.5 million, an increase of 30 percent for about the same number of ships moved. When I began, the average ship was 600 feet by 105 feet. When I retired, the largest containerships were 1095 feet long and 150 feet wide but have increased in size again. Another comparison: during the Battle of Jutland, the biggest sea battle of World War I, the Germans sank 117,025 tons of British warships, which was considered a catastrophe. Now that could be one ship, not a whole fleet.

As far as piloting is concerned, changes were inevitable after the NTSB, the Federal Government, and the Coast Guard ruled against Captain Cota. Only one month after the spill, California Senators Feinstein and Boxer initiated legislation, giving more power to VTS and $20 million more to those who were part of the problem! Politicians think they can legislate safety, but accidents still happen.

Talking safety is cheap. For example, many ships have huge red letters painted on their bulkheads reading: THINK SAFETY. Does this do any good when the very same ships have gangways that are basically just planks with loose ropes for handrails? Those gangways put out by Third World crews were subpar to say the least, and they are very dangerous. I not only hated those gangways, but feared them.

When I was a college senior, instead of attending a management class, I helped write a thesis about moving floating cargo-stowed barges that could be loaded onto ships like containers. This made it possible for Third World countries without expensive port infrastructure to be able to receive cargo more efficiently. A school alumnus who worked for the

United Nations Transportation Section asked my school for help, so two classmates and I visited the U.N. many times, not as tourists, but as collaborators. We had parking privileges under the U.N., which in Manhattan is a big deal. Working there was also a nice break from the regimen of school, especially when we visited the Delegates' Lounge, where Mr. Trout treated us to cocktails. Since I was usually broke, that was most welcome. I got a kick out of seeing delegates from around the world in their countries' native attire sitting next to us, and I wondered what they thought of our naval uniforms.

The first ship containers appeared in 1956, but containerization was still in its infancy in 1969. Containerization is very capital-intensive, requiring specialized ships, very expensive shore cranes, thousands of containers, truck carriages, and semis to haul them. The barge concept was thought more efficient because ports needed very little infrastructure.

These cargo barges could be loaded anywhere there was access to a port in the developed world. Once the barges were packed, they could be floated out to a ship, then hauled aboard using the ship's heavy-lift rolling gantry crane. Once loaded, they would be taken to countries without modern facilities. The barges didn't take up precious dock space or need special shore side equipment. The beauty was the ship didn't need a dock because the barges could be floated off while the ship sat at anchor and towed away using small boats, and unpacked later.

That system came to be known as LASH (*Lighter Aboard Ship*). It took a while, but eventually the concept failed because in the end it was more expensive to operate than conventional container ships. Many LASH ships were converted to full containerships, but we still called them LASH ships because of their design. In the beginning of my career, I piloted several true LASH ships such as the *Edward Rutledge,* the last one ever built in the U.S. at Pascagoula's Avondale Shipyard in 1980. She changed owners many times, becoming *Sea Land Reliance*, then *CSX Reliance,* and finally *Horizon Reliance,* captained by another golfing buddy, Jim Kelleher, who retired to Hawaii's Big Island to grow coffee! The last LASH was MV *Rhine Forest,* which was scrapped in 2007. Because they were all stem-winders, with their bridges located forward near the bow, they were not my favorite type of ship to handle.

On January 13, 2012, the Italian luxury liner *Costa Concordia* sank off the Italian coast with the loss of thirty-three passengers and one recovery diver in a needless tragedy. Apparently, her captain, Francesco Schettino, deviated the ship to salute a fellow captain who lived on the Island of Scole, west of Tuscany. The captain's poor judgment put his ship too close for safe navigation and touched the rocky bottom, opening a huge hole in her hull.

Obviously, this wasn't the first time a passenger ship sank, but in 2012? In terms of passengers on board and the size of the ship, this tragedy supplants the *Titanic*. Almost exactly 100 years after her sinking, when a plethora of rules had been implemented to ensure that this type of tragedy wouldn't happen again, it did. *Costa Concordia* met all these safety provisions, but stupidity, poor training, and limited language skills can sink any ship.

With ECDIS and modern GPSs accurate to a few feet, this sinking seems insane. What made this tragedy even worse was the crew's reaction (or lack of same), starting with the captain on down. Judging by news reports, the crew didn't act in a professional manner.

The panic among the crew and their unseamanlike conduct didn't surprise me. This was highlighted when the captain left the ship before his passengers, a violation of Italian law. While technically it may not be a violation of the Safety of Life at Sea (SOLAS) convention, Captain Jans-Uwe Schroder-Hinrichs, at the World Maritime University in Sweden and former master mariner, stated it's understood within the industry that captains must stay on board to direct evacuation. Schettino never heard of the expression "The captain goes down with his ship," because he had to be ordered back aboard by Italian Coast Guard Captain Gregorio De Falco, who didn't buy his explanation of why he deserted his passengers. Schettino actually delayed making the initial distress call by forty-five minutes, postponing the Coast Guard from going into action; and, according to court testimony, the Coast Guard first heard about this tragedy from a passenger's cell phone! The sooner you get help the better, forget your embarrassment!

Many shipping lines now hire multinational crews, which can lead to problems. As an example, on the night of the grounding, Captain Schettino testified that the Indonesian helmsman had trouble understanding his orders, and it took him thirteen seconds to respond to a rudder command. Worse, he put it the wrong way just prior to the first grounding. Thirteen seconds is a lifetime when trying to maneuver away from danger.

The shipping industry has been dumbing down the seagoing trade for decades, especially with the advent of computers, GPS, and other electronic aids. Ever since the space program brought about a quantum leap in technology, the level of professionalism among seamen has suffered with the skills necessary to go to sea weakened, such as knowing celestial navigation, something no longer taught at the U.S. Naval Academy.

I think some shipowners believe computers can do all the thinking and would rather pay for equipment than pay their crews a decent living or teach them the necessary skills, especially in emergencies that happen on ships frequently.

Flags of Convenience (FOC), sometimes called "Ships of Shame," are ships not registered in a company's home country. Thirty-four countries, mostly in the developing world, offer FOCs. Seventy-three percent of the world's fleet operates under this system. Companies do this for a variety of reasons: They have no obligation to the FOC state; they want to avoid higher taxes and skirt state or international standards; and they can pay much lower wages. This is not only bad for pilots who have to deal with them, but also for the crews themselves, many of whom aren't paid a decent wage and are forced to live under substandard conditions. There is such concern for FOC crewmen that Australia regularly monitors crew conditions because there are so many deaths on FOC ships. In October 2012, three crewmen died on the *Sage Sagittarius* while in Australian waters.

FOCs have had a particularly devastating impact on U.S. flag shipping, as the number of U.S. sinks shrunk because they couldn't compete with foreign ships, particularly ones from the Far East. So unless an American ship is trading solely in the U.S. or carrying U.S. government cargo, it's difficult for American companies to survive. Of the 7,863 ships trading with the U.S., only 89 are American bottoms! Only about one-third of the ships I piloted were American, with fewer and fewer as time went by. My first year, I moved 480 American ships, while during the last year I only moved 41!

The crews changed also. For example, over time, Japanese ships replaced their crewmen with Filipinos. Eventually the Japanese officers were also replaced, but with Indians, and now there might be Korean officers with crews from Bangladesh. The search for cheap labor in the shipping business is relentless.

Mixing nationalities has also made the crews' living conditions worse. At least with one nationality, they could speak to one another. I've been on ships where the captain and chief engineer were the only people from the same country. For the length of their contract, which can be as long as eight months, the captain would only be able to converse with the chief, and captains and engineers are famous for disagreeing. What if they didn't get along? What a long voyage that would be.

Here is an example of how diversified ships, crews are today: on March 17, 2014, the USS *Roosevelt*'s seal team boarded a North Korean tanker, *Morning Glory,* owned by a United Arab Emirates company. Her crew consisted of six Pakistanis, six Indians, three Sri Lankans, two Syrians, two Sudanese, and two Eritreans. How anyone can control a ship full of oil with so many nationalities on board is mind–boggling. I saw many mixed crews, but this one takes the cake, and I'm glad I never piloted a North Korean ship.

One winter day in 1988, a storm was approaching the Bay Area, so the wind was blowing like stink out of the south. Unfortunately, my job was to sail the *Ocean Commander* berthed at Oakland Berth 24. Normally, I turned ships at that berth to the left, but due to the gusty winds, I decided to turn the bow toward the dock to help counter the wind on the superstructure. Also, Outer Harbor is a dead end, so I didn't want to get two-blocked if the ship didn't turn around as planned. I could have refused to sail because of the wind, but I always got all my ships in and out of port, no matter how bad the weather, so I came to regret that decision. The captain spoke Chinese talking to the forecastle, so I never knew what they were saying. As I was backing the ship away from the pier, he said we had enough clearance when we really didn't. The bulbous bow didn't swing clear of the underpart of the dock, and a few piles were broken, but there was no damage to the ship. Thankfully the bow didn't knock over the crane dead ahead when the ship was perpendicular to the dock. This miscommunication cost $250,000. This sounds like a lot and monetarily it was, but on a $50 million ship, this is like replacing a taillight. Of course, nobody thought that except me, especially the Commission, which regrettably put a "Pilot Error" letter in my file. I may have made a mistake, but when swinging multi-million dollar ships in front of costly container cranes, it helps to have everyone on the same page.

One thing I do miss on ships is drinking different types of coffee from all over the world, especially Greek, medium sweet, so strong and delicious. Once I was with Perry Stiltz on a Greek tanker when they served coffee made their traditional way, where if you drank all the coffee, you were in for a surprise because the grounds are on the bottom of the cup. He surreptitiously threw his over the side, while I savored mine and came to love Greek coffee. Brewed coffee might still be poured on passenger ships, but some serve it in paper cups! When I think of all the beautiful china coffee cups I received as gifts from cargo ship captains, embellished with the ship's name and picture, it's a sad commentary about the white fleet.

Once I boarded a PAN Ocean tanker in Richmond, traditionally manned by Koreans, who were replaced with Bangladeshis. I was greeted at the gangway by the dirtiest crew I'd seen in my life, dirtier than the former crew who were no great shakes, either. The captain confided his crew received 30 percent less pay than the former crew. No wonder they didn't wash! That was one ship I didn't have coffee on.

Over the years, even the coffee changed, with brewed coffee served in china cups replaced with Nescafé Instant which I wasn't fond of, but I was addicted to coffee so I drank it, like it or not. Most Third World crews don't drink coffee, they drink green tea, usually out of an old jelly jar, so they don't know much about coffee, often making it with two heaping spoonfuls of Nescafé in a small cup. That made for a *really* strong cup of coffee, which I called "Filipino cappuccino," because half the world's crews were Filipino. I drank too much coffee and smoked too many cigarettes to kill time during long night trips up river. Eventually I quit smoking because it kills more than time.

As the years went on, other small changes transpired. Once, around lunch time, I was piloting a Wallenius Line's car carrier registered in Sweden when they served me what they called "sandwiches," which were really gourmet canapés, a real treat.

Compare that to years later when I piloted a Liberian bulker all night up river. Around 0700, I was hungry, so I asked for breakfast. They served me a fried egg topped with cabbage and grape jelly on stale white bread, which wasn't in the same league as the Wallenius ship, but I ate it anyway. I came to miss those European ships for many reasons.

CHAPTER 13

DAYDREAMS TO NIGHTMARES

The saying "Hours and hours of boredom punctuated by a few seconds of sheer terror" can easily be applied to ship pilots. Most of the time while on a ship's bridge, I was at totally ease and in control. However, there were a few times when things got way out of my comfort level, and thankfully, I got myself out of almost every jam I ever got into.

It may be hard to believe, but when I piloted ships 1,000 feet long, sometimes it seemed easy. The reason I am writing about these relaxing times is that there were other times when things didn't go exactly as planned. Piloting can be routine, but if a monkey wrench gets thrown into the works, your knees will buckle and your stomach will tie itself into a knot until you get the ship back under control, because when a ship gets squirmy, it can be downright frightening. Piloting is very demanding, but there is always a chance something out of your control will change a routine job into a nightmare. Of course, this can be self-induced if you make an error.

Whenever I piloted ships north and east of San Francisco, I called this "going up river." On most of those ships, if the old man went below,

I was alone except for the helmsman and the Mate on watch, which could make for a long night if the Mate didn't speak English. So basically, when I wasn't maneuvering the ship, I was alone with my thoughts.

Piloting involves hours of standing on steel decks, which can be tough on your legs; so whenever it was safe, I'd look for the pilot's chair, get off my feet, and relax a bit, which always included a cup of coffee and a long lingering smoke.

After my ship passed between the Brothers Island Lighthouse off to starboard and the Sisters Islands off to port in Marin County, it entered San Pablo Bay. The Brothers Light is built on a granite island about 900 feet off of Point Richmond. When the Coast Guard automated the light house, a BB opened in the lighthouse keeper's home. Whenever guests waved at my ship, I blew the ship's whistle for them, just as I did for tourists looking down from the Golden Gate Bridge walkway.

San Pablo Bay, thirteen miles across, is an immense expanse covering ninety square miles, but it's fundamentally shallow with a six-mile channel in the middle. Richmond's suburbs stretch out to the south, while Petaluma and Napa Valley sit to the north. There used to be only a few homes scattered across San Pablo and Pinole's beautiful grass-covered hills, but now you can see traffic lights out in the middle of the bay!

The first three miles of San Pablo are wide open and fairly deep, and all I had to do was point the ship at mid-channel buoy "E." If I was going to relax, this was the place to do it, as long as there was no small boat traffic or down bound ships to contend with. In thirteen miles, the relaxation would be over when I entered the Carquinez Strait, where I'd have to deal with five bridges within five miles. And the channels got smaller and smaller the further east I went.

This stretch was also a good place to hit the "Head" because it's impossible to use it when a ship has to be maneuvered. There aren't many safe areas to do this when piloting sixty miles upriver, but sooner or later nature calls. As Captain Gregg Waugh once opined, "Pilots are the master of the one-minute crap," and he wasn't kidding.

At the east end of the bay is Mare Island. The Napa River flows out of the famous wine region up to the north and empties into San Pablo Bay after passing by Mare Island Naval Shipyard, which began operations in

1854 under command of David Farragut, later famous for the Battle of Mobile Bay. It was the first navy yard on the West Coast and produced over 5,000 ships during WWII. After the war, it became a nuclear submarine base, which I liked because I got to pilot a few subs into the shipyard.

In 1945, the U.S.S. *Indianapolis* (CA-35), commanded by Captain C. B. McVay III, sailed from Mare Island to Hunters Point Naval Shipyard in San Francisco, then raced across the Pacific carrying the world's most lethal cargo, the first atomic bomb. The bomb was bound for Tinian Island, then to Hiroshima. After making its delivery, the *Indy* was sunk by Japanese submarine *I-58* as she steamed to fight in what was hoped to be the last great sea battle in history. Disastrously, only 317 out of 1,196 *Indy* sailors survived the sinking.

Ships don't stop like cars or airplanes; there are no brakes. Also, per Sir Isaac Newton, the sheer mass of a ship, which is built to go forward, once moving doesn't want to stop. When a propeller is going astern, it will not always stop, or slow down a ship. When a ship is moving above a certain speed, the propeller doesn't "grab," it cavitates, meaning it spins ineffectually in a bubble of air and the ship keeps right on moving. The best way to stop a ship is to stop the engines long before you want the ship stopped. The ship must scrub off the speed on her own. On heavily laden tankers, I often stopped the engines several miles from my destination. I only started and stopped them to control the ship's direction, letting the ship drift toward my objective. I approached an anchorage with too much way, and I used the engines at the last moment, the ship would just torque, then shoot out of the anchorage and possibly go aground.

When a ship is going astern, its stern moves in the direction the propeller is spinning because of the pressure differential between the propeller's top and bottom. The stern moves like the prop is digging into the ocean floor, called "Walking." If anticipated, it can be used to your advantage, but if it happens when you don't want it to, the results can be ugly. Many pilots have torqued the bows of ships into docks because of this phenomenon.

My first experience of not being in total control happened when I made the common rookie mistake of going too fast, which is probably the number one cause of maritime accidents. Until then, I thought I was a decent pilot, but my ship didn't slow down as I anticipated. Not only was I going too fast, but my berth was at a dead end with no bail-out room. It was a Catch-22 moment for me. If I didn't get her stopped in time, I would hit the dock straight ahead, but if the ship's engines went astern, and the ship torqued, it could have hit my berth and maybe knocked over a very expensive crane.

I already had an assist tug tied up on the ship's port quarter ready to work. Unlike some pilots, I always tied my boats up long before I needed them. I was running out of room with few options, so I had the quarter tug push Full Ahead just prior to backing the engine up. Fortunately, I was going slowly enough for the tug to have effect, and the ship didn't hit anything. After that scare, I never approached a dock with more than three knots of headway. This doesn't sound very fast, but piloting is all about control.

The Benicia–Martinez Bridge refers to three almost parallel bridges crossing the Carquinez Strait just west of Suisun Bay. The original 1.2 mile truss type auto bridge consisting of seven 528-foot spans opened in 1962, replacing the last automotive ferry in the Bay Area. On August 25, 2007, a 1.7-mile highway bridge was added east of the old highway and railroad bridges. Caltrans built the new bridge literally over our heads because we never stopped moving ships during construction. Talk about inflation, the new highway span cost $1.275 billion more than the old one!

The Southern Pacific Railroad sits between the two other bridges. After SP merged with Union Pacific in 1996, I referred to all three bridges as the Union Pacific Bridge or UPB. It's well used, and trains crossing the bridge was something we always had to take into account.

Nothing in my career gave me the willies more than going through this lift bridge, where the railroad tracks are raised vertically to allow ships to pass. I wasn't the only one who got edgy because at least one of our pilots pulled his name every time he was assigned a ship going through the UPB.

The railroad bridge worried me most because of its narrow width, vertical clearance of only 135 feet, and the way the current didn't set fair through it. I moved thousands of ships all over The Bay, and let's say I had a few "interesting times," but nothing compared to the experiences I had with the UPB.

It wasn't just the act of getting a large ship through the UPB. We also had problems communicating with the bridge's lift operators, so we formed a committee to deal with them! There has been a lift bridge there since 1930 (when there weren't even two-way radios!), so why we needed a special committee at this late date was beyond bizarre. Our main concerns were the bridge not opening when requested or trains taking longer to get across the bridge than the bridge-tender led us to believe. Because ships have the right-of-way over trains, pilots can stop them from crossing if it interferes with a ship move. It's easier to stop a train than a big ship sitting in moving water, especially if the current is pushing the ship toward the bridge.

Because bridge tenders work for the railroad, naturally they want to get their trains across without delay. I only regretted doing a bridge-tender a favor once. He scared the crap out of me by not lifting the bridge when he told me he would, so I advised my apprentices not to have any sympathy for them or their trains, they might regret it as I almost did. Also, there are electronic stops preventing the lift from rising if a train is anywhere on the bridge or its approaches, so the bridge-tender can't lift the bridge once the train starts moving across it. Coming through the Carquinez Strait from the west, you can see the ends of the bridge passing Port Costa, a former grain-exporting port that now is a little touristy town. If a freight train wasn't already moving across the bridge, it could mean there wasn't enough time for the span to lift in time. If you got too close, you had to go to *Plan B,* meaning aborting the approach, making a U-turn, or fighting to keep the ship lined up. If you made a U-turn, it was almost impossible to get a ship back in position to go through without tugs. If the span wasn't rising fast enough for my comfort, my voice would always rise an octave when I asked, "When are you going up?"

The UPB was hit or bumped into numerous times over my career. I came too close for comfort a few times. Most of the incidents didn't involve much damage, unlike the most famous one that involved Captain Leo Wuestoff when his ship rammed the bridge in thick fog, something I was always worried about.

Then, ships' agents hired river pilots directly so they were at their mercy to do things like dock in fog. This type of economic pressure caused many accidents, like this one, not just here but around the world.

On January 22, 1975, Wuestoff was piloting the tanker *Norfolk* drawing 36 feet 3 inches bound for Amorco, which is just west of the bridge on the Martinez side. It's so close to the highway bridge, if a ship overshoots the dock, it can easily hit the bridge.

Wuestoff was coming upriver in fog and ran aground near Anchorage 25, causing the ship to miss her tide window for a starboard-side-to landing. After refloating the ship, still in fog, Wuestoff tried approaching the dock again, but by then it was too late: the current had already changed. The flood tide overpowered the ship, pushing her into the bridge's fendering system and resulting in $750,000 of damages, which was a lot in 1975. The ship only weighed 17,000 tons, tiny compared to ships piloted to the refineries there on a regular basis. Wuestoff made two poor decisions: attempting to dock in fog and docking at the end of a tide cycle.

Captain Wuestoff experienced fog called Tule Fog, named for tule grass growing in wetlands lining the river banks. It's quite different from sea fog, being denser, and often hovers low to the ground or water. It's also peculiar because sometimes you can see the sky, but not the river in front of a ship. A few times, I was caught when I could only see the tops of buoys, but not the river itself, which is eerie. It's prevalent from November to March, can form at any time, especially after rain, and is the leading cause of traffic accidents in California, and a few ship accidents, as well.

When a pilot gets caught in fog in a tight spot, such as the middle of Suisun Bay, he has no choice, he has to safely anchor or keep going. Anchoring isn't always an option due to the lack of safe anchorages or contrary currents that can easily shove a ship aground. East of the UPB, there are few safe anchorages, even for small ships. One winter night, I got to use one.

At 0100 on December 21, 1986, I was assigned to sail the *Goldbond Conveyor* out of Domtar's dock forty-eight miles downriver. As soon as a ship was done discharging her cargo of gypsum rocks, which are used to make wallboard, Domtar wanted it moved out to sea. Gypsum is imported from an island in Mexico's Sea of Cortez, which is literally made out of the stuff.

Goldbond had specialized self-unloading ships that dumped the rocks onto a pier-side conveyor that ran into Domtar's plant.

After my driver dropped me off at the gypsum plant around midnight, I felt like Neil Armstrong when he landed on the moon, because as I walked to the ship, I left footprints in the fine talc-like gypsum powder that had fallen off the conveyor belt that went into the plant.

We never had a choice when ships sailed, but I never cared for sailing out of Domtar on moonless nights. It was the proverbial "Black hole of Calcutta" because that part of the river was inky. Except for light coming from the plant, there wasn't much of it, which made it hard to distinguish the sides of the river in such an isolated spot. During daylight trips you could see the shoreline, and it was quite pretty.

After I arrived on the bridge, in my white boots, I met a Canadian captain, and after introductions we discussed how I was going to take his ship downriver. Then I checked all the ship's particulars. I always double, checked empty ships' air drafts to be certain their masts would fit under the UPB because several ship masts whacked it and the Commission didn't like that.

The first time I sailed the *Exxon Baytown* from Martinez Terminal, I asked her captain about his air draft. He assured me that everything, including his radio aerials, was lower than 135 feet, so I took him at his word. However, as we passed under the bridge opening, all the ship's antennas hit the steel above us at the same time! They didn't do any damage because they were flexible, but they made a hell of a racket. I just grinned, knowing I had warned the captain.

I alerted VTS we were about to proceed down New York Slough. They replied no vessels were moving but didn't mention the visibility down river. I assumed it was safe to get underway, so off we sailed down the dark slough. Even though it was as clear as a bell, something told me I should have called the UPB directly because VTS omitted things in the past. Five miles downriver in New York Slough, I radioed UPB with my ETA. To my regret, he replied the bridge was socked in with tule fog. That was the last thing I wanted after getting an 800-foot ship underway, so I relayed the news I was going anchor the ship to wait for the fog downriver to clear. I sympathized with him when he got upset because I also wished

I had stayed at the dock. Tule fog can last for hours or even days, so eventually I would be relieved. I told him fog had not been a problem earlier, VTS hadn't reported it, and I didn't want to sit at anchor any more than he did. I came to regret sailing because it would have been preferable to the fun I was about to have.

I radioed the tugs running ahead to wait for me. It was ebbing so hard in New York Slough that I knew it would be a bitch dropping an anchor without help from a tug. I could lose an anchor and chain if I tried anchoring with that much current without a tug. I needed to get to a wide spot in Suisun Bay about a mile from where the San Joaquin and Sacramento Rivers join forces at N.Y. Point. An unbelievable amount of water leaving California rushes by a point that looks nothing like New York.

One tug put up a tow line through the stern's centerline chock. Once it was up, I had the tug pull straight aft to slow the ship so I had better control. Then I backed the engines, taking the rest of the way off. As the ship slowed, I had the after tug pull the stern downstream. Once the ship was facing into the current, the old man dropped the hook. I told him to pay out just enough scope so we wouldn't move. I wanted it short if we had to a chance to get underway again. We were pointing almost due east toward Sacramento, which felt silly. We were in clear visibility.

I thought it would be a long wait. Well, typical of a commercial freighter's captain who wants to maintain a schedule, it didn't take him long to ask when we could get underway. It was so clear he thought we should get going. Unfortunately, we were facing east but needed to sail west. Unlike the captain, I was in no hurry to move his big ship down Suisun Bay with a following current, in fog, and go through a small lift bridge, even with an empty ship. As I stated before, I didn't move ships when captains wanted, rather when it was safe. This is what I got paid for.

About an hour later, UPB reported the visibility had improved slightly, which unfortunately the captain overheard. This just made him even antsier to get going. Looking west toward Port Chicago, six miles away, I could just barely make out the base's smoky lights. I thought I had enough visibility, but I had a premonition I should wait longer in case the fog dropped again. Against my better judgment and knowing how fickle tule fog could be, I reluctantly agreed, "Okay Cap, heave up, let's go."

It's difficult to turn a ship around with a strong current in the tight space where we were anchored, so I used the after tug to pull the stern up river as the crew weighed anchor. Once it cleared the bottom, she started down Suisun Bay almost on her own.

Well, the visibility cooperated for about two miles, but as soon as we passed Mallard Island, the fog rolled in with a vengeance. I could no longer see Port Chicago's lights only four miles away. I was committed to going west in a narrow channel in zero visibility with only one possibility to anchor up ahead. I told the exasperated captain we were going to anchor off the Weapons Station, the last place wide enough to drop anchor and it wasn't that wide, before the ship entered a series of narrow channels forming a big arc in the bay with little wiggle room for error. It's hard enough to keep a ship in that channel with the crosscurrents, even in good visibility, no less with none. Approaching Port Chicago, the captain of the largest ship I ever piloted above Avon told me I was doing a fine job and to keep going. I was glad he was so confident, but I didn't bother informing him I never steamed down Suisun Bay in such thick fog before. I thought he was nuts to proceed when we couldn't see. I radioed UPB again. They gave me the same report, which still didn't change the old man's mind.

Once past Port Chicago, there is a series of short channels that form a horseshoe south of Roe Island. While in that bendy section, the ship never stays on one heading for very long. To stay in the channel, I had to make a series of left-hand turns and course corrections, which in fog is a neat trick.

I hardly moved from the radar. I stood glued to the port side radar while the captain, off to my right, stood over the other. As we proceeded, I tried kissing each port hand buoy with the hull because the strong ebb was shoving the ship right or away from them. If I made even the slightest error, the ship would slide directly out of the channel. Whenever I thought we were cleared a buoy, judging by the radar data, I'd peer down the hull at the water. In the drifting mist I could barely make out each buoy's red blinking light as we missed it by mere feet. As I cleared each one, I'd turn away from the old man, quietly letting out a sigh of relief.

The end of the big curve is a one-mile run straight down Point Edith Range, which has range lights ahead and astern that help vessels stay in the channel. However, without being able to see them, it's extremely difficult to judge if the ship is setting, especially with the cross crosscurrent runs across the channel.

The last turn before the bridge was about 20 degrees to starboard after passing #9 buoy, about 1.5 miles from the bridge. The strong ebb was setting the ship to the right toward the buoy, so I delayed my turn until the hull almost touched it, then ordered hard right rudder and Full Ahead, shoving the stern away from the buoy. Looking in the radar, I pointed the ship at the #7 up ahead, steadying on 250, which put the ship almost parallel to Avon Wharf.

As we slipped past the tanker dock, the only thing I saw was the glow of a few amber lights off to port. I called the bridge-tender one last time, hoping to hear good news. Instead, I received the same comeback, "Bout a half a mile, Cap," which didn't help my nerves.

The ebb, at maximum strength, was pushing the ship from directly astern, creating too much speed, so I ordered Dead Slow. I hoped that wouldn't cause loss of steering control, but I liked having one or two bells up my sleeve in case I had to give the ship a big kick in order to get the bow swinging in the current.

Just then, VTS advised that *Solana,* towing a barge, was approaching the bridge from the west. They said she would stay to the north, but this was just something else to worry about. I hoped she would, but who knew? Boats were always saying one thing, then doing something else.

I was running out of sea room if I couldn't see the bridge's center lights, but by then it really didn't make any difference. I had to go for the bridge opening because the tug was now blocking me from rounding up into the current if I decided to bail.

Because of all the problems with ships and tugs touching the bridge, the COTP mandated a minimum of a half mile visibility to transit through the three bridges. As much as I hated Coast Guard rules, I wished he made it a one-mile rule because you need to be lined up well before half a mile to go through properly.

Doubting the bridge-tender's eyesight, I asked *Solana* for her visibility because it didn't seem as if there was even one-tenth of a mile and I hadn't seen a thing since heaving the anchor, except Avon's lights. Why would I doubt the bridge-tender when we had to have a committee to deal with them? Then again, why would he give me the wrong visibility? It would be his ass if I hit the bridge and his little house fell down.

I was looking into the radar when the *Solana* radioed that he could see my bow, which perplexed me. I radioed back, "How the hell can you see my bow? I can't see it myself!" I was less than a mile away and on edge. Entering the bridge with an underpowered ship with ebb can be tricky even in clear weather. If the current pushes on the ship's quarter, you can lose control. It's as if a tug were pushing on the ship at the wrong time.

The bow had to be slightly north of the entrance or the current would set us right down on the south tower. Even with radar it isn't that easy hitting the center of the small bridge opening.

With my heart rate up and doubting the tug, I raised my eyes from the radar to see if indeed the fog had lifted. There dead ahead were the bridge's center lights as clear as crystal. I also saw *Solana*'s running lights off to starboard. The ship, despite my doubts, was perfectly positioned. In mere minutes she slid directly under the middle lights, much to my relief. My heart rate corrected itself because I could see all the way to Ozol several miles ahead through the bridge opening. Once past the bridges, I didn't care if we had more fog because the next thirty-five miles were nothing like going through Suisun Bay.

I slumped into the pilot chair, asked for a cup of coffee, lit a cigarette, and asked for more speed. I had had enough and wanted to get the hell off as soon as I could. At least the old man was happy.

CHAPTER 14

OTHER TALES OF THE UNION PACIFIC BRIDGE AND SAM DAVIES

I cannot believe the number of mishaps that occurred at the Union Pacific Railroad Bridge, especially several close calls that happened to me. Ships ran aground approaching it, turning off it and in the middle of the channel near it and two did major damage to it We had one ship lose her engines, scrapping it, on the way through, and another that landed on it. This does not include the ships that hit it with their masts!

I had two other events that, quite frankly, scared me. The interesting thing is both of them had to do with Samuel Davies. I wouldn't exactly say they were his fault, but it was strange that twice when I was scared out of my wits he was involved.

When I first started my quest to become a pilot, there were two groups of pilots: San Francisco Bar Pilots Association and California Inland Pilots Association (CIPA). The CIPA was a loose association that did most of the ship docking and moved ships upriver to Sacramento and Stockton until 1984, when the two groups merged. The CIPA came into being after a tug boat strike in the '70s. Because all the tugs were idle, the Red Stack

Tug employee pilots started docking ships without tugs, so after the strike, some of those pilots decided to be independent. This docking pilot system is still prevalent on the East Coast, where sea pilots bring ships into port and docking pilots come aboard and park them. The docking pilot is often an employee of the tug company supplying the tugs for the ship.

In 1984, all the docking pilots were absorbed into the Bar Pilots' Association, so all pilots had to pilot ships in from sea and dock them no matter what their final destination was except those going to Stockton and Sacramento.

Before the merger, river pilots competed to get Stockton/Sacramento jobs because they paid well. After, some of those same pilots thought the trip from the central bay to Sacto/Stockton was too long, especially in winter with tule fog. I was always a sea pilot, but I agreed with them, except I always thought I'd rather be stuck on a ship leaning on a river bank in fog than have had some of the hairy moments I had getting on and off ships at sea in raging seas. Chesapeake Bay Pilots pilot ships for up to twelve hours, so it's not unreasonable to move a ship with only one pilot from Stockton down to the Bay. Also, no river pilots were ever, to my knowledge, hurt changing pilots at New York Point, unlike at sea, where guys regularly fell into the ocean and were injured, maimed, or even died. The only river pilot who ever fell into the river was Dennis Welch, when his ladder parted in two. He got wet but was unhurt.

To give the river pilots a break, the Association agreed to buy and locate a new run boat, *Pittsburg,* in the Pittsburg Marina fifty-three miles from the sea Pilot Station. After that, about twelve of our pilots specialized in piloting ships above NYP. I called them the *River Pilots.*

Prior our apprentice program, no one was paid to ride for experience. Not only did we have to find out who was taking what ship where, we also had to bother individual pilots and convince them to take us along. It wasn't easy, but it was part of the system if you wanted to be a San Francisco pilot. Today's apprentices are well paid, transportation and schooling are covered, they earn paid time off, and the Ops pilot schedules them.

Before the merger, ship agents hired specific docking pilots for specific ships. Pilots like Gar Long even worked for specific companies like APL, while Swede Anderson did Delta Lines' ships.

Because I wanted to become a docking pilot, I thought working in the CIPA office was ideal to get my foot in the door, so I took their dispatcher's job. Dispatching turned out to be tougher job than I anticipated. Some pilots thought that they were getting screwed by not getting enough jobs, or whined about those who got more jobs than they. I got caught in the crossfire. I couldn't figure out this sort of bickering, so I didn't last long. For the first, and only, time, I was fired. I didn't see it coming, so naturally I thought my pilot future was over.

The day I was canned, Captain Clarke, whom I considered a friend, walked into the office after he finished a ship move as I was cleaning out my desk. When I told him I was sacked, he was as surprised as I was. I don't know if it was pity, but being the great guy he was, he took me to a waterfront bar overlooking Pier 35's passenger ship terminal, where we had had a few a "heave-aheads" in the past. I was certain my drink with Al would be my last one with him, but like many other things in my pilot quest, I was wrong. Al tried consoling me, but I got loaded feeling sorry for myself. Despite the fact that I was fired by his company, he always supported my efforts, writing me a letter of recommendation, and attended a party I threw when I became a Bar Pilot. I was sorry when he went out with the tide.

Notwithstanding Al, I thought I had run hard aground, but what really happened was the CIPA pilot who fired me did me a favor. Of course, I was disappointed, but with Captain Sever's assistance, I changed course toward becoming a sea pilot. Getting into the Bar Pilots was a huge step up the pilot ladder from docking pilot, because the Bar Pilots had been in business since statehood, so they had more prestige, had a stronger organization, and earned a pension; and agents never chose which Bar Pilot moved their ships, so we never fought over jobs.

In 1984, the state mandated all docking pilots had to buy into our company, so there was only one pilot organization. The day of the merger was wonderful for me. The docking pilots had to buy into my corporation, so I always felt the CIPA pilot who instigated my firing gave me the buy-in money himself. I always wondered what that SOB thought when he paid me, but by then I didn't care, he was ripple on a vast ocean. I bought my first Mercedes with his money!

To be a pilot you need a Coast Guard unlimited tonnage first class pilot license for the entire Bay, which covers about 200 miles of waterways and 184 different docks. Because of my piloting experience with the Corps, I was serious about becoming a pilot. That experience allowed me to sit for many parts of the exam, but I wasn't finished. I needed rides into places like Redwood City, Richmond Inner Harbor, and Stockton. To obtain this, I rode along with any pilot who let me. I had a few favorites who taught me the art of piloting and were nice, but there were also jerks, like Captain Samuel Davies, who tried to discourage me by saying, "Why on earth do you want to be a pilot? The hours stink and your life is not your own." I kept my mouth closed because I thought it was the best job in the world, and I still do. Nothing compares to being in charge of moving a huge ship.

Davies was a Brit who had this cheery exterior personality, but I don't think he liked, or trusted, the other pilots. He was nervous they might steal his jobs because all the pilots were literally at the mercy of the ships' agents. The CIPA tried keeping out competition, and I didn't exactly blame them, I just wanted to be a pilot, so I did whatever it took to get a leg. I learned one thing from the CIPA. That was they would kill their own young to get jobs, and Davies was no exception.

I rode with any pilot who allowed me to, and I mean *any,* and occasionally that meant Davies. I stayed away from him because I wouldn't learn much with him because he didn't want to teach me. Sometimes I had no choice because he was the only pilot going where I needed trips. I rode with him no matter what I thought of him personally, just as I'm sure some of my apprentices did with me.

He was strange for many reasons. Once on a Japanese chip-ship he didn't say a word to me the entire seventy-six miles up to Sacramento. It wasn't as if he didn't like to talk, because he talked nonstop to the crew, he just didn't like talking to me, so that eight-hour trip was a long day. Pilots are famous for spinning sea stories, and I told plenty myself if the crew understood me. The longer I worked, the fewer conversations I had with Third World crews, unlike Davies, who'd talk to the windows if no one else was listening.

My first professional run-in with Davies happened when I was piloting the *Transatlantic,* a car carrier, into Richmond Inner Harbor. Car carriers have a lot of freeboard, and the navigation bridge is located near the bow, not the stern, like most other ships. This can make for some interesting piloting because it's trickier to tell when a ship is swinging, since most of the ship is aft of the navigation bridge.

That night as I passed Alcatraz, VTS informed me that Unit 30 (Davies) was in Richmond Inner Harbor ready to get underway. Because of the strong currents, sharp turns at the entrance, and how narrow it is, two ships cannot pass safely in Richmond except near a no-longer-used dock called Parr 3, where an outbound ship could wait out of the channel. I called Davies on Channel 13, telling him I was already committed and for him to wait inside and not get underway. I had the right of way, but as it turned out, I should have waited for him. He replied he wanted to get underway, but he would stay by Parr 3. I agreed, except he lied.

I kept my ship moving into Southampton Channel until I was off Chevron Long Wharf, where I made a wide swing to the right so I wouldn't get set on red Buoy #2, which was marking the entrance to the Inner Harbor. Once I straightened the ship out, the strong ebb from astern caused the ship to pick up speed, and at the same time she moved bodily to the right of the range lights I was using to guide me in.

My next move was to swing very close aboard green Buoy #3 on my port hand, or the ship would slide south right out the channel. Just as I was getting ready to turn, I saw a green running light and a white mast head light moving quickly out of Richmond. This threw me a curve ball, because I'd never heard of two large ships meeting in Richmond before, and two were about to meet at about the worst possible place imaginable!

Davies hadn't waited, and instead he came out heading directly at me like a game of Chicken; but instead of cars, it was big ships! He shouldn't have gotten under way, but the least he could have done was move as far over to his right as possible to avoid hitting me. Instead, he stayed in the middle of the channel. I was so intent on maneuvering around him, I couldn't yell at him. Boom! The wicked current took control, shoving my ship out of the channel and sliding to an inglorious halt as Davies steamed past me. He took his half out of the middle, which I'm convinced he did on purpose! I couldn't believe he risked two ships to save time or whatever he was thinking.

As the ship sat in the mud, I fruitlessly tried using the engines and the two tugs I had with me, but nothing budged the ship. The ebb had her pinned. Despite my vain attempts, she never moved an inch. After I gave up, it dawned on the Chinese captain, who was wearing a bright red hat with "Captain" embroidered on it, that we were not proceeding.

Looking at me as if nothing were wrong, he said, "No moving?" A slight understatement!

"Nope Cap, she's hard aground," I said in disgust, thinking of Davies.

With that, without asking me, the crew turned on all the bridge's fluorescent lights and started playing Mahjong right on the chart table. Turning on the bridge lights destroys night vision, so you can't see outside, but the crew could not have cared less we were aground. In fact, they didn't even plot our position or ask what was going to happen to their vessel. I sat there with egg on my face feeling like it was one of the worst days of my life while the crew happily played their game. Contemplating my predicament, I thought, *This is okay. They don't seem the least bit upset about being aground!* I had only been aground with Captain Sever, so I wasn't quite sure how the crew was supposed to behave. *Not like this,* I thought.

I only ran aground one other time in my career, in 1989 in N.Y. Slough. She, the *Sun Rose,* was also Chinese-crewed. I experienced this same sort of naïveté from the crew, who didn't seem the least bit concerned their ship might have a big hole in her hull or be taking on water. Thankfully, there are no rocks there.

During that episode, despite being aground, the old man disappeared without telling me. Once I was certain the ship was stuck until another tug showed up. I radioed Traffic, telling them that we were blocking N.Y. Slough and for other ships to stand clear. Not seeing the old man, I asked the Mate where he was. He just shrugged. I was stunned that any captain would leave his bridge with his ship aground. Frustrated, I went below to inform him that the Coast Guard might be coming to inspect the ship. Instead of finding someone concerned about his ship, I found the captain with his feet on his desk, holding a water glass of brown liquid with half a bottle of Johnny Walker sitting near his feet. Even though he thought it was happy hour, I asked him if he was drinking. He smiled, "Whiskey!" like it was a big joke. I hadn't had a cigarette in two years, but I was so furious at being aground, and seeing him having a cocktail only made it worse. I asked him for a butt and went right back to smoking full steam ahead and didn't quit again for several more years.

With *Transatlantic* sitting on South Hampton Shoal, I felt helpless, so I called Captain Clarke for words of wisdom. All Al said was, "Get her off the way you got her on."

When the tide finally changed, I refloated the ship, headed into Richmond Canal Industrial to the dock, turned her around, and parked her just like a normal day. When we finished, the captain's mood changed; he wanted me to sign a bunch of papers, which I politely refused, telling him to talk to my lawyer which (I didn't have one then).

The grounding got me a nasty letter from the Commission. In those days, there were no drug tests. Today, I would self-test, then go to a certified lab to get drug-tested. Now you would also call your lawyer, even before the Coast Guard. If you contacted them first, they might get you to admit to something, knowing you are under duress. I carried a list of admiralty lawyers with me just in case.

I took all the blame and learned you couldn't always trust what pilots told you.

Sacramento and Stockton once exported logs and wood chips before the tree huggers put a stop to that. Unfortunately, the lumber industry lost a number of its jobs. Ships once full of logs are no more, and a state full of trees imports wood from New Zealand.

I just went where the dispatcher sent me, but I wasn't crazy about changing pilots at New York Point, especially in the middle of the night, when it seemed most of the Sacramento and Stockton jobs took place. NYP was also a long drive, particularly during commute hours, and it could be very foggy in the winter. Also, I wasted too much my time waiting around on our small boat when the river pilot's ETA was wrong. I prided myself on giving accurate ETAs.

At 0200 in November, 1991, I jumped onto the *Pittsburg* and motored out to relieve Davies from piloting the fully loaded Indian log carrier, *Lok Priti,* out of Sacramento.

The first fun part about a log carrier was trying to get up to the ship's bridge over all the logs that were lashed 20 feet high above the main deck using wires, chains, and turnbuckles. There were also large vertical metal stanchions that helped prevent logs from going over the side. Once aboard, I had to climb over the wet logs via a crude wooden walkway the longshoremen built out of rough lumber. No matter how primitive they were, they were better than walking over wet logs.

After Davies and I exchanged information, I learned the ship was deeper in the water than I'd been told by our office. It was also ebbing like hell, and the water level was falling quickly due to a full moon. If I had known she was going to be so deep, I could have refused to take her down, which was always my call. This wasn't the first time an agent fudged the ship's draft to help the ship get more cargo on board.

The tidal conditions meant the farther west we sailed, the closer the ship got to the bottom and the closer we got, the more difficult it was to handle or slow down. I wasn't worried about slowing down so much; I was more concerned about touching the bottom, or if I could control an under-powered ship full of heavy logs. The ebb would also be at full strength just when the ship was approaching the UP Bridge, the narrowest point of the journey. It couldn't have been worse timing.

After Davies left, I headed the ship due west, where there are roughly three miles of deep open water until the ship enters Middle Ground, a fairly straight, but narrow buoyed fairway with 35 feet of depth. When the ship exits Middle Ground, it passes Port Chicago Naval Weapons Station, where the channel is wider and deeper. After Port Chicago is the big curve in the Bay I wrote about when I moved the gypsum ship.

It was pitch-black, but at least I had great visibility. About an hour and a half later, the ship was flying along with maximum ebb, and every buoy we passed was being pulled over on its side. Because bulkers don't have very powerful engines—in fact, some have less than 8000 HP, which on a large ship is nothing—I didn't have any reserve power to help control the ship. Also, because of low water, the ship was "smelling the bottom," so it was harder than normal to keep the ship headed the way I wanted.

I remember the Jordanian captain wasn't on the bridge at this critical stage of the transit. Like too many bulker captains, he was probably asleep, but he should have been with me because we were about to go through two bridges, one of which is very narrow. It astonished me how captains thought nothing of disappearing to their cabins in the middle of the night, so after this incident scared the crap out of me, I always demanded all captains be on the bridge approaching the UPB.

As we flew by Buoy #7, which was almost submerged, the ship was situated where I wanted her, pointing slightly to the right of the lift span's north tower. I was expecting the ship to slowly drift left in the current, and when the bridge was a half a mile away, I'd swing the bow slightly to port toward the center. All things being equal, the ship would slide over and go under the middle of the bridge.

I only wanted to change course 2 degrees to port, so I told the helmsman to alter course to 242. Because all ships handle differently, depending on their draft and trim, I always believed helmsmen knew more about steering than I did, so I usually gave them a course to steer. However, I always watched them like a hawk because too many of them couldn't steer very well. In this case, it almost turned out to be fatal because I should have given him a helm order. In any event, it should have only taken a few degrees of rudder to turn the ship to port. After I gave the course, I was glad to hear the gyro make its "tick . . . tick" sound, meaning the ship had started turning. As always, I looked up at the rudder angle indicator to be certain the helmsman had turned the wheel correctly, but immediately I did a double-take. To my horror, the fool had turned the wheel full to starboard, causing the ship to swing in the wrong direction! His mistake was putting the current on the starboard quarter instead of square on the stern, where I needed it. Looking with trepidation, I thought, *If we hit the bridge no one will believe it was his fault!*

I yelled, "Hard-a-port, hard-a-port!" cursing under my breath as I stared at the quickly approaching bridge as my mouth went dry. As the bridge towers grew larger, I thought, *We are going to hit this old goddamned bridge because of this idiot on the wheel!* My stomach was in knots and I was certain my career was about to end as the ship turned away from the green navigation light of the span, where it needed it to be. At least it was green, not red, meaning the lift was up.

I fumed at the Mate standing by the engine-order-telegraph with his head slightly bowed, as if he were dozing, "FULL SPEED AHEAD!" I needed all the rudder power I could get. I didn't care how fast the ship was going because hitting the bridge on Full or Half Ahead would have the same catastrophic effect on the bridge and my career. The Mate, a young Indian kid wearing a turban, startled by my yell, grabbed the engine-order-telegraph's brass handle and slammed it against the stops to FULL. Immediately the bells in the EOT clanged, but how much extra power I received out of that sorry old ship, I have no idea, but at least it was comforting to hear those bells go off.

The startled Mate must have been daydreaming because, after ringing up Full, he looked forward at the fast-approaching bridge and literally started screaming something in Hindi as he covered his face with both hands, as if he were about to be executed and he didn't want to see the firing squad. I didn't know what to make of his hysterics, but it wasn't helping anything. I prayed his shouting didn't rattle the helmsman any more than he already was. What was truly astounding, with all the ruckus going on it didn't disturb the old man's sleep. I thought a competent captain would have rushed up to the bridge hearing all the bells and screaming. So much for due diligence.

Squeezing the grab rail so tightly that my knuckles were turning white, I gazed at the old rusty railroad bridge coming right at us, wishing I was someplace else. Just when I was certain the ship was going to make a U-turn and end my career, I heard the compass start clicking as the ship started to roll back to port. *Holy crap! Thank God Almighty she WAS turning!!* If she hadn't, I wouldn't have made the opening, or for that matter be writing this book. In what seemed like an eternity, the forward mast passed directly under the center of the railroad bridge dead center, and somehow the rest of the ship followed through. I let out a huge sigh of relief, ordering, "Half ahead," as the ship had picked up too much speed with the ebb current pushing us as if we had a tug back aft pushing Full Ahead.

I'm not too sure how many cigarettes I smoked after that escape, but that was too close. Sometimes pilots need a little luck, and I sure did that night. Like a cat, I lost one of my lives. I don't think I could have done anything differently. The helmsman's simple error almost cost me my career, and on nights like I wondered if Davies was right. Maybe I made the wrong career choice.

Another catastrophe I narrowly avoided in regard to Davies happened in 1990, while I was piloting the empty Russian bulker M.V. *Gregori*.

Many bulkers go upriver to load cargos like rice and grain. Others import cement and large items like windmill parts, which you can see erected on the hills above the Sacramento River. The bulker fleet is like the backwater of the Merchant Marine. While very important because of the vast quantities of cargo moved, their crews aren't always the cream of the crop. To make my point: there are roughly 5,000 containerships and 5,000 bulkers worldwide, yet 42 percent of *all* ship accidents involve bulkers. That's not counting tankers, etc.

I vividly remember one of my worst piloting nightmares like it was yesterday. It was a fresh, clear New Year's Day with a strong westerly wind blowing. Winds can be quite strong because cold sea air is sucked into the San Joaquin Valley in central California by rising hot air, especially in summer. In general, prevailing winds follow ships from sea all the way up to Stockton and Sacramento. Wind was something I paid close attention to. In fact, a sailboat wouldn't have to adjust her sails all the way in from sea to Sacramento because the trip would be entirely downwind.

My closest near-miss occurred when I was following Davies on a loaded tanker directly ahead of me in San Pablo Shoal Channel. Davies was going to Shell Oil, about a mile east of the UPB opening, I was going thirteen miles farther on to N.Y. Point. Eventually I'd pass him, but I wanted to do it before we got anywhere near the UPB because; he had to turn around to dock, and turning a heavily loaded tanker can take up to half an hour. In half an hour, I would be six miles closer to him. I wanted to pass him as soon as possible, so I radioed, asking permission to overtake him. There was ample sea room to go around his ship after Pinole Shoal, but in his usual selfish way he refused, saying there was plenty of time for him to turn around and for me not to worry. I should have worried.

Davies had three assist tugs, which was unusual because normally two tugs are sufficient to help a ship dock at Shell. I had a bad feeling that his turning around might take more time than he was leading me to believe. I also didn't like slowing ships down unnecessarily, especially with the current pushing me from behind. I had no choice I ordered Slow Ahead so I didn't get close to his ship.

My ship was completely empty, so her propeller was partially out of the water, meaning the propeller wasn't efficient. Also, the propeller wash didn't hit all of the rudder, which affects a ship's ability to turn. This wasn't ideal with strong currents and a lot of wind.

As I passed Port Costa, I saw that Davies was almost parallel to Shell and slowly moving sideways toward the dock, so I knew that he was far enough along for me to get my ship back up to speed.

Most Sacto and Stockton jobs are bulkers, and most of them have gigantic swing cranes on the ship's centerline, which block the view so things like small boats or the center of a highway bridge can't be seen if you stand in the center of the ship's bridge. You must stand to the side, making them much more difficult to pilot. At least they were for me. It was just one of the things I got used to, like piloting from bridges that were forward on some ships. The *Gregori* had extra-wide cranes obstructing more of the view than usual. It's like driving your car with a refrigerator on the hood. I thought how much I disliked naval architects who designed bulkers in general, and her in particular.

I planned on being about 600 feet off Shell, but as I approached Davies's ship, I could see all of his tugs were pushing full, so I anticipated their prop wash shoving my ship to port, as a crosscurrent would. I knew, even from 600 feet, that his tugs would still have an effect on my ship. I never thought that he'd stop his tugs because if he did, my ship could suck his right off the berth, or break mooring lines that weren't fast.

About a mile from the bridge opening, I made a series of small course corrections, gradually turning the ship to port toward the opening. I used green Buoy #7, a mile on the other side of the bridge, as a lead mark. When it was directly under the bridge's center, I could, more or less, head toward the lift opening. The flood current and the wind tend to set ships right toward Martinez, so I had to allow for that.

My ship was in good shape, holding up against the tugs' prop wash and the wind that was gusting at about twenty knots toward Shell.

I thought I had all these forces balanced when, without warning, Davies stopped all three tugs! Maybe he thought he was doing me a favor when, in fact, he had just screwed me. In a heartbeat, the 600 feet I needed to be off his ship disappeared as the wind and current pushed me toward his ship. I never had an empty ship slip sideways so quickly, so I had to react to get my ship back in shape or she wouldn't make it through the narrow opening. In seconds I was too far right of where I needed to be. When the green buoy I was using disappeared behind the south bridge tower, I knew I was in dire straits, so I started barking helm orders like a crazed person. No ship of mine had ever been so far off course approaching a bridge, or at such a God-awful angle to it. I wasn't sure, even with my years of piloting, I could get her through, and the worst thing a pilot can do is lose faith.

I should have passed Davies earlier to avoid this situation, but it was too late. I was in deep shit all because he hadn't let me pass. Knowing him, I think he did it on purpose, just like running me out of the Richmond Channel.

"Hard-a-port, no, hard-a-starboard, no, no hard-a-port," I barked, giving so many orders I'm not sure the confused Russian helmsman actually turned the steering wheel. Frustrated, I ran out to the starboard bridge wing to get a better handle on the situation since I couldn't see the opening from the middle of the ship. On a normal approach, the opening would be only a few degrees one way or the other from my intended course line, but the ship was at an angle of about 15 degrees to the bridge! Despite the helmsman screwing up my orders, I was never this messed up before. My stomach was in my throat.

With the flood current, I didn't have enough time or engine power to make a U-turn away from the bridge. Even with the comparatively slow ship's speed, dropping the anchors was also pointless. I'm quite sure the crew wouldn't have dropped them in time anyway. Horrible thoughts raced through my mind. *What if I hit the car bridge. Would it topple on top of the railroad bridge?* Who knew how many would die if their cars fell into the river? If by some miracle I cleared the highway bridge and only plowed into the railroad bridge, there would still be a horrific amount of damage, but preferable to killing innocent people driving home.

I thought, *Well, if I'm going to hit the G-D bridge, I might as well get as much rudder power as I can. If I hit it, more speed won't make much difference.* I was on Slow so as not to disturb Davies's ship, but I had no choice, so I yelled as loud as I could, "FULL AHEAD!" hoping to get more rudder response. The screw was half out of the water, but I had to do something. I barked, "Hard to starboard!" hoping to swing the bow away from northern highway tower into the 291-foot gap between the railroad bridge's towers, and at the same time miss the highway bridge with the ship's starboard quarter. I was fairly sure the ship would miss the wider highway bridge, but I still wasn't convinced I'd make it through the much narrower second span.

All of a sudden, the gyro compass started clicking as the bow swung right, fighting the wind and the current. I ordered, "Midships!" swinging the rudder hard over one last time. Throwing the rudder hard over actually slows a ship because it acts like a brake by stopping water from going by it. To my amazement, the bow squeaked by the north tower by a few feet. Seconds later, the bow swung into the lift bridge's span. The ship was sagging like a greased brick toward the south side, but she was making it! If I could get parallel to the wooden fendering protecting the railroad bridge, I wouldn't care if I hit it so long as I didn't hit it at an angle, equally distributing the ship's weight. As the ship slipped through the opening, I leaned over the side of the wing looking straight down at the fendering less than six inches off the hull. We were moving parallel to it, and I hadn't touched anything despite my cockamamie approach.

I wondered what the bridge-tender, who lives in a little house at the top of the lift span, was thinking. Whenever the lift span goes up, his "office" goes up also, so he was high above looking down at us, and I swear he was laughing. Usually I waved, but I was too embarrassed to bother. I wondered how many other crazy approaches he witnessed in his career.

This episode made me think about Captain Perry Stiltz, who I often rode with. On a similar day, he was docking an empty ship at Port Chicago. As usual, Suisun Bay was very windy. As Perry approached the dock, the ship fell sideways with the wind and the single screw tugs weren't able to hold the ship up, so she landed quite hard. Fortunately, the ship was parallel to the dock, so the stress was equally divided along the dock. Landing like that makes an agonizing sound as the wooden dock face compresses. Because nothing broke, pilots say: *That was another good landing.*

Perry turned, "You know, Paul, if you are going to hit a dock hard, hit it flat." I never landed as hard as he did, but I hit hard a few times with no damage.

As my ship exited the bridge I let out a huge sigh of relief, ordering, "Slow Ahead." I was feeling cocky, as if I had cheated death and destruction again, but I still don't know how I pulled it off. I lost another of my cat lives that day.

A day later, I was riding a tug over to the *Arco Prudhoe Bay* at Amorco. I plopped into a chair to BS with her captain as he drove across the Straits. Having been on every tug on The Bay, I knew all their skippers.

"Hey Cap, did you see the show the other day with me going through the bridge sideways? Weren't you helping Davies?"

He laughed, "Oh yeah, we sure did!"

"What'd you think?"

He replied bluntly, "I thought you weren't going to make it!"

I replied, "Me either!"

Maybe because I didn't heed Davies's advice about becoming a pilot, he had it in for me because too many things went wrong around him for it to be a coincidence. I can still see Davies in his funny little porkpie hat, cheap rain coat, and those ugly shoes people with bunions wear.

To misquote Twain again, "I didn't attend his funeral, but I sent a nice letter saying I approved of it!"

CHAPTER 15

GREAT ESCAPES OF OTHERS

Ship masters are schooled to stay far away from shallow water and other ships. As we are not pilots, we are near hard objects and close to the bottom often. Because so many things go wrong, and in so many different ways, I witnessed many close calls. You could say getting out of hairy situations is a pilot's stock-in-trade. Piloting the world's largest movable objects definitely has inherent risks, especially when landing them on concrete docks with wood facings or moving oil tankers within a few feet of the ocean bottom. Also, sooner or later ships in port will be within feet of others during dockings, especially when berthing between two others. Even small miscalculations can lead to two megamillion-dollar ships colliding, causing untold damages as well as possible injuries to personnel.

Massive amounts of petroleum is transported along California coast coming from Alaska, foreign countries, and between West Coast ports. Los Angeles and San Francisco Bay have some of the highest-volume oil facilities in the U.S. Unfortunately, collisions or ship groundings happen. Except for the *Cosco Busan,* there were no oil spills caused by San Francisco Pilots during my career.

Intertanko, a trade association of independent tanker owners, i.e., nonoil companies or state-controlled tankers, is the world's chief critic of pilots. Their main complaint is that most accidents happen in pilotage waters! Of course, they fail to emphasize that most of the danger in moving ships, especially tankers, happens when they enter port. They fail to mention that most of their ships are manned by Third World crews.

Pilots move thousands of ships every day without problems, but when something goes wrong, someone usually gets hurt, damages are in the millions, and, of course, it winds up in court and in the newspapers. Unfortunately, we had our fair share of such events.

In a TV documentary, Captain Bill Meyer said, "You're only as good as your last job," and "We can't turn the pencil upside down and erase our mistakes." Just ask John Cota.

We must be one of the few businesses that, when we appear in newspaper articles, whether for good or bad, they always mention our salary. Not many articles about other professionals mention theirs. For example, a tanker touched the Bay Bridge in January of 2013. The next day our income was in the papers.

"Traffic, I need some help!"

Fifteen percent of the nation's crops and 7 percent of all revenue from livestock originate in California. This is billions of dollars. California imports a lot of anhydrous ammonia used in fertilizer. Especially Stockton and Sacramento.

At 2100 on June 14, 1995, the LPG tanker *Mundogas Europe* was inbound from the Pilot Station bound for Stockton. She had 36,000,000 pounds of one of the most toxic chemicals on earth, liquid ammonia, on board. Captain Donald Hughes was piloting her. She was approaching the Golden Gate at fourteen knots with flood current when she suffered a steering casualty. Approaching any bridge with following current without steering or power is the worst scenario a pilot can face. The following current pushes the ship forward, regardless of whether the engines are stopped. If Hughes's tanker rammed the Golden Gate or ran aground and ammonia leaked out, it could have been a catastrophe. Ammonia must be kept frozen because it boils at -28 degrees Fahrenheit, and if a tank ruptures, ammonia oozes out like toothpaste, then vaporizes into a deadly cloud. Ammonia is extremely toxic. If you breathe it, your larynx explodes and the insides of your lungs burn. San

Francisco's prevailing winds are westerly, so a lethal cloud of gas could have enveloped the Golden Gate Bridge, then drifted toward The City. I've had the unpleasant experience of getting a tiny whiff of the ammonia on ships, and it made me gag. In January 2014, the New Zealand Port of Taranki was evacuated when a 200-liter drum of aluminum phosphide on *Poavosa Wisdom* leaked.

Obviously unnerved, Hughes radioed VTS, "Traffic, I need some help! Our steering just went out on us and we're approaching . . . we're approaching . . . " This is the dreaded equivalent of, "Houston, we've had a problem!"

"Do you have an escort tug?" Traffic replied.

"We don't have no escort!"

It's impossible to anchor in the 300 feet of water west of the Golden Gate, so it was imperative that Don move his ship into the shallower water south of the channel near Baker Beach, or she could have drifted into the bridge. The ship still had power, but he couldn't steer. Her rudder was stuck 5 degrees to starboard. This turned out to be a good thing because by judiciously going ahead and astern, Hughes miraculously maneuvered the ship out of the channel and dropped both anchors, saving the day.

After the *Valdez* mess, laws were enacted to stop future spills. OPA 90 was one, and like most well-intentioned laws, it's flawed because it doesn't require LPG tankers to have escort tugs despite their lethal cargo!

Nothing makes a pilot's heart race faster than losing the plant, unless, of course, the rudder stops moving. The UP Bridge not opening in time was another. I always made it through, unlike Captain Peter Crowell. In his case, the lift opened, but the empty bulker *CSL Trailblazer*'s engine quit as the ship approached from the east. To make matters worse, it was ebbing. Have you noticed how often the current is going the wrong direction when the shit hits the fan in piloting?

When Crowell realized he wasn't going to make the entrance, he ordered hard-to-starboard, trying to run aground. Unfortunately, with the ship's light draft she never did. Grounding is always preferable to hitting something, but it's strange that when a pilot wanted to, he couldn't! As the ship got out of control, Peter dropped the starboard anchor to slow the ship down by dragging it in the mud, and also to turn the ship away from the bridge.

At Port Revel, we learned stopping a ship with too much speed by using the anchors is impractical because when they come out of the chain locker, they accelerate as more weight goes into the water. It's the weight, not the anchor itself, that moors a ship. Anchor windlass brakes are not strong enough to arrest a chain madly running over the side. Also, accelerating anchor chains will jump wildly over the windlass. In all probability, the anchor detail will run for their lives. Luckily for Crowell, the crew stood fast as the anchor chain paid out to the bitter end, lost over the side.

As the following current pushed the ship broadside toward the bridge, Peter dropped his last hope to stop the inevitable crash, the port anchor. When it hit the bottom, it took a solid bite. Due to the slower speed, the bow pivoted into the current against the chain. Peter thought he was saved until the stern started swinging sharply toward the bridge, pivoting around the anchor. Luckily, the engines came back on line. Peter threw the rudder hard to port and gave the engines a kick. A wall of water from the prop lifted the stern just enough so she landed parallel to the railroad tracks without a scratch! Crowell could have also ripped up the underwater oil pipelines buried east of the bridge. To have all those problems working against you and not lose your cool was amazing. His quick thinking earned him a commendation.

One blustery day, I was in the South Bay. I noticed a ship cockeyed underneath the Bay Bridge pointing at Yerba Buena Island. The ship's rudder stuck hard over, but her engines were still working, which wouldn't have been so bad if the ship wasn't near the bridge. The pilot backed the engines full to avoid hitting the bridge, another near miss. The ship's rudder motor eventually came back on line, so the pilot anchored her for repairs.

Captain Edgar, aka "Dead Slow Ahead Ed," Carlson, a retired Panama Canal Pilot, worked with us. Ed was on an outbound Matson ship when she lost her rudder approaching the Golden Gate, so Ed ordered Full Astern. When that didn't stop the ship, Ed ordered a "Double Jingle," which is when the engine-order-telegraph is quickly moved from Full Ahead to Full Astern twice, letting the engineers know there is a major crisis.

Full speed astern didn't stop the ship, so Ed ordered both anchors let go. Unfortunately, there was still too much momentum. The ship didn't stop, so she plowed into Marin County. Regrettably, the anchors also tore up telephone cables crossing from San Francisco to Marin, which disrupted telephone service.

These cable areas are clearly marked on nautical charts, and we were always careful never to drop anchors in them for fear of pulling them up like Ed. However, when the crap hits the fan, you don't have many options other than dropping the pick. We were also careful not to drop anchors onto the BART tunnel buried just off Oakland Berth 35.

A Marin County stock broker sued Matson and Edgar, testifying that he lost money because he couldn't make any trades. Who knew a pilot could get sued for that? We were always getting sued even if it wasn't our fault.

OPA 90 required loaded oil tankers to hire tug escort once inside Mile Rocks. In the 1990s, tractor tugs were becoming more widely used, but when it was enacted, San Francisco only had two.

Tractor tugs are much better suited for escort work than twin screw tugs because they can trail behind ships on a long hawser. Tractor tugs can help stop a ship or swing the stern with great effect in an emergency. They are much safer than conventional tugs, and you can move faster.

One day, Captain Tom Hand was on a loaded tanker north of Alcatraz Island using the deep water channel, which is contrary to outbound traffic flow. At the same time, a sailboat owner—who invited a neighbor, who didn't know a thing about sailing—was sailing around the same area. In any case, the yachties, or what pilots called WAFIs (Wind-Assisted Fucking Idiots), were having a fun time until Captain Hand's tanker came through the Golden Gate, putting them on a collision course. An infinite number of sailboats have sailed directly in front of the mammoth ships I piloted, not seeming to care in the least bit about being in harm's way. This reckless disregard for their safety and their crew, not to mention putting something very valuable at risk, always astounded me. From a small boat's perspective, it might look as if there were plenty of sea room when there really isn't. Also, large ships aren't very maneuverable, especially when moving slowly, and they take eons to stop. When Tom realized the sailboat had a zero CPA, he immediately started blowing the danger signal of five short blasts on the whistle. At the last moment, the sailboat tacked clear of the ship, but as the sailboat crossed from under the ship's bow, he saw the escort tug near the ship's quarter, which was running free of the ship. Harbor tugs can be 100 feet long. They put out huge bow wakes, being very beamy. Further, their stems are covered with massive rubber mats, and immense truck tires hang over their sides.

When the WAFI saw the tug, he panicked, tacking back across the ship's bow. This time, the sailboat didn't make it across, and the tanker rammed the boat because of her momentum. Down onto the sailboat's deck crashed the mast and sails. To make a long story short, no one was hurt, but being California, the land of lawyers, the frightened guest sued the sailboat's owner, the ship, and Tom for "mental anguish." Fortunately, the guest lost the case.

On fair weather days with small seas, it's a real pleasure being on Station. It was easy to read or get some shut-eye while waiting for my arrivals. And the food wasn't bad, either, because we employed two fantastic cooks named Klaus Lange and Ray Pinochi during the last part of my career. I wish I could make Ray's salad dressing. The meals they prepared in all sorts of weather was truly amazing. I was always grateful for their dedication.

I remember one particularly perfect afternoon when I was reading while the sun was slowly sinking into a rare flat, calm Pacific. Whenever it was that calm, I tried savoring the moment because when winter arrived, we had to batten down the hatches as calm days became a rarity.

I was wondering what was for supper, when I heard the cook banging around in the galley after his afternoon siesta, getting supper together. Relaxing with my feet up, I heard the engines engage as the boat steamed south toward an inbound Japanese containership. Once *California* cleared the ship's stern, she would turn around and go up her starboard side and put Captain Jim Nolan aboard. It wasn't my ship, so I just stayed in the saloon. Having seen thousands of pilots jump on ships, I seldom went into the wheelhouse unless it was something special, like a sub or a liner. As I was daydreaming, through the wheelhouse's door came words that got my attention.

"*Nippon Maru*, please repeat! Did you say man overboard?"

I could hear the concern in the Japanese captain's voice when he radioed, "Roger, pilot vessel, man overboard starboard side!"

"Man overboard!" At that, I jumped and went up into the wheelhouse. Nolan was already up there in his float coat waiting to go to work.

Naturally, we thought a crewman had fallen into the sea, which didn't seem possible, as all ships have guard rails and it was almost flat calm. Also, no one would be working on deck this late in the day, and the crew was standing by to receive a pilot.

Everyone in the wheelhouse had binoculars to their eyes looking for a body. Bob Porteous passed the ship, driving down her wake in the fading light, anticipating that whoever was in the water must be astern of the ship. Scanning the horizon was akin to the proverbial needle-in-the-haystack except the needle was a man's head and the ocean—a vast place—was the haystack. When I raced sailboats, we practiced man-overboard drills because with the frantic activity of racing offshore day and night, someone could easily fall overboard. Even if you see someone fall, you quickly lose sight of them. During drills one man was assigned to keep shouting the victim's direction and keep pointing at the body so the helmsman knew where to steer, while the rest of the crew turned the boat around. If you didn't have a "pointer," you could sail around and miss the victim.

"Over there, over there. Two points to port!" someone cried, pointing at a black head bobbing in the ocean some distance off.

"Man, that doesn't look like a sailor," someone else remarked.

Nolan, standing on the boarding platform, started yelling in Japanese at a man bobbing in the sea. Baffled, I thought, *I didn't know he could speak Japanese!*

Someone else chimed in, "That ain't no Jap!" I didn't take that as racist, just as a startled observation. I didn't know about other pilots, but I liked piloting Japanese ships. They spoke English, their ships were impeccably clean, and they could steer a straight course. That may sound trite, but those things were important to me, especially a clean ship.

"What the f . . .? That guy has on a wet suit and goggles! What the hell is he doing way the fuck out here?"

Bob deftly maneuvered our 85-foot boat over toward a guy who we assumed was Japanese, but turned out to be an American in an old black neoprene wet suit, waving the whole time despite suffering from the beginning stages of hypothermia. When the boat drifted next to him, the crew tossed him a line and pulled him over toward us, then yanked him out of the water over the stern like a big fish, using a davit we used to put our Avon in the water.

In another hour he would have been alone in the dark, and it was very doubtful anyone would have spotted him until sunrise, if sharks and hypothermia didn't finish him off first. When we got him aboard, he was shivering so badly he couldn't help himself, so the crew cut off his wet suit with a fishing knife, then carried him below and threw him into a hot shower. After that, he put on some clothes a crewman had rounded up. Andy Anderson, our cook, fed him a big meal that he gobbled down.

Curious how the hell he managed to be floating around in the Pacific when no one had radioed "mayday," he told us a sea tale about how he and his dog were solo sailing south of the Bar Channel, where a big wave flipped and sank his boat. That sounded fishy, since he had the forethought to put on his wet suit and goggles. Also, there was only a big glassy swell, not something that would flip a boat. That was a dangerous way to collect insurance money if that was his game. We never found out if he was dumb or clever or if there really was a dog. He was also very fortunate how alert our Japanese crew was, because seeing someone's head in the water from one hundred feet above the sea isn't easy, even on a calm day.

We gave him a few bucks to tide him over, and as soon as time allowed we transferred him ashore. The ironic thing about this bizarre incident was the man we saved from certain death never bothered sending a "Thank you," a bottle of booze or anything, to the crew that gave him their clothes, and money, and to whom he owed his life. Some people are just ungrateful or maybe he was up to no good after all. Some of us thought he purposely sank his boat and his scheme would have failed if we hadn't found him floating around.

CHAPTER 16

MY GREAT ESCAPES

Most pilots don't like discussing their errors or miraculous recoveries, but I will because if something can go wrong in piloting, it probably will. This isn't always caused by pilot error; rather, there are so many things entirely out the pilot's control, such as equipment failure; misinterpretation of a pilot's orders; putting the rudder the wrong way; weather incidents such as unexpected wind shear, heavy rain, or fog; published data being wrong; events happening out of the pilot's sight, e.g., the crew letting the anchors go at the wrong time, not at all, or putting out the wrong amount; or actions of other pilots, as when saying they will remain at the dock, then running you out of the channel.

I had my fair share of close calls, and thank goodness I got out of almost all of them. Yes, I did have a few incidents such as going aground three times and twice touching docks hard enough to do some damage. This makes my accident rate about .0006 percent based on how many ships I moved, so in general I had a normal career. However, when you move massive ships, sometimes things get broken.

I liked when other pilots discussed jams they got themselves out of. I knew I could always learn something from their experiences, and if nothing else, they made good sea stories. When someone goofed up and went before the Commission, you read about it in their monthly minutes; otherwise, the pilot might never mention the incident.

This chapter is about incidents that happened to me that didn't involve the UP Bridge, where I had three near-misses. After reading this chapter, you might think I had a lot of interesting experiences, and I did, but I'm not so sure I was the exception. Either I had crazier things happen to me, or I was very good at extricating myself out of trouble, which Al Clarke counseled me to do when I was only twenty-six.

In front of Antioch's Riverview Lodge, between Kimball Island and Antioch Point, is the only place wide enough to turn around a ship after passing New York Point three miles downstream. From here the San Joaquin River turns east toward Stockton another thirty miles upriver. Riverview is also a good place to dine unless you're eating when a ship crashes into the restaurant, which happened once. Too much speed will do that every time.

One of my more bizarre "near misses" happened on my way up to Domtar on *Goldbond Trailblazer* loaded with Gypsum rock. These particular ships had cargo doors on the port side near the stern, so they had to be docked port side to. We had to turn them around at Riverview, then backed them up more than a mile to the pier.

That day, it was clear with flood current. I wasn't concerned about the job because daylight always made jobs easier, especially upriver ones, and flood was ideal to go backwards because the ship would be facing into it. I actually liked backing ships into berths because their pivot point moves aft as the ship gains sternway, so you can control the bow more easily. *Trailblazer* had a small bow thruster, which is a propeller in a tunnel perpendicular to the hull near the bow that pushes the bow left and right. Thrusters have less power than tugs, but when going astern they are effective if the ship is moving slowly.

American Navigation Company's tugs, *Bobby Jo* and *Marauder,* assisted me. *Bobby Jo* was a small single screw tug, but she was handy, meaning she could move around quickly. She put up two lines through chocks on both sides of the stem so she could work both bows. Acting like a "rudder" in front of the ship, her bow to mine, she could push the bow either way as the ship moved up the slough backwards. *Marauder* was tied up on the port quarter laying alongside until I needed her. Using the ship's engine and the current, I slowly moved the ship from Riverview up the last stretch of slough.

I thought it was slick that AmNav owned another tug named *Lobo* and was thoughtful enough to give me the tug's name board when I retired. I have it proudly displayed at our Cape Cod home.

As ships traverse this little waterway, the river bends in a slight arch on the portside. When I was about two shiplengths away from the berth, the bow started sagging slowly toward the portside river bank. I wanted the current dead ahead, not only on one side, which could affect the ship. I had to react quickly. I assumed the current was a little stronger on the starboard side and I could control the swing using only the thruster. The bow was only moving slightly, so I put the bow thruster lever all the way over to starboard. When that didn't do anything. I radioed *Bobby Jo* to push full into the port bow. Even at 90 degrees and Full Speed, she didn't budge the bow in the slightest.

When the swing increased more, it really got my attention. Something was terribly amiss. I let out all the stops, ordering *Marauder* to come up to Full Speed into the quarter, hoping to swing the stern back toward the dock. I was certain *Marauder*'s two several-thousand-horsepower diesels would do the trick. Well, they didn't. The bow kept accelerating toward the shoreline and I wasn't the least bit comfortable, hollering into the wheelhouse, "Half Ahead" as I raced out to the port wing. I had to stop the ship from going backwards and stabilize the situation. Even Half Ahead didn't slow the ship or slow the turn that had started involuntarily. I didn't have much left up my sleeve, so I ordered "Hard right!" trying to help *Marauder* push the stern in and stop the ever-increasing rotation. I'm sure I was praying, anything to help, but nothing had any effect. I was edgy, and the last thing a pilot can be is nervous. I had piloted thousands of ships, but I was in uncharted waters, so to speak. Not only was it bizarre that the ship had a mind of her own, but I felt helpless. I only had one bell left, which I was reluctant to order because I didn't want to headway and drive the ship into the bank or, worse, the fast-approaching dock. I was running out of options; I yelled, "Full Ahead," into the wheelhouse. It didn't matter, the bow swung faster and faster toward the end of the pier. Water pushing on the side of a ship has a tremendous effect, especially if a ship is deep in the water like she was.

I never had a ship this much out of my control, nor had one even come close to making a 180 degree turn I didn't initiate! I waited for the swing to stop as she made a big counterclockwise turn with the bow doing most of the swinging. As the legendary Captain Don Hughes often opined, "She's in the hands of God now," and he was so right.

My last option was to drop an anchor, but I feared the ship's crew might drop the wrong one and flatten *Bobby Jo*. This happened once when a pilot panicked, forgetting his tug was under the hawespipe and the anchor almost hit the tug's wheelhouse!

Full Speed wasn't only *not* stopping the swing, but soon, if she didn't hit the pier, she would be perpendicular to it. If the ship had too much headway on, I might very well wind up ramming the pier I was praying to miss. I also had no idea how much water was outside the channel. As far as I knew, no one had ever turned a fully loaded ship off Domtar.

I was rapidly getting myself into "irons." Either I was going to run the "expensive" end of the ship (the propeller) into the mud or the bow would flatten not only into the pier, but also the expensive un-loader sitting on it. No matter what I did I was screwed, and I didn't want to join the "Million Dollar Club" just yet.

I had nothing to lose. I was so certain the pier was a goner, I stopped both the ship's and the tugs' engines, thinking, *Well, it's probably better to run the ship aground than to hit the damn pier.* I was sure it would explode into a million splinters at any second. The lesser of the two evils would be the aground, but the ship continued spinning like a whirling dervish, and it still looked like we were going to knock down the bloody dock.

As I gazed at the unloader, like a deer in headlights, the bow went flying by without making a sound. It was the sweetest silence I can remember. Momentarily the ship was perpendicular to the dock, something I was certain I shouldn't have been able to do. I assumed that the ship was longer than the river was wide off the berth. The ship wasn't aground; instead, it was facing upriver just as if I were going to dock the ship starboard-side-to. Thinking back, it was good she spun around or we might have drifted upriver sideways until I ran out of the wet part of the river.

The stunned captain hadn't said a word the whole time. Guiltily, I asked him, "Captain, are you sure you don't want to go starboard-side-to?"

He looked at me with this solemn expression. "No, Pilot, we must dock portside-to," which I already knew!

Just because the ship was facing upriver didn't mean the current took a break; it was still shoving us toward Gaylord's pier. I had to back all the way back to Riverview against the current, which wasted more than an hour. How embarrassing this was I cannot tell you, but I was glad the old man took it in stride.

At Riverview, I turned the ship around (again) and dragged it back up the river, repeating what I had just done without all the extra turning. The entire time I was nervous I might replicate the harebrained stunt that had almost been a disaster. It never crossed my mind to turn the ship off the dock, but I had been too lucky already. The ship acted like a real lady the second time, adding to my confusion. I'm not even certain how I screwed up in my approach or if I learned anything, but no ship ever got of my control again. The only damage, other than to my ego, was all the standby time my car service charged me.

Every pilot fears engine failure or a rudder casualty, but pilots never know if or when they will happen. Like cops who never draw their weapons, some pilots have never experienced failures, but pilots must be vigilant at all times. Once a ship's anchor chain broke just as I was leaving anchorage dropping into The Bay. I'm glad I wasn't near a dock or had a tug alongside, because that could have been ugly.

When I started piloting, I never expected so many bizarre events to happen to me, but surely one of the strangest happened October 25, 2004, on the containership *Nuevo Leon*. Not only did the captain warn me about his jinxed ship, but the engine failed just as he was talking about it! We were shooting the breeze, which not only kills time, but it was fun learning where different captains lived and what was happening in their countries. The *Leon*'s captain was a pleasant enough guy, except my ears perked up when he said how unlucky his ship was, how many times she had grounded, where it happened, and other things I wasn't too happy hearing. Since I had to move his ship into Oakland and turn her around, hearing how jinxed his ship was disconcerting. Losing the engines or the rudder can lead to disaster, especially if a ship is near something hard. After my near misses, I was always ready to go to "Plan B," but no one ever warned me about it. I have no idea how many other pilots lost the plant, the rudder, or both, but I did.

As the ebb flowed out of the South Bay like a river, we stemmed it heading toward the Bay Bridge. As if preordained, the RPM gauge dropped to zero and immediately I felt the loss of power in my feet. The good news was I had sea room ahead and two assist tugs waiting for me near the bridge.

When the propeller quit I didn't hesitate, I radioed my tugs to get to me pronto because I was in a jam. The tugs' captains didn't even answer, but I could see by their black exhaust that they had already given their engines the bullets coming to us. I radioed Traffic requesting vessels stand clear because my ship was powerless and I was about to dead-stick into Anchorage 7 just east of us. I told them my tugs were coming to help.

Anchorage #7 was the perfect spot to aim for because it was close, shallower, and easier to anchor in than in middle of The Bay, which has deeper water. I thought if everything went just right, I would be clear of all ship traffic and wind up in a designated anchorage.

Even without the propeller turning, the ship was moving at about ten knots, so she still had headway, meaning I could still steer until the ship lost her speed. A ship with no power will slow down quickly when you start making turns because once the rudder is out to 40 degrees maximum, it's like a barn door blocking the water.

I waited a few minutes to lose some speed, then ordered, "Hard-a-port." The ship responded, turning toward Treasure Island. I gave several more rudder commands as I guided the ship into the shallower water. I knew it would be easier to stop using the anchors without pulling them over the side. Anchors have more holding power in shallow water because there is more of an angle between the hawsepipe and the sea bottom. Ships usually drop five times the depth of the water the ship is in.

As the ship slipped sideways, I checked with VTS one last time, confirming what I already knew she was inside the anchorage. Once confirmed, I hollered from the bridge wing, "Let go the starboard anchor!" Watching it slam into the water was like a lead high diver performing a gigantic cannon ball. The ship had a little way on as she gently rode up on the anchor chain, dragging it on the bottom for a short time until her momentum ceased. With that, *Leon* started drifting backward with the current, so I told the old man to pay out more chain until five shackles were in the water or 450 feet. When they were paid out, you could feel the anchor take a big bite into the sea bottom, causing the bow to swing wildly southward as she fetched up. The ship twisted in the current, lining up with the stretched-out chain. The ship settled down exactly where I wanted her as if I had used the engines. It was a relief it went so well. I never even used the tugs but was glad they were standing by.

The ship wasn't going anywhere soon, so I was relieved of duty, went back to the office. They repaired the ship and I never heard another word about it. Unlucky is right! I was lucky the ship was on the down current side of The Bay Bridge or we might have landed on it. If we'd been turning near a berth when the engine quit, I'm not sure what would have happened.

I didn't know a ship could get pooped entering port, but I was sorely mistaken. I read about ships being "pooped" in the middle of the ocean in great storms when a wave comes over the ship's stern and crashes onto the "poop deck," but never ones entering port, as happened to me. Ships' bows are pointy to drive into waves and reinforced to take the heavy poundings they endure. Bows also take waves over them, called "green seas," but the stern seldom gets inundated, so most ship sterns are round or flat. Taking green water is common, but it's very dangerous, so in extreme weather, ships must face into heavy seas or can lose control. Large ships have vanished in the Southern Ocean after punching a hole in a huge wave that rises high up and lands in the ship's mid-section. The tremendous weight breaks the ship's back with horrid consequences.

When Exxon first started hauling crude from Alaska to their refinery in Benicia, they thought the misnamed Pacific Ocean wasn't going to be as tough as the Atlantic; but Exxon was wrong about the Pacific, just as they were about a lot of other things. I boarded a few of their ships after they'd been in storms and seen ship parts bent like pretzels. Once, one of their lifeboats was dangling precariously from a davit arm after the ship took a beating.

Early one evening on November 22, 1977, I boarded the American tanker, SS *Santa Clara,* as a weak sun slowly sank astern of the ship. After arriving on the darkened bridge, I got my bearings, then took the conn from Captain Church, swinging the ship southeast toward the Main Ship Channel.

The wind wasn't particularly strong, but the seas were fairly large, the aftermath of an early winter storm. The *Santa Clara* was drawing 33 feet, so I anticipated a cushion of about 22 feet under the keel, more than sufficient water to enter port even with the tall swells running. I still wanted to be in the deepest part of the Bar Channel, which is maintained to 55 feet. Despite the failing light, I could see waves building up on the north side of the channel near Buoy #1, where, if the bar broke, it would there first. Two miles farther east the bar could also break near Buoy #7, so I didn't want to be anywhere near either of those buoys.

As the ship slowly picked up speed, her bow wake started flowing smoothly down the black and rust-colored hull as I looked down from the bridge as the ship slowly rolled from side to side. There wasn't a thing to worry about, it was going to be a routine transit. There I went not worrying again!

While shooting the breeze with Captain Church, I heard an eerie sound I never heard before, or for that matter since. A sustained rumbling noise reverberated through the portside door, faint at first, then increasingly louder. I'd never heard of a wave building and making noise, but the commotion was undeniable, sounding like a freight train getting closer. Confused, I nonchalantly strolled over to the open door as if nothing were wrong and glanced aft for myself. That's when I saw it! A great wave with spume on top building up and overtaking the ship. I can only assume a rogue wave was following us and rising higher because the water gets much shallower near the Bar Channel!

I spun around, certain the immense wave was going to swamp the ship.

"Do you have a lookout forward, Cap?"

"Half Ahead," I ordered as he faced me with this quizzical look.

"Half Ahead," The Mate answered, quickly moving the EOT lever up to Half.

"Sure Mr. Pilot, the AB's on the bow, what's wrong?"

I said, "Crap, you'd better get him off there, we're about to get pooped!"

He grabbed his radio and yelled, "Tony, get your ass off the fo'c'sle, right now!"

We watched with growing apprehension as the lookout slid down the forecastles' hand rails like a fireman down a pole landing on the main deck near a bunch of valves and pipes. I prayed the deck equipment might somehow block the brunt of the wave that was outracing the ship.

As I gazed at the boiling water overtaking us, SMASH! Up and over the middle of the port side of the hull rose a huge wall of green and white water rising straight up into the air, as if it had punched the side of the ship. The next second the wave fell en masse onto the foredeck with a loud *whoosh* as if a giant had emptied an enormous bucket of soapy water onto the foredeck. The water rushed across, sweeping from port to starboard at a thirty degree angle to the keel and completely submerging the forward part of the ship. As the water raced, we could still see a single white light coming from the AB's flashlight going up and down with his swaying arm. He knew what was about to happen and was hightailing it for all he was worth up the starboard side, trying to get into the lee of the main house before the deluge.

It was too late. The foredeck became totally overwhelmed with frothing water as if the ship were a submarine. When the white light disappeared, I thought, *Man, what if that poor bastard goes over the side? Would he survive in the freezing Pacific and would they blame me?*

With that, the ship heeled sharply over to starboard, causing most of the green water to cascade over the bulwarks and through freeing ports—holes in the bulwarks—which allow water to escape over ships' sides. Ships' decks are also built with a slight arch in them, called camber, which allows water to flow to the ships' sides, relieving the deck of its weight.

Just when I was thinking the AB was a goner, a lonely flashlight reignited, except now the motion was more like a police car's twirling lights as the AB ran like mad. Happily, the next wave just rolled harmlessly by and no more green water came over the bulwarks. The old man radioed, asking how the AB was. He replied that he had grabbed onto a stanchion and held on for mercy, getting soaked, but was okay. I brought in some deep ships with some terrible seas, but I was only pooped once.

The freighter MV *Cotopaxi* was named for an Ecuadorian mountain. Her former master, Alberto Dillon, is retired and living on a beach named

"Farallon Dillon," where he owns a hotel. Alberto and I struck it off from the first time I piloted his ship. I looked forward to seeing him whenever his ship returned to San Francisco, and we would have him over for dinner whenever he could get away, especially if his wife, Yolanda, was aboard. Why we were such good friends after what I put him through on April 16, 1990, is a testament to our camaraderie.

The *Cotopaxi* traded along the Americas, west coasts. She was a real working ship, not sterile like modern containerships, where you never knew what cargo was coming aboard because it's hidden in containers. The *Cotopaxi* had booms and masts looking and feeling like ships I first sailed on. I always like boarding ships like her. She was handy-sized and fun to handle. She always berthed at Pier 80, also called Army Street Terminal, which is used for general cargo and some container trade. If a ship had containers and didn't go to Oakland, it probably docked there. Pier 80 has three berths: the north, the south, or Islis Creek side, and the side facing the bay, or the face. The south side had room for two to three ships, but the dock only had one container crane that was rolled around to work both berths. Across, and south of Pier 80, is Pier 90-92, where small tankers loaded vegetable oil. The easiest maneuver I ever performed was docking at Pier 80's face because all I had to do was stem the current, then push the ship sideways until it stopped.

Docking the Islis Creek side was much different from the face because Islis Creek is only about 400 feet wide and there was shoal water opposite the pier, making it tricky getting in there. There also was a small berth directly across from 80's corner, where dredges discharged sand dredged up from The Bay so they took up more of the creek! Aggregate sand is also imported from Canada to Pier 94, a no-longer-used container pier. I still can't believe San Francisco imports sand.

Getting a ship alongside the south side was always challenging because strong crosscurrents run perpendicular to the channel and have a tremendous effect on a ship as it slows down. When we piloted straight in, that was a "Ferryboat landing." It's a very delicate maneuver. I calculated how strong the current was and how much it would set my ship constantly adjusting my approach, so as the ship entered the creek, it wasn't at an angle to it. This was nerve-racking if the ship didn't behave. I landed many ships there, but as the years wore on, I wasn't comfortable ferry boating in the larger ships, so I always dropped an anchor outside the entrance and dragged about 90 feet of chain, which helped stabilize the bow.

On the night I scared Alberto (and myself), something was wrong with the current tables. Either they were misprinted or I misread them. At most berths I knew the current just by observing how the buoys were leaning or even how the birds were sitting in the water, but going into 80 south, I couldn't guess. I had to know precisely because the current along the city piers changes earlier than out in The Bay. So it could be flooding in the middle, but ebbing at the dock.

Positive it was flooding, I anticipated that the current would push the ship south as I turned toward the dock. I turned a little early to account for it. I envisioned slowly drifting south as the ship slipped into Islis Creek. Out in The Bay I thought my approach was okay until I noticed the ship wasn't drifting south at all; instead, she was turning toward the pier face and with the angle toward the dock, I knew she wasn't going to clear the corner!

I knew something was seriously wrong. "Bingo!" It wasn't flooding, but ebbing! Unfortunately, I was already committed and quickly running out of sea room. We weren't going to make the entrance if I didn't react quickly. If I put the ship on Full Astern, she would have stopped, but there was also a good chance she would have drifted onto a shoal across from Pier 94, so I decided to keep going.

To make matters worse, as we drifted toward the face, I noticed another ship tied up on the south side, something the dispatcher failed to mention. Now I had to go around another ship, which reduced the channel width by about 100' feet, and I needed all the room I could get. There was also the container crane working over the ship.

I had to get the ship into a narrow channel, but now I had to go around another one loading containers and I could only go so fast or I'd rip the other one off her berth, or, worse, pull the crane over on top of both of us. The situation would really get ugly if I didn't do something, so I backed my port bow tug, which pulled the bow away from the pier, giving me a little more time before I dove for the entrance. When the bow was pointed where I wanted it, I ordered hard right rudder and Half Ahead to get her moving again because the tug pulling on the bow was acting like a brake. Thankfully, I could see I was gaining on the entrance, but would I make it? The ship was slowly picking up speed, but I didn't want to slow down too much and lose rudder control. My second tug was single screw, so she was useless until the ship was almost stopped. Because she couldn't get out to a 90, she also couldn't back me away from the pier. Just as the *Cotopaxi*'s bow passed close aboard the docked ship, I told Alberto, "Drop the starboard anchor!" I didn't say how many shackles to put out. I just wanted its weight on the bottom.

Instantaneously, it crashed into the water, as if the crew knew I needed their prompt attention. An anchor hitting the water with the chain rumbling out has a very distinctive sound as clouds of red dust go flying everywhere and the chain links clank over the windlass. That noise is a sweet sound to a pilot in a jam.

"Full Speed astern," I yelled from the bridge wing as I looked at the docked ship only a few feet off to my right. The ship had too much speed, so I needed to slow down fast. Islis Creek is only about three shiplengths long and I would hit the Third Street Bridge if I didn't stop her. The astern bell made the stern torque south, where there was no water, toward a sand barge sitting there. But it also threw the quarter tug out to 90 degrees, which was good because now the tug could push the ship toward the dock.

"*Sea Cloud* give her the bullets," I yelled into my radio.

By then the effect of the ebb stopped as most of the ship was in Islis Creek. I ordered, "Drop the port anchor." I wasn't taking any chances, I wanted both anchors firmly on the bottom. *Clank, clank, clank* went the other anchor. With two anchors on the bottom, a ship's pivot point moves straight to the stem, giving maximum control. I should have dropped them sooner. I thanked God that Captain Dillon's crew was so professional and did everything I asked of them.

"Stop the ship! Stop the ship!" I cried.

"*Parar maquina*," came the response from inside the wheelhouse.

Bam! I'm not sure how, but the *Cotopaxi* was stopped and sitting in her berth next to the BRIDGE sign with 50 feet to spare to the other ship that was still loading containers as if nothing had happened. Somehow we had wiggled around the containership without pulling her off the berth, or hitting the dock or the sand barge. What a rush!

I told both tugs to work easy pinning the ship to the dock as I began to relax, lighting another cigarette. Whenever I got myself out of a jam, I was always amazed how quiet it was when it ended.

Captain Dillon looked at me unsympathetically from under an old salty captain's hat. "*Capitan* Lobo, don't ever do anything like that again!"

I looked at him sheepishly, "Alberto, amigo, don't worry. I never will." And I never did.

Getting out of that near miss reminded me of Mark Twain when he had to get his steam boat over a shallow spot in the Mississippi. No one, except him, thought he could bring it off. Being a lightning pilot, he did it. I sort of felt like a lightning pilot myself that night.

About every hundred years, The Bay Area gets punished with terrific cyclonic winds. Winds stronger than 72 knots are considered a hurricane, so it's very unusual to have such strong winds along California's central coast, and it only happened twice when I piloted. We had plenty of storms, but none was ever named a hurricane, but maybe they should have been. I remember those stormy days very well because I worked during both of them.

Besides Peacock rescue in Chapter 20, the other time we had near hurricane force winds happened one late winter afternoon when I sailed the *Mathilda Maersk* disembarking around 1800 at the Station. The wind and sea were normal for a winter day, but it wasn't awful when I landed on *California*'s deck and waved goodbye to the ship.

I remember I ate a delicious dinner and felt fine. Rough weather rarely affected me other than to make it uncomfortable reading or watching TV. My next arrival, *Kanata Spirit*, into Richmond wasn't due for a few hours. I wasn't particularly tired, but *California* wasn't riding very comfortably, so I decided to get some shut-eye to be more alert when I got up.

I enjoyed having the boat to myself as if it was my own yacht, so I had no trouble finding a bunk because shipping were slow and no ships sailed that afternoon except mine. The cooks always made up the bunks whenever pilots used them, so we always had fresh linens, which was nice.

I lived through many storms, but I was usually successful at sleeping in any weather. Even though all the bunks had lee boards, you could still get thrown onto the deck if the boat slammed violently into a ship. It was the high pitch from the engines that was more of a problem for me than the motion, especially if they were revved up chasing ships, so I always used ear plugs. Unless I had a short wait, I always undressed and got under the covers unlike some pilots who laid on top of a bunk with a blanket. A few pilots wore pajamas, but they got kidded.

A few hours after sleeping soundly, Yutaka "Tak" Kuwatanik, the boat captain, knocked on the bulkhead above my head, waking me up. The operators knew I liked being called when my ship was four miles away. Some pilots wanted more to wake up, not me; I only wanted enough time to get dressed, walk up to the saloon, put on my float coat, and get on my ship. I also didn't like sitting in the wheelhouse waiting if the boat was heaving and pitching, which was fatiguing.

When I sat up in my bunk, I didn't feel right. I put on my shirt and slacks okay, but when I tried to tie my boots, my stomach went into a knot. I rushed into the head, becoming violently ill. This was very odd because I was seldom seasick during my whole career. I couldn't figure out why I felt so crappy until it dawned on me that the boat was in a raging "sou'wester" that had come up unexpectedly. While I was asleep, the boat was crashing around, which must have upset my dinner.

I cleaned up as best I could, trying to finish dressing before I became ill again. I knew if I fought off the seasickness until I got on my ship, everything would be fine, but I needed some air fast, so I stumbled up the ladder to the saloon. I struggled getting on my float coat because the boat was tossing me around like a Mixmaster. When it's that rough, you really have to hold on. Once I squared awa, I walked up into the pitch-black wheelhouse, no small feat, as the door swung wildly with every jump of the boat and Tak drove the boat into a brewing storm that no one had forecast.

Once Carol and I sailed on *Black Prince* from the Canary Islands to Madeira Island, when we ran into a big Atlantic storm. Because I witnessed so many others getting seasick, I was nervous she might get violently ill. I knew she could not only be very uncomfortable, but become incapacitated, so I warned her, "Whatever you do, don't throw up or it won't stop until the ocean calms down!" Once you start vomiting, you momentarily feel better after emptying your stomach. However, it's only a matter of time before you will heave again. Repetitive seasickness leads to the "dry heaves," which are actually worse. I was proud of her during that storm because she willed herself not to get sick. Seasickness is awful and to be avoided at all costs.

I had to steady myself from falling over as I peered at the approaching ship lights that looked like blurry stars through the rain-covered windows. The three windshield wipers, working in unison, were pathetically trying to remove the torrential rain in addition to walls of sea water flying over *California*'s bow as she dove into one wave face after another. When a small boat is in huge seas, it's like riding up and down a moving mountain side. As *California* climbed up a wave face, Tak would add more throttle to keep her moving up what seemed like a vertical wall that was trying to push us over backwards. When we got to the crest of a fifteen-foot sea, Tak backed off the throttle and let the wave move under us as the bow came out of the water. Momentarily, we would sit weightless as the bow hung over the wave top. The next instant the boat would slide down a wave's backside, feeling like Coney Island's Cyclone that we rode on as kids. *California* would accelerate at an angle into the next trough as we fought our way toward the ship. Over and over again, we went up one wave, then down another, but it seemed as if the ship wasn't getting any closer.

I tried with all my might not to be sick again, but I wasn't having much luck with the advice I gave Carol. The first rule of going to sea is "Never pee into the wind," but I couldn't figure out which side of the boat was the lee side, so I rushed over to the port watertight door hoping I could get outside because my stomach had had enough. Two "dogs" held the door tight against rubber caskets keeping the raging water surrounding the boat outside. I flipped them up, then pushed against the steel door with all my might, but the wind was so strong the door wouldn't budge. Seeing my predicament, Tak put the wheel on auto-pilot, helping pry the door partway open against the hurricane force winds. Unfortunately, I never made it all the way out. Instead, I threw up on my shoes. As Tak went back to the wheel, the door slammed, shut just missing my soiled shoes.

Soon the boat went around the tanker's stern going down her lee side, which took us out of the worst of the storm and allowed me to open the door now that the wind wasn't pushing directly on it. I gladly stepped outside into the driving rain, getting soaking wet, but I also got some badly needed air. As the boat neared the ladder, I watched as it swung in the wind, thinking that relief was only 30 feet above me, but I had to steady myself gripping a hand line hanging down from the gallows above me, or I'd have gone over the side with the motion.

The *Kanata* had lots of freeboard and I wasn't in any mood to climb up any more ladder than I had to, so I waited for her to take a big roll toward us. When she did, *California* quickly rose up against her hull just as if I were on an elevator making the big truck fenders screech from all the friction between the rubber and the steel hull. During the roll, the pilot ladder fell by me, piling up on the boat's deck just below my feet. I hoped the ladder didn't get snagged by the tires, but I wanted the boat to rise up as high as possible before I transferred over. I also didn't want the pilot boat chasing after me if the ship took another big roll while I was climbing. The pilot boat can actually hit and flip you into the sea, as happened to Columbia River Bar Pilot Kevin Murray, who was killed. As *California* rose up as high as she was going to, I leaned over, grabbing the ladder with one hand as I stepped onto a rung, then let go of our boat at the same time. As I did, *California* dropped more than ten feet from under me, slamming into the hull as she tried pulling away. The ship took a big roll the other way, which briefly made me lighter, so I quickly pulled myself hand over hand to get away from the boat.

As soon as I stepped onto the ship, I started feeling better and was trying to ignore my boots. When I reached the house, the rain and sea water flowing back and forth across the tanker's deck had washed off most of the mess. As I looked down 35 feet at the pilot boat's deck lights receding into the torrential rain, I was glad it was them not me staying at sea. I radioed Tak saying I was sorry if I had made a mess, which made him laugh. He had seen plenty of seasick men before, but never me.

I entered the ship's bridge soaking wet and forgot about my stomach. I didn't even take off my float coat when I assumed the conn because the empty VLCC was in dire straits in the southwesterly storm. She was losing the fight against the wind because we were going too slowly, and I needed to get her straightened or we would be blown toward shoal water up to the north. In addition to more speed, I needed to get her pointed far to the south of the intended course line just to get her into The Bar Channel. The massive empty tanker was slipping sideways in the wind and swells as if she were made of paper.

Up ahead I could barely make out the entrance buoys' lights that kept submerging in the enormous swells blinking on and off as the waves forced them onto their sides. At least I had something to aid me; without them I be guessing where the channel was because both radars were useless in the high wind and hammering rain.

I couldn't give the ship too much speed or she might drive her bow into one of the mountainous seas and cause a tremendous amount of damage. I had to balance between going too slowly and drifting out of the channel, or going too fast and punching the bow into a wave. My plan was to try to point the ship's bow outside of the channel to fight the wind until we were almost on top of a red buoy. Then I'd throw the rudder hard-a-port and rev up the engines to Half Ahead to help swing the bow away from the buoys. If I didn't crab the ship, she would be blown north out of the channel onto the famous Potato Patch Shoal, named for a Schooner filled with potatoes that was lost there. It was breaking as usual. I didn't make this type of maneuver very often, but the wind was extreme.

As I entered the Bar Channel, VTS advised that the Captain of the Port had closed the port and for me to proceed to any anchorage, but not my berth. As much as I hated VTS telling me to do anything, I was very glad to hear that. I was also pleased that Traffic hadn't told the ship to stay at sea. If they had, I would have spent a very uncomfortable night. That took a lot of pressure off me because I wasn't quite sure how I was going to dock a huge empty ship safely in so much wind. The gusts were so strong earlier that day that Captain Steve Wallace lost control of a containership. Even after dropping two anchors paid out to the bitter end the ship still punched a 105-foot hole into the Pacific Container Terminal. The Commission ruled it "An act of God."

The next day I was outbound again when I observed the power of the terrible storm. Hundreds of trees all over The Bay—including Angel Island State Park, which looked as if a giant with snow shoes had flattened all the trees—were knocked over. The newspapers called it one of the worst storms of the century, and it sure was, as far as my stomach and shoes were concerned. If I felt that sick on a daily basis, I'd have quit. Thankfully, storms this big were rare, but there were plenty of times when I didn't feel terrific bouncing around on the Station Boats.

In October 1986, I went to Terminal #4, the northernmost pier in Richmond, to sail the American tanker *OMI Yukon*. She was the only American ship I ever sailed from there, or ever saw docked there. It was used mostly by small foreign tankers. The dock is near an abandoned whaling station once burned down by anti-whaling protestors.

She was portside-to facing south, which wasn't ideal for sailing with an ebb because of shoal water immediately south of the berth. Deep draft ships never departed that way. Several ships had run aground on that shoal. I once "smelled the bottom" passing there, so I never went through there unless I had light draft. Therefore, I had to turn the ship off the dock directly across from the solid granite Brothers Island. There was just enough turning space for a medium-size ship, so I had to be careful not to get set onto the island.

After I went up the gangway, the ship's agent cornered me. This was unusual because most often I saw them in the captain's cabin. He seemed agitated, asking me if I'd sail the ship if she was on the "Bottom." Then I noticed the ship had quite a starboard list, leaning away from the dock. Her mooring lines were straining at their bitts. Looking around, I didn't know what I had gotten myself into, but I told him I'd have to see what it looked like after I talked to the old man. I wasn't about to do anything for the agent that would risk my license, no matter how much I liked him or the crew, so I made no commitment to him.

When I arrived on the bridge, I met the captain, who looked tired from worry. Maybe he didn't want any witnesses to our discussion because he took me aside explaining obviously the ship was aground on the port side.

I said, "Okay, what do you want to do about it?"

The tide was dropping rapidly and he was afraid waiting would put a tremendous strain on the mooring lines and they might part, so he was desperate to sail. He knew if I refused (which was my right), the ship might break away or he would have had to hire several large tugs to pin her to the dock if they arrived in time. In any case, he'd have to inform the Coast Guard that the ship was aground, a big NO-NO, especially with a loaded tanker. I saw his predicament, so I agreed to sail.

It was only going to get worse. It wasn't my fault the ship was over-loaded. They should have sailed sooner or called my office to get the depth at the pier before loading so deeply. We had to act swiftly, so I asked the captain to get the crew to their mooring stations and take the tugs' lines. I had already told both tugs to push full on the hull to help relieve some of the strain on the mooring lines. If we got underway soon, it wouldn't be much of a problem getting the ship moving because only part of her was on the bottom and the strong ebb would do most of the work. My main concern was the ship getting into irons and not turning around quickly enough. I also thought if I didn't get an ahead bell at the right moment we might drift onto The Brothers or drift down onto the shoal water. That wouldn't be too good for the ship, or me. I told the captain I didn't want to hang if the shit hit the fan because as far as I was concerned the ship was already aground. He agreed that he would take all the blame if something went wrong. Whether he would or not, I'm sure the Coast Guard would have hung us both if anything happened.

The crew tied up the boats and quickly singled up the mooring lines. Then I asked for all lines, except for two forward spring lines to be cast off. As I expected, once the stern lines were clear, the stern started moving off the pier as the current overpowered the after tug. Immediately, the ship groaned as she was shoved forward along the dock by the current, which caused the two spring lines to stretch as taut as any lines I had ever seen. Crews always had to be attentive to lines parting. They are an ugly sight when they whip-lash across the deck, sometimes killing men. The forward springs stopped the forward motion as the stern lifted off toward the Brothers. That crappy dock, which even had holes in it, moaned in protest as the weight of the bow slowly rolled into it, compressing the ancient worn-out pilings. If they broke it wasn't my fault, because rolling a ship was common practice and that dock should have been condemned.

When the ship angled to about 30 degrees to the dock, I ordered, "Slow Astern." Immediately, the strain eased off the two last lines attached to a bollard as the ebb crowded between the ship and dock. As more angle opened up, the ship began moving toward the Brothers. The springs weren't doing anything, so I told the captain to take them in freeing us from the dock. I didn't bother telling him I'd never turned such a large loaded ship off Parr 4 before, but piloting involves improvising, as every job is different.

Even with the after tug pushing full, the stern fell downstream like a son-of-a-bitch, so I stopped the engines as the forward tug came up to full power to pin the bow against the current. The stern whipped around on her own until we were pointed squarely into the current parallel to the dock, facing north, just as I wanted. On Half Ahead, the ship was almost neutral in the current, so I ordered Full. With that, the ship started slowly moving along past the Brothers. When I was certain I would clear that massive granite rock, I swung the rudder over to port and around she went. Once the current was behind us, the ship quickly sped up. I was quite happy how well the whole thing unfolded as we sailed out to sea.

The next day I received a peculiar phone call from the *Yukon*'s agent asking me weird questions about the sailing and if I thought the ship had been aground when I boarded. I said, "Are you kidding?" I didn't answer any more questions, as I didn't know where he was going with the conversation. Then he wanted to know if I told anyone else that the ship was aground. Instead, I asked him if he thought I was nuts sailing a ship that was "technically" on the bottom. He agreed. He seemed relieved, but I wondered if there was anything else wrong with the ship they hadn't told me. This is the first time I am telling this story all these years later.

The sad part of this saga was that on October 28, 1986, not long after I sailed her, she had a huge engine fire and explosion en route to Ulsan, South Korea, and sank. Two of her sailors were never found and four others were injured. Japanese fishing vessel, *Shoichi Maru*, rescued the crew that day. Maybe their luck finally ran out, and I'm glad I wasn't aboard when this tragedy struck. Being aground is nothing compared to a ship fire or sinking with loss of life or going to jail for spilling oil.

If you've ever heard the expression "Have you ever had the shit scared out of you?" then you know how I felt when I came within inches of running a fully loaded tanker over a solid granite rock. Other than just missing the UP Bridge twice, nothing even comes close to this event.

A bulker in the New York Slough, fifty-three miles from the Pilot Station.

Approaching the Golden Gate Bridge.

Getting ready to board a Chevron tanker.

The author at home—on the bridge.

More than a Bay.

A Maersk containership passes under the Golden Gate.

Tight squeeze. The 180-foot-wide tanker *Denali* approaching the Interstate 80 Carquinez Bridge.

Tighter squeeze. A bulker about to pass under the Union Pacific Railroad Bridge.

New York Maritime reunion. The author with his classmate Captain Bob Groh.

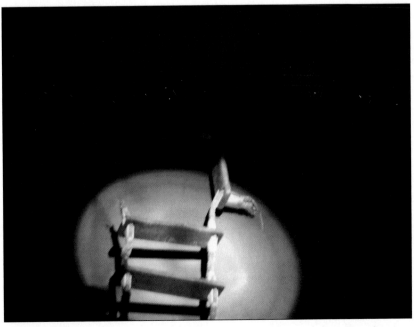

The perils of boarding—a broken ladder. This time the pilot made it on board.

The tanker *Puerto Rican* leaking oil after a fire and explosion at the Pilot Station.

A MSC Post Panamax container ship entering Schnitzer's Turning Basin.

The "Big E," the USS *Enterprise*, one of my challenges.

A helicopter hovers over the carrier USS *Boxer*.

A Wallenius Lines auto carrier at Port of Richmond.

People have asked me how modern radar could have failed when Captain Cota hit the Bay Bridge. I just tell them shit happens. As I've written, I've had engine and rudder casualties and far too many helmsmen who couldn't steer worth a damn. When equipment fails, you pray it comes back on line quickly before you have an accident, or you go to Plan "B." At the beginning of my career I didn't have a Plan "B," and on the horrifying day I am writing about, it almost sank it.

After 1990, we were required to take Bridge Resource Management classes, where we learned a series of events usually leads to an accident. In my case, this turned out to be true. However, BRM didn't even exist when this near miss occurred. Also, I didn't attend manned model training until 1991, when I became a big endorser of it.

I was a relatively new pilot when I piloted the fully loaded American tanker SS *Exxon San Francisco* with 41 feet of draft. Her keel was more than four stories below sea level. Back then, 41 feet was very deep for most ships. Years later, we piloted fifty-footers regularly, but we could only do that at high water to safely pass over a shoal northeast of Alcatraz.

Coming in from sea I had clear visibility, so I wasn't thinking I needed radar to navigate and wrongly assumed the Exxon officers had properly tuned them for entering port. Plus, it wasn't my job to tune ships' radars. These assumptions were the first two links in the chain. If I had just looked at the radars, I might not be writing this hair-raising story.

As the years sailed by, the less I took anything for granted. In my business, being too relaxed is a terrible idea. Even being a little on edge never hurt, and I wish I had been more so on that day. Years later when I was a senior training pilot, I advised my apprentices, *Never take anything for granted. Always double-check everything!*

This story is also about a lookout who failed to see a big sea type buoy directly in front of the ship as he stood guard on the bow. He was the third link. These mistakes almost led to an ecological disaster with a capital "E."

The entire trip in from sea, we had a low ceiling of gray clouds, or what I call high fog, but it wasn't foggy. San Francisco's famous fog often drifts into The Bay through the Golden Gate toward Alcatraz, where it usually dissipates. When it clears, it does so first north of Alcatraz Island, where I was heading after passing under the Golden Gate. I was relaxed as

I could be, considering I was on a ship weighing 32,450 tons fully loaded with toxic Alaska crude. I was so relaxed, I was quietly talking to the helmsman, who happened to be a pilot's daughter. Normally, I didn't talk to helmsmen. I wasn't inattentive, as far as the navigation was concerned, but I should have looked at the damn radars. After this event, I never made that mistake again.

After the *Valdez* disaster, many pilots, including me, hated going on Exxon ships because of all the piloting regulations they implemented about speeds and times they wanted ships to be at certain points. This nitpicking was strange because if they had hired a pilot at Valdez, that accident would never have happened! In any case, we were stuck with Exxon's idea of how to pilot ships, which to my way of thinking wasn't correct, nor was it safer than how we handled other tankers. When this near miss happened, Exxon's officers weren't so uptight because the *Valdez* tragedy was ten years in the future. They were so laid back, in fact, that some Exxon ships replaced their engine-order-telegraph handles with beer keg handles, like taverns use for pouring beer. It was a joke because American crews are forbidden to drink. I bet Exxon's First Engineers replaced those beer handles five minutes after oil started gushing out of the *Valdez* after she ran over Bligh Reef!

Once the ship neared the Golden Gate, she was still going along about twelve knots, so my plan was to slow her down as we entered The Bay. Then, as the bow passed under the bridge, I ordered a new course of 075 pointing at Angel Island about three miles away, which I could still plainly see. The very next instant, what had been high clouds suddenly dropped down, enveloping the ship in zero visibility. I had never seen this happen before, and it really threw me off guard. I thought we were past having fog.

Up ahead on the starboard bow was Harding Rock Buoy (HR). Buoy #1 on the opposite side from HR marks the entrance to Richardson Bay. Together they mark the sides of the deep water channel. HR guards a very pointy granite rock only 34 feet below the sea surface, which was 7 feet less than the draft of San Francisco. HR must be kept to starboard to stay in the channel north of Alcatraz Island. Before ships reach HR, they must start turning east or they will run into Angel Island only a mile beyond the buoy. When large ships are turned, they don't turn like a car; instead, they slide, sometimes as much as a half mile forward (called transfer) even when the ship is at full speed. I always anticipated large turns well in advance because the ship could drift over buoys, or worse.

As soon as the fog dropped, I asked for Slow Ahead to get more of the way off the ship as I nonchalantly walked over to a radar to get ready to pilot without being able to see, something I did all the time. To my horror, the screen was all orange. I thought maybe that radar was tuned for sea, so I stepped over to the other one. Again I was speechless. I couldn't distinguish anything on that one, either. Radars manufactured by Raytheon in the '70s had black screens. Any targets, or land, showed up as orange blips. Instead, both were a big blur of orange. I couldn't differentiate a thing on them, not even Angel Island, which has a small mountain on it! It was like watching TV when a station goes off the air. Instead of white noise, I was getting orange fuzz.

To adjust radars, you use the gain dial, which is like a radio's volume control. At sea, ships turn up the gain to see objects farther away. In piloting grounds, you want more clarity for small close-in contacts like boats, so you use less gain.

As the ship started losing some of her way, I vainly tried tuning the radars. I also asked the dumbstruck captain to have someone else tune his faulty radars immediately because I could have made them worse by meddling, as all radars are different. If there is a major problem, the go-to guy is the radio operator, so they rang the radio shack to have him come up. I was blind without the radars, and moving loaded tankers in fog with three granite rocks and two islands nearby is a lame idea.

In only about one mile, I needed to make a 35-degree course change or we would crash into Angel Island. At twelve knots, it takes six minutes to go 1.2 miles, so I should have waited five minutes to start my turn. Instead, I miscalculated and started turning too early, which was one of the biggest errors of my career. (The fourth link in the chain.) Because loaded tankers take so long to turn, I assumed I needed to start my turn. I was more concerned about Angel Island ahead than Harding Rock, and I shouldn't have been. Being in fog can be disorientating, but with a good radar it's usually a routine operation. Without it made me feel as helpless as I've ever felt on a ship. Being in confined waters with granite rocks to my right and an island dead ahead only made it worse.

Because the radars were useless, binoculars were glued to my eyes, which were straining to find HR in the mist. When I finally eyed a buoy, I couldn't see what color it was, so I frantically asked the captain to radio the bow to find out what color it was. The lookout hadn't bothered reporting the buoy. What he thought his job was I don't know, but he certainly didn't do it. I was 650 feet (more than two football fields) farther away from the buoy than he was, so he should have seen it long before I did. In any case, it was too late. When I heard the lookout's voice, a chill went through my entire body like I never felt before. Momentarily, it paralyzed me. I'll never forget that sick feeling to my dying day, and thinking of it still brings back that same terror I experienced then. The lookout, who obviously wasn't very fluent in English, never said the color. Instead, he said, "*Si*, dere iz a buoy." Just then, I saw HR's quick-flashing red signal warning me to keep it to starboard. Then I knew the ship and my career were doomed because HR should have been on the starboard side; instead, it was fine on the port bow, meaning I was heading for one of the sharpest, hardest rocks in the whole bay. I was hoping it was Buoy #1 across the channel from HR, where there was deep water, but my eyes confirmed what my mind didn't want to believe. This lookout screw-up was ironic because prior to the *Valdez* hitting Bligh Reef, the *Valdez*'s lookout kept telling the Third Mate that Bligh Reef Buoy was on the wrong side of their bow. In my case, the bow lookout didn't see or report it to the bridge.

I think my heart stopped as I hopelessly asked for Full Astern, thinking we were about to run over a solid granite rock pointy like a pyramid. I knew Full Astern wouldn't stop the ship, but I had to do something, so like a condemned man, I lit another cigarette. I wasn't too sure I could extricate myself from this jam, as I had from a few others I had gotten myself into. Not only was the buoy on the wrong side, but we were swinging toward two other granite rocks.

Luckily, it takes a long time for a steam plant to reverse the propeller shaft, so nothing happened for a few minutes. At the speed we were traveling, reversing the propeller wouldn't have had any effect. It would have just spun helplessly in the water, called cavitation.

Desperate to act, I asked the captain to let go both his anchors. I hadn't attended Port Revel Shiphandling School yet, so I didn't know that dropping an anchor going more than five knots was useless. With all the ship's momentum and the anchor's weight, no anchors, no matter how big, would ever stop a ship, especially a loaded one. They would just go over the side and be lost.

To my utter consternation, he calmly told me no one was on the bow. We were going to anchor, we were already two miles inside the Gate in fog, and no one was manning the anchors except for the useless lookout! Then I noticed several men frantically racing 600 feet up towards the bow. Seeing them hopelessly sprinting didn't help my stomach, which was already in a knot. If I hadn't been so occupied, I might very well have vomited because I was literally afraid for the ship and my career.

I didn't think so at the time, but I was actually blessed that the anchors weren't ready because in all likelihood they would have been lost over the side for no reason and we would have plowed over Harding Rock anyway. It was just dumb-ass luck they weren't manned and that the engines never went astern. I lost another of my pilot lives right then.

When I realized that slowing the ship wasn't working and the anchors weren't ready, I went to Plan "B," deciding to pass as close to Harding Rock Buoy as I could and hope for the best. I knew I didn't have enough sea room to get it on my starboard side or make a U-turn in front of it, but I wanted to get as close to it as possible, so I ordered hard left rudder. Then I asked for Full Ahead to get maximum rudder effect. The captain, who was as confused as I was, ordered Full Ahead, then stared at me without getting out of his chair.

I'm not sure if I showed it, but my hands were shaking as I tried to maintain my composure. Losing my cool wasn't going to help anything, but I'm sure I had at least three cigarettes going by then.

I raced out to the end of the port wing by myself. I didn't care if I looked frantic. As I looked down, the big buoy passed down the black hull, almost chipping the paint off. I'd have gladly settled for snagging HR's anchor chain. That would have been bad, but not as horrible as running over Harding Rock, which would have split the ship open like a ripe watermelon. In all likelihood, oil would have filled The Bay up to about one foot with smelly Alaskan crude oil. A 1990 Coast Guard study estimated an oil spill of four million gallons would cause $232 million in damages.

This is what San Francisco had on board. Not only that, but The Bay Area was years away from having oil recovery equipment on standby.

I turned toward the doorway and hollered as loud as I could into the fog-shrouded wheelhouse, "Hard Right, Hard Right!" Now that I was almost clear of the buoy, I was afraid the ship might keep swinging in the current toward Angel Island less than seven shiplengths to the north. It seemed to take an eternity to start swinging back around as I waited alone on the wing for a shudder from the impact, but to my everlasting relief nothing happened. Looking aft again, I watched Harding Rock Buoy slowly recede into the fog, just as it had appeared what seemed like ages ago.

The captain never came out on the wing, he just sat inside the wheelhouse. Maybe he didn't want to see the end of his career out there with me.

NOAA's chart of the central Bay indicates Harding Rock is directly adjacent to the buoy. I thanked the Lord, it was farther away for some reason! I'm not sure what I would have done if the ship had been holed. Years later, my wife and I joked if I made a *special call* that she was to meet me where we got married in Mexico with all our money. I never made that call.

When I knew we were finally clear and safe, I shouted into the bridge for Slow Ahead, calmly walked back inside, and steadied the ship on 090. I knew I had some time before we would hit anything on that course, so I tried to get my heart to stop racing. I also needed to extinguish some of those damn cigarettes I managed to light. Today some ships forbid smoking, which just makes smoking pilots edgier.

Once everything calmed down, the ship exited the fog bank and I could see the entire Bay to the east. Just as she had entered it, the ship left the fog bank, quickly and silently. The ship hadn't traveled very far, but those were the most petrifying, longest five miles of my career.

Later on, the old man, who was probably twenty years older than I, made some snide remark about how I should have known better and not gotten his ship into such a predicament, which I agreed. In my defense, I reminded him that his lookout didn't speak English, and wasn't a lookout to begin with. I also told him he didn't have an officer on the bow, which in pilot waters is a must, especially when you already know you are going to use the anchors. In fact, the ship could have been considered unseaworthy for improperly manning the bow, just as when a ship's whistle doesn't work you cannot sail until it's fixed. Because he was on my case, I reminded him his radars were pieces of crap. In essence, nothing happened, so what could he say? He should have thanked me for saving the day, since I had no radars to work with and everything was going just fine until that point. I don't think he realized how close we came to destroying his ship and both of our careers, but I didn't bother to emphasize this point.

Nothing ever came of it, but there was talk in 1996 of spending $43 million to blow up Harding Rock, which wasn't the first time the Federal Government wanted to do this. In 1871, the Feds thought HR was such a hazard to navigation that they hired a contractor to blow it up. The newspapers wrote that all of San Francisco sat on Telegraph Hill to watch the big explosion, which never happened because the contractor lost so much money, he gave up. HR's granite was too tough for dynamite and I had almost hit it!

After I anchored the ship, I explained what happened to the Port Agent and waited for the Exxon shit storm, but nothing ever came of it. I just assumed the old man didn't want anyone at Exxon to know what happened. After the John Cota accident, I know the crew would have testified the radars checked out fine (after the fact), when I knew they were useless.

Many times I re-ran what happened in my head, and because God had spared my career, I developed better ways to pilot, even if a ship had poorly performing radars. That dreadful day gave me nightmares for quite some time. It still makes me anxious writing about it, but, to paraphrase Frederich Nietzsche, "What doesn't kill you, makes you stronger." I was stronger after that and I never put a tanker in danger ever again, which was a good result.

CHAPTER 17

MAN, IT'S DANGEROUS OUT THERE

Loss of a Pilot-boat and Seven Men at San Francisco.

SAN FRANCISCO, Cal., Friday, April 12.

The pilot-boat *Caleb Curliss* and crew—A. A. BUCKINGHAM, HENRY VAN NESS, JOHN F. SHANDERS, pilots, and four sailors—were lost yesterday while attempting to cross the bar.

The New York Times, 1867

The Bar Pilots are members of the International Maritime Pilots' Association (IMPA), which is headquartered in London and represents over 8,000 pilots from fifty-four countries promoting professional standards of maritime pilotage and safety. Every two years, a different port city hosts pilots from around the world with discussions, exhibitions, and regional social events. The country or port holding them opens the congress with great fanfare, and local color is added during these occasions, like when King Juan Carlos of Spain opened the 1986 Madrid congress after we made him an honorary pilot because of his interest in the sea. The opening ceremony includes a moment of silent prayer for pilots who died working in the last two years. It always seemed at least one of us was killed during the previous two years, indicating how hard getting on and off ships is.

Going to sea is inherently dangerous, especially for pilots. For example, during 2006–07, five U.S. pilots and one pilot boat captain died while engaged in piloting, and one pilot boat was needlessly destroyed by a ship.

Here are their stories. On October 24, 2006, Boston Harbor Pilot Captain Robert G. Cordes, a thirty-year veteran, was killed after falling more than 20 feet from a 28-foot ladder while attempting to board the 803-foot *Baldock* moored at a Chelsea, Massachusetts, salt terminal, showing that pilots can get injured or killed even at the dock.

The ship could have moved farther down the dock to allow the gangway to be lowered onto a barge that Cordes boarded from. Instead, he had to climb up a Jacob's ladder, which is far more strenuous than a gangway.

Another tragedy happened at 2130 hours on January 9, 2006, when fifty-year-old Columbia River Bar Pilot Captain Kevin Murray was lost at sea during a forty-knot gale with 18-to 20-foot seas while disembarking from the loaded log carrier *Dry Beam*. Murray fell while attempting to get off when the ship took a deep roll toward the Pilot Boat *Chinook*. No one knows why he fell into the 47-degree Pacific Ocean, but the *Chinook* couldn't immediately locate him, and he disappeared. A Coast Guard Jayhawk helicopter started searching in the wrong location because they thought Murray had fallen off a different ship. Four ships crossed the Bar that night, despite the conditions, but it was too rough for the Coast Guard's 47-foot rescue boats to get out to sea until the next morning. Captain Murray was a new pilot with only one year of service on the Bar. His body wasn't recovered for three days. He was found seventy-five miles north the accident site!

Cape Disappointment, on the north side of the Columbia River, was named by Englishman Captain John Mears in 1788 when his ship failed to find the river. In 1805, Lewis and Clark were also disappointed, hoping a ship might be anchored at the mouth of the river when they arrived on the West Coast. Cape Disappointment lighthouse is the oldest lighthouse on the West Coast, standing guard over "The graveyard of the Pacific," named for the severe weather that regularly pummels the Oregon coast. Disappointment could also be applied to the brave pilots who work the Bar, because in 163 years, some two dozen of them have perished in the line of duty.

The Columbia River Pilots are the only pilots in the U.S. using helicopters to board ships 24/7, even in harsh weather. Wind and low visibility can restrict the use of helicopters, whereas a traditional pilot boat can board a pilot in any visibility and in almost any weather. Helicopters don't necessarily make transferring safe, because several helicopters world-wide have crashed hauling pilots out to ships. The night of his death, Captain Murray didn't use their helo and maybe he should have.

On January 20, 2007, the 57-foot Pilot Boat *Galtex* sank in heavy seas in the Gulf of Mexico while transferring Galveston-Texas City Pilot William R. Kern III. Allegedly, she was hit and rolled over by the much larger, offshore oil-support vessel *Sanco Sea*. Kern and boat captain George Robert Frazier (55) were trapped inside the overturned pilot boat for twenty-five minutes until Kern was rescued by another pilot boat. Captain Frazier, a seventeen-year veteran skipper, died in this needless tragedy. Kern was lucky he didn't drown because he wasn't wearing a floatation device.

Ships can easily smash into pilot boats, and being so much larger can roll them over, which is all too common. Captains with any nautical savvy are always out on the bridge wing watching the pilot safely get off, not just taking the word of his deck officer, before ordering more speed or turning their ships. Too many times I swung off a pilot ladder and looked up to wave goodbye only to see the bridge wing empty. When a ship is about to cross the Pacific, a few minutes don't amount to much wasted time.

On January 29, 2007, another horrific accident occurred when my friend, thirty-year Hawaii Port Pilot veteran Dave Lyman, fell into the ocean after disembarking from the passenger liner the *Island Princess* while departing Nawiliwili, Kauai. Dave was lacerated by his own pilot boat's propellers. The pilot boat captain, who was alone, was unable to rescue Dave in time to stop him from bleeding to death. This is the reason we have deck hands.

Dave and I sailed together as Third Mates on one of my first ships, an old tramp steamer with the peculiar name S.S. *Surfer*. One of our regular ports was Honolulu, where Dave told me he was going to be a Hawaii Port Pilot one day. I thought he was dreaming because that didn't seem attainable, especially when I was twenty-two.

He was a hell of a character with a huge handlebar mustache and always sported a straw Panama hat, like he was a plantation owner. He was also an ordained "Sky Pilot," performing marriages all over Hawaii until his early demise. He was a fun-loving partier, and he would have loved the farewell party thousands of his friends threw to wish him a fond aloha at his sea burial in Honolulu Harbor. He, like many other working pilots, died too soon.

Another calamity happened on February 4, 2007, when Chesapeake & Interstate Pilot Lynn Deibert fell into the Atlantic off Cape Henlopen, Delaware, and was never found.

The number of our guys who went into the drink was like a *Who's Who* of pilots: Carlson, Gans, Mauldin, Sever, Thomas, Welch . . . , but it's the pilots who were severely impaired, not just wet and scared ones, I am talking about. When sailors get hurt it's called being on the *Binnacle List*. I can't recall all the pilots who made the list while I worked, but I remember the seriously injured ones: Al and John Carlier, Filipaw, Johnson, Moran, Mauldin, Nolan, O'Brien, Shandower, Spry, and Winterling all required hospitalization except Captain O'Brien, who fell into the ocean and was lost.

Once, I badly bruised my leg disembarking in a storm and I was self-conscious of hitting my head walking around dark ships, because on New Year's Day 1985, I walked into a steel beam at head level on the *Hoegh Duke* when the mate escorting me to the bridge didn't have a flashlight, as required. Due to the darkness, I almost knocked myself out! These two incidents aside, I was extremely lucky, especially compared to the pilots I write about.

Captain Joe Moran went on the binnacle list for hand surgery. I can only assume he returned to work too soon, because on his very first job back on duty, he lost his grip at the top of a pilot ladder, falling over backwards onto the Station Boat's truck tire fenders. Luckily, Joe didn't hit the boat's steel deck, but he was seriously injured, going right back onto the List.

Our engineering gang makes Station Boat fenders by stuffing one semi-truck tire inside a bigger one, then hangs them from the Station Boats' decks using chains. Even these massive truck tire fenders get flattened when our boats smash against ships' hulls.

Veteran Captain Ted Filipaw once became exhausted climbing up a swinging ladder on an empty rolling ship. He, like Moran, lost his grip, falling 15-20 feet onto the Station Boat's deck and earning him a trip to the hospital, as well.

Captain Winterling was returning from a job using a tug boat like a water taxi—something we often did—and as the tug approached our dock, John stood on the bow ready to jump off. Unfortunately, he didn't jump in time and because it was low water, the tug slid under the dock, catching John's foot, which was severely injured, and he almost lost the use of it.

When you are standing on a tug's bow waiting to jump onto a pier, there is nothing to hold onto, so you must balance yourself or else when the tug stops, it can throw you forward, as happened to me once at the Benicia Industrial Dock. As the tug was about to touch down, I was thinking about the tug's inertia throwing me forward, so I jumped off the bow too quickly, catching the dock's stringer piece with my toe, planting my face into the dock's rough asphalt surface, and cutting my face and hands. I didn't blame anyone except my clumsy self. It also didn't help I wasn't wearing the thick leather gloves I usually wore. A few macho pilots never wore gloves, and sometimes they came onto the boats with bleeding hands from the manropes, especially if they were synthetic.

Captain Al Carlier was with Captain Nancy Wagner and me on what was supposed to be his last job before his retirement. All Al had to do was ride out to the Station and pilot in a Sea Land ship just as he had thousands of others, then swallow the anchor. Early, we rode out "light" on the run boat *Golden Gate (GG)* to rendezvous with the Station Boat *San Francisco (PVSF)* that was waiting for us and bobbing in the swells facing The City near Mile Rocks Light. When we neared the *PVSF*, the *GG* raced around her stern to get on her lee side, which provided some protection from the sea when we jump over. The *GG* puts out a big wake and when she slows down, eventually it catches up to her and moves her around and lifts her up, so it's best to transfer over just before the two boats came together before her wake makes her squirrelly. If not, you had to wait for it to subside.

Al was between Nancy and me out on deck holding the grab rails and waiting to jump over to San Francisco. There was no way I was going to jump across the gap at that moment, because the GG was moving around too much as the boats got closer together. For some reason, Al leaned over and let go of the railing just as the *GG* rose up on her own wake, sending him flying across with her momentum, which was like watching a slow-motion movie. Al's leg dropped between the two boats while the rest of his body went flying across, landing him on his face with a terrible thud. I was stunned that he didn't roll into the water, but I thought, *If he goes into the sea he will have more problems than his hurt face.* I also thought if I leapt over then to help him, I might also fall into the drink, so there would be two pilots in trouble. To my relief, just as I was about to jump, our deck hand Mike took a giant leap of faith over to the Station Boat, and held onto Al so he didn't roll into the sea. After Nancy and I got onto the Station Boat, we helped Mike carry Al, who was moaning something awful, into the saloon. The boat rushed Al back to The City, where an ambulance was waiting. He retired, but not as he had planned.

Al was a great shipmate, and I never tired of his sea stories about when he was a Red Stack docking pilot before becoming a Bar Pilot. He spoke about the "Old Days" when pilots joined the "Million Dollar Club," after accumulating a million dollars in damages. This sounded like twisted logic to me because pilots never want any damages and he was the only pilot I knew who bragged about being a member. What it really meant was you had piloted many ships. Those old-time pilots must have done a lot of damage to get up to a million bucks in those days.

Al told stories about when The City's piers would ignite in flames whenever a ship backed out of them during big tides. This wasn't the pilots' fault, rather the result of San Francisco's strong currents pushing against a ship so tightly that as she moved out of a finger pier, a tremendous amount of friction was created between the steel ship and the wooden dock. That would have been a strange sensation, indeed, seeing the pier you just departed from erupting in flames! Over my career, fewer and fewer ships used San Francisco's finger piers, so I only piloted a few ships into them, which was always a tricky proposition.

Pilots pride themselves on not being seasick, something everyone, especially new pilots, had to get used to, but some fared better than others. One rough day, Captain Sever, Al, and I were on the Station Boat at dinner-time when the cook called us to eat, so John and I sat down at the dining table. Al didn't get up from his seat, he just sat there smoking. Many pilots smoked then, but today it's not permitted on our boats.

John liked controversy and needling people. That night, John thought he had a victim in newly appointed Bar Pilot Al and mistakenly thought Al was seasick, despite the fact he was smoking! After we finished dinner, John lit up a big black cigar and blew a cloud of gray smoke in Al's direction, just as you might see in a cartoon, hoping to annoy Al. Then John asked Al why he wasn't eating, thinking the thought of food would make Al feel worse. Al just grinned, blowing a perfect blue smoke ring right back at John and telling the cook to fix him a plate with all the trimmings, showing John his kidding wouldn't work on him. Al had been captain of ocean-going tugs moving barges up and down the Pacific Coast, so I know he saw his fair share of rough weather. Nothing fazed him, much to John's annoyance.

Captain John Carlier, Al's son, fell off of an empty bulker one day when he made a lousy lee and became exhausted holding onto a twisting ladder while attempting to land on the pilot boat. Eventually, he lost his grip, injuring himself quite badly. At one time I thought it was the older and heavier pilots who got hurt on ladders, but in John's case, he was young and very fit. The longer I worked, the harder it was to climb on and off ships, so I was pleased when I retired and no longer put myself at risk. I felt lucky I didn't wind up in the hospital, like many of my partners.

Captain Jim Shandower was a retired Coast Guard captain and graduate of the Coast Guard Academy. After retirement, he joined the pilots and we worked together for many years. Once I asked Jim, who was older than I, when he was going to retire. He replied, "When piloting was no longer any fun."

One of our more serious accidents involved Jim, who was primarily a river pilot, piloting more upriver than on the ocean. This might have accounted for his foot getting smashed while disembarking from the Cypriot tanker *Cleliamar* on January 8, 2005, at 0315 during bad weather. Jim endured many painful surgeries to mend his mangled foot. After all his trauma, he emailed me, "This accident took the fun away," ending his blemish-free career.

The next story is not about a pilot injury, but what Jim witnessed while docking a ship at the Benicia Industrial Dock. Spring lines are mooring lines that run fore and aft along the ship's hull, as opposed to being perpendicular to it. Their main function is to prevent the ship from moving laterally along a dock. They are the first lines put ashore and last ones cast off. Pilots also use them to position a ship by heaving on them hauling a ship up and down the dock until it's in the spot the wharfinger wants. Occasionally, they get stuck between the ship and the pier. When this happens, the tugs must be stopped to clear the lines.

This exact scenario happened to Jim on a Chinese bulker. Prior to stopping his tugs, Jim specifically told the captain to slack all the spring line to release any tension on them. Jim never knew if his order was carried out correctly, because the captain spoke Chinese to his crew and unfortunately the lines weren't slackened. Like a bungee cord, one shot up in the air, looping over the neck of the ill-fated Chief Mate looking over the side. When the line resumed tension, it yanked him off the forecastle, pulling him down onto the concrete dock, and he died on the way to the hospital. Sailors get hurt and killed far too often because of this type of miscommunication, and it's so unnecessary. Jim was never in any danger, but witnessing a tragedy like this must have been traumatic.

One day, Captain Woody Johnson, who started going to sea as a kid during WWII, was boarding a Chevron ship at Richmond Long Wharf when the gangway collapsed, throwing him to the steel deck and severely injuring him. I walked up many unsafe and wobbly gangways in my time, but I never expected ones at the Long Wharfs to collapse because they are permanently attached to the dock and substantially made of steel. Chevron prides itself, almost to a fault, about safety, but their lawyers fought Woody tooth and claw not to pay for his pain and suffering when it was so blatantly obvious whose fault it was. Chevron owned the dock, the ship, and the gangway that failed. Woody never piloted again, either, and another great shipmate was needlessly taken out of service.

Captain Edgar Carlson, whom I wrote about before, had the unenviable job of piloting a sea-going tug—the kind used to tow huge barges up and down the coast—out to the Pilot Station one lumpy night. Getting on, and especially off, sea-going tugs is a very tricky proposition because, unlike ships, they don't have flat sides that there isn't a very good place to hang a pilot ladder or a manrope, so they aren't set up well to board pilots. Another consideration is that seagoing tugs don't make very good lees because they are so small compared to ships and usually they are pulling big barges. Most of the time, we just jumped across from one boat to the other and prayed we would make it safely, so they weren't my favorite vessels to pilot.

That night, Ed did his best to make a lee, but when he leapt from the tug, he missed *California*'s deck and plunged into the frigid Pacific Ocean. Auspiciously, neither the tug nor *California* ran over him, but he wasn't out of danger because he also had to clear the tug's towing wire and her barge trailing a few hundred feet astern of the tug. These barges can be hundreds of feet long and 100 feet wide. The Station Boat went flying around the barge's stern, desperately searching for what they were sure would be a floater. What they saw instead was a tiny pinpoint of light waving erratically at them. The Energizer bunny people should have had Ed in one of their ads because Ed's penlight saved his life. He should have been killed, either by the tug or its tow, but the sea gods were smiling on him because the crew brought a very cold, soaking wet "Dead Slow Ahead" Ed aboard without too much damage.

After that close call, all the pilots attached whistles to our float coats, and our shore gang made web belt harnesses with "D" Rings for us. These belts made it easier for us to be pulled out of the water. There were no such things as built-in safety harnesses, strobe lights, water activated lights, EPIRPs, or 3M reflective tape, and newer two-way radios are waterproof.

If a pilot fell into the sea and was still conscious, the crew threw him a lifeline that he attached to the harness and was lifted over the stern of the boat using a large davit. A fully clothed, soaking wet, and very cold pilot trying to climb up the boat's built-in ladder would be very difficult, especially if the boat was pitching and rolling, which it usually was. The Station Boats also have Avons ready to be launched off the stern. If necessary, a crewman can pull an injured man aboard the Avon, and then they can be pulled back aboard together. The *Golden Gate* has a ramp on the stern. The operator, using an after steering station, can winch a pilot out of the water more easily, because he can see him.

Pilot coats were once made only in navy blue, but we liked them because they didn't show dirt from the pilot ladders. Later on, I didn't care about the dirt and had mine made in bright orange or Day-Glo yellow so I could be seen more easily in the water.

Float coats are waterproof foul-weather jackets specifically designed to keep us from sinking. Of course, pilots never think they will fall into the sea, but I was always prepared for the worst because so many pilots fell into the drink. I never got wet except for getting on and off submarines. When I found out SeaSafe Ltd. on the Isle of Wight made coats for the North Sea Pilots, I thought, if their coats are good enough for North Sea conditions, they were good enough for me. They're very expensive, but what is your life worth? Ask O'Brien.

My coats had two water-activated lights (one was a strobe light); a built-in EPIRB; reflector tape on the arms, back, and chest; a neoprene crotch flap like a wet suit to keep my "private parts" warm; and a whistle and a built-in safety harness. My float coats were custom-made with big inside pockets—called Booze Pockets—to carry newspapers, tide books, and of course any liquor or smokes that were kindly given to me by captains. I had so much Johnny Walker Red that I gave it away, and I never bought cigarettes when I was a pilot. Ships gave me all kinds of gifts, like a tip, so I have a huge collection of coffee cups with ships' logos from all over the world, as well as plaques, ties, cuff links, hats, and shirts. Over the years, these lovely logoed cups disappeared from ships and were replaced with paper cups or plain old white ones. I always appreciated captains' generosity.

Captain Donald "OB" O'Brien was longtime pilot, whose main occupation I thought was fishing; piloting was just something he did to get out to the fishing grounds. Like many pilots, he fished for salmon while he waited between ships, but no one fished as much as he did. This must have made his neighbors very happy because he could never have eaten all he caught. OB often traded places to stay at sea to fish longer. Not me, I always wanted to go home as soon as possible, so whenever he asked me, I always jumped at that no-brainer. I also think he fished on calm nights, which is illegal.

I often wrote Herb Caen, the San Francisco *Chronicle*'s gossip columnist, whenever I thought he'd be interested in an item about the waterfront. He must have liked them because he put in every one I sent him.

One day, I was about to send Herb another one as a joke. I was going to tell Herb that if there was a shortage of salmon, it was because "OB" had caught them all. When OB fell into the ocean after getting off the Liberian bulker *Friendship,* I ripped up my note.

The day of the accident, Captain Wally Campbell was on deck helping OB land safely onto the Station Boat. After OB landed, Campbell didn't look back as he walked back into the wheelhouse. The boat operator, looking away as he peeled the boat off the ship's side, also didn't notice anything, either. In that short amount of time, OB disappeared.

When OB didn't come into the saloon, someone asked, "Where's OB?" With that, the boat sounded the man-overboard alarm and made a mad dash back to where they thought OB might be floating. When the crew found him, OB was helplessly floating with his head bobbing just barely above the sea. Unfortunately, he was never recovered because his float coat failed him and, he sank below the waves as they reached him. That was sad because we fished guys out of the water all the time. If they had seen him stumble, perhaps they could have saved him. I never thought anyone would die just by falling into the ocean. They might be hurt and cold, but no Bar Pilot had died, to my knowledge, falling from a ship. I was more concerned about being hit by a ship's propeller.

OB was known to be frugal and didn't buy new float coats as I did every other year, so mine were always reasonably new, unlike his, which were old and worn-out. It had lost its buoyancy, in other words, the ability to hold his head above the sea, as life vests are designed to do. Frugality might have cost him his life.

Aside from OB drowning, our biggest pilot disaster happened on Halloween 1984 at 0324 when the American oil tanker, *Puerto Rican's* number six center tank ignited, sending flames hundreds of feet into the air. At the exact same time, Bar Pilot James Nolan was standing on her deck ready to go down the pilot ladder accompanied by Able-Bodied Seaman (AB) John Peng and Third Mate Philip R. Lempiere. Nolan and Lempiere were literally blown through the ship's steel guard railing into the ocean, sustaining severe injuries and massive burns. It was recognized that the AB was vaporized because he wasn't in the ocean, and his body was never found.

What a horrible mess for the injured men, the environment, and my classmate, Captain Jeff Spillane, the ship's master, who never sailed skipper again. The Coast Guard never determined the cause of the accident, but I think static electricity ignited vapors created in the ship's slack tanks. Today, tankers have inert gas systems that pump smoke stack gases into the cargo tanks, rendering them inert so this type of accident doesn't happen.

The Pilot Boat *San Francisco* was underneath the pilot ladder when the ship detonated, forcing her to escape the flames. Her crew valiantly returned, in the tradition of the sea, saving the two injured and helpless men despite the ship being engulfed in flames while oil gushed into the sea.

Both men were pulled from the sea using the "Jensen Pilot Retrieving System" invented by Newt Jensen, one of our pilot boat captains, just for this type of situation. Instead of lifting victims over the stern, Newt's device allows our boats to get next to incapacitated persons and roll them up the hull onto the deck, like rolling up a rug. This usually works well except in the case of Nolan, who was in agony because his femur was sticking out through his skin as they lifted him up.

San Francisco rushed both men to the Presidio, where an ambulance met them at the Fort Point Coast Guard Base, then drove them to Letterman Army Hospital. Nolan, like Jim Shandower, walks with quite a limp, like Chester in *Gunsmoke*.

The ship eventually broke in two. One part was towed into a San Francisco shipyard, while the other half was deemed a total loss and sunk further west in the Pacific, spilling 1.47 million gallons of oil into the Gulf of the Farallones National Marine Sanctuary and killing 2,900 birds.

Our boat operators are the best in the world, living day-in and day-out enduring all sorts of weather in some fairly cramped quarters on our Station Boats. They work four days on and four days off, but those days on can be very draining as well as dangerous.

The pilots put their trust in each operator to keep them, their crew mates, and our boats safe. This includes running around in fog finding ships and not getting in a ship's way no matter what the ship does. Knowing how

to use radar is an essential part of this, and all ships' officers and boat operators must have a Coast Guard Radar Observer license.

Once in a while, we hired the wrong man, and a guy named Ray filled
that bill. He reminded me of a tubby frog wearing thick glasses. He made
me very uncomfortable when he was on watch, especially when I was trying to sleep.

One day, Ray had the watch when I entered the wheelhouse ready
to go to work. I couldn't see anything outside the windows as we slowly
steamed toward an inbound Exxon tanker in zero visibility. Normally, I
sat behind the operators while I waited to board my ship, letting them
do their thing. I never micromanaged them because they did a better job
chasing ships than I could.

A fundamental rule when using radar is if a target maintains the same
bearing and is getting closer, either you will hit it or it will hit you. From
my chair, I noticed this was exactly what was happening as we got closer
and closer to the tanker. I didn't like what I was seeing, so I stood up and
moved over toward Ray, asking him point blank if we were going "port-to-
port," because the blip on the radar screen was on the radar's left half. Back
then, radars only used relative motion, so what was displayed on the screen
wasn't necessarily what was happening.

Ray replied that we were port-to-port, and I believed him even
though I had an odd feeling about what was happening. Just then, out of
the smoky fog popped a massive red bulbous bow pushing a huge bone
in her teeth coming right at the middle of the Station Boat. We weren't
port-to-port after all; instead; we were crossing directly in front of the
ship's bow, the worst possible place to be in fog, perpendicular to another
moving ship! Almost paralyzed, I stared at the immense white wave coming straight at us, and just when I thought with any luck we would steer
clear, Ray slammed both engine throttles into reverse, which was exactly
the wrong thing to do. Stunned for a second, I knew I had to act quickly,
so I leapt over him, shoving him out of the way and slamming the engine
control levers back to Full Ahead. Then I threw the rudder hard to port.
As we started to accelerate again, the tanker's bow slid by, barely missing
our port quarter by only a few feet. As the tanker turned, her big bow wake
shoved us away from her, as we slid down the tanker's port side just barely
clear of her, but we were out of harm's way, no thanks to Ray.

As we moved away from the ship's hull, Wally Campbell slammed open the wheelhouse door, yelling, "What the hell's going on up here?" The engines going from Full Ahead to Full Astern, then back to full, got his attention. Breathlessly, I told him we were almost cut in two by the Exxon tanker.

"And I don't have on my float coat!" he said, shaking his head and knowing Ray needed to be replaced (and eventually was, much to my relief).

That was one of the few times I feared for my life when was I wasn't on a pilot ladder.

I was nervous plenty of times, but only injured twice, and luckily not seriously. I am very thankful I wasn't disabled, or worse, like many other pilots. Piloting is a very dangerous profession, and every time the steamship companies complain about our salaries, I wonder if they fathom how perilous our line of work really is.

A TOUGH WAY TO GET TO WORK

There are many ways pilots get injured or killed, but the principal risk is the way we get to work, climbing up pilot ladders. Every time I left home, I never knew what kind of pilot ladder or gangway I'd see or if I'd be safe. Ships can tell their position to within a few feet using GPS, but pilots still climb aboard the same way they've done for thousands of years. Today's pilot ladders may be synthetic and very strong, as opposed to older ones made with manila side ropes and hardwood steps, but it's the same concept as in the Bible. When disembarking at sea after I left the bridge, I hurried down to the main deck so I wouldn't lose my lee. However, when I got on deck, I seldom knew if the ladder was too high, or too low, or if it would break. All I had was the crew's word it was properly rigged. Can you imagine getting into an elevator and not knowing if it would free-fall?

Today's ships are enormous, and getting up to the main deck from a pilot boat is harder than ever. However, if all ships were like Germany's *Hapag-Lloyd,* I may have continued working because their ships have side-ports with relatively short ladders. After climbing through the outboard side-port, I was shown through another smaller watertight door leading into the engine room, where it was always interesting to look at gigantic, two-story engines slowly pumping away, waiting for me to give them the bullets when

I got up to the bridge via an elevator. Boarding like that was as good as it got. It was fast, safe, and much easier on older pilots like myself, but this arrangement is expensive and impossible to build into break-bulk ships or tankers.

No matter how hard pilots worldwide try to inform ships' representatives or Coast Guards about rigging safe ladders, in the end it's up to the ship. Regardless of the number of IMO regulations or what country the pilots came from, it was the same story: pilots continue to be injured because ladders are not being properly rigged or are of inferior quality.

Some regs are quite simple: the pilot ladder must be well lit, an officer must be present with a radio and flashlight, and nothing should block the pilot access point. These regs are constantly ignored. One of the biggest problems was the pilots themselves knowingly getting on second-rate ladders because they didn't want to waste time. Occasionally I did this, and I shouldn't have.

An IMPA representative attends all IMO meetings to ensure they don't change pilot ladder regulations or make them less effective. From what I gather, ship owners would like to have pilot ladder regulations simply state there must be a means to "Board a pilot," and forget the safety requirements. Getting ships to rig their ladders in the middle of their vessels and not aft by the deckhouse would be a good start. No matter how often we instructed ships by radio or pilot information cards, too many put their ladders just forward of the deck house, which on most ships is located near the stern. IMPA publishes pilot posters with IMO boarding requirements asking ships not to put the ladders aft, but it happens continuously.

As ships have gotten larger, so have their freeboards. What might have been a climb of 10 or 20 feet can now be one of 50. By treaty, ships with freeboards over 10 meters (33 feet) must rig a "Combination pilot ladder." That is, they must lower a gangway that joins up with a traditional pilot ladder hanging next to it. If the freeboards are less than 10 meters, pilots still have to climb as much as a three-story building, straight up, on a ship probably rolling. No ship is immune to rolling, not a cruise ship, battleship, or an aircraft carrier. They all roll in big seas.

Combination ladders made it less stressful as far as not having to climb hand over hand; however, they're not always rigged properly. If not properly attached to the hull, as required, they can swing away from the ship, which can be extremely dangerous.

SeaRiver Maritime have the best combo rigs for pilots. Their gangways have a trap door built into them with a Jacobs's ladder suspended below it. They also use a giant pneumatic suction cup to hold the gangway tight to the hull so it doesn't swing away. SeaRiver's ships are huge, but their combo-ladders are very stable even 40 feet below the main deck.

During my career, quite a few ladders broke when pilots jumped onto them. I witnessed Captain Bruce Alden holding on for dear life when his ladder, broke in several places when he stepped on it. Luckily, one side held long enough for him to cross over to the gangway. No gangway, and Alden is in the water hoping the ship's screw doesn't chew him up.

Occasionally, our pilot boats broke a ladder due to rough seas, but too often ships put out ones already broken.

Both sides of Denis Welch's ladder let go at the same time while he was transferring pilots in Suisun Bay. After he drifted past the ship, the PV *Pittsburg* rescued him. The Coast Guard investigated this accident, but as far as I know they didn't fine or punish the ship.

A pilot falling from as little as fifteen feet can result in serious injury because water does not compress. Some pilots in warmer climates think float coats are too hot and have drowned as a result of not wearing one, paying a hefty price for comfort.

Despite all the pilot injuries, Americans are not covered under the Merchant Marine Act of 1920, commonly called The Jones Act, an extension of similar legislation for railroad workers. It protects seamen, allowing them to make claims for negligence against ship owners, captains, or fellow crew-members, but not pilots, because we are not members of the crew.

One day, Captain Mike Sweeney and I took the *Golden Gate* out to his ship waiting in Anchorage #8, which was on the way to mine in Oakland. When we arrived shipside, Rory Sheridan, the boat captain, gently nudged the boat against the ship's hull adjacent to a gangway that was lowered to the height of our deck. Gangways are suspended from cables and are much easier to walk up because you don't have to climb hand over hand like with a hanging pilot ladder.

As Mike put his weight on the gangway platform, the support cables above him snapped with a big *clang* and it started sinking into The Bay while still attached on the main deck. Mike had no choice. He had to climb hand over hand, grasping the gangway's hand lines as if he were on a regular ladder as the gangway turned into a vertical climb. When he reached the main deck, I yelled up to see if he was all right, and he gave me a thumbs-up as the Mate escorted him toward the deck house.

I thought, *I bet that Mate never led a pilot dripping seawater into the wheelhouse before!*

If a pilot falls into the sea, he is automatically relieved of duty no matter where it happens, per our working rules. This came into effect when Captain Mauldin fell into the ocean and still piloted his assignment despite being sopping wet.

Rory radioed the dispatcher about Sweeney's problem. She never asked if Sweeney was okay, she just told Rory to bring him back to the office, per our rule. Rory hadn't told her Sweeney had made it onto the ship, so she had no idea if he was injured or not. So much for sympathy.

At 1715 on May 7, 2007, I boarded the Ukrainian tanker M.V. *Voidomastis*. As I did, both sides of the ladder parted at the same time, with everything below my feet falling away into the sea, leaving me hanging on what was left of the ladder. Luckily, twenty feet of ladder was still secured to the ship's railings above me, and I was strong enough to pull myself up using only my arms. If I hadn't, I'd have followed the bottom part of the ladder into the sea. It took thirty years to have a ladder break on me, but it finally happened.

Naturally, I was steamed about the ladder's poor quality, so when I met the captain on the bridge, I told him in no uncertain terms that his ladder was a piece of crap and unacceptable. It only got worse when he lied, saying it wasn't the ship's fault!

We carried Commission-issued *deficient ladder forms*. On them, we recorded pilot ladder defects or problems, then explained to the master why their ladder had to be fixed or replaced. We filled them out all the time and still had problems. I filled out one, but the *Voidomastis's* captain refused to sign it. Instead, he made a cell call to his office. After I finished parking his ship at Oleum, he finally signed it, but I noticed he wrote in the comments section that our boat broke the pilot ladder and they weren't responsible! I explained that this was impossible because it was broken above where the pilot boat could have possibly hit it. He kept arguing with me until I got exasperated and called him a liar. After that it got ugly. He was the third captain I ever swore at for good reason, and I didn't care what he thought. He complained to the office, but the Port Agent backed me up, explaining that maybe I was a little upset because I almost fell into the ocean and the captain's explanation was ridiculous.

On the evening of December 15, 1977, I was outbound on the car carrier *Sovereign Accord* during a full gale, something not unusual for December. Even though I hadn't been a pilot very long, I usually made good lees and never had any trouble getting off ships.

A is created as a ship turns through the weather, creating a slick or flat spot on the downwind or lee side. Once the ship steadies up on one course, there is a brief lull when the ship is relatively stable. If you wait too long, the lee quickly disappears and the ship will start rolling because she has lost most of her speed. Usually, I was at the bottom of the ladder before the ship started rolling like hell, but on that stormy night I made a critical error, turning the ship too soon, which didn't give *California* enough time to get into position before the ship started to roll her guts out.

At 2200, I left the bridge and hurried down to the main deck and waited in torrential rain for the Station Boat to come alongside. Usually, only one pilot waiting around on the Station Boat came out to be sure pilots got off their ships safely. That night, as I looked down far below, I noticed not one, but several out on deck wearing their float coats and looking back up at me in the glow of the pilot boat's yellow flood lights, which are designed to cut through fog and rain. I don't remember the other pilots, but I wasn't expecting Captain "Smiley" Norm Wainwright to be there, nor did I particularly want him to be. I called him *Captain Smiley* because the entire time I knew him, he never laughed once. Maybe he just wanted to see me plunge into the ocean because he was one of the ringleaders who tried to blackball me, so he was no friend of mine. He had never come out on deck to help me before; then again, I never helped him, either. So I was more than a little surprised, or maybe anxious, seeing him because he gave me the creeps even on calm days.

As I waited, the ship began to take some serious rolls back and forth, which gave me pause for thought. I didn't have a choice—I had to go down the ladder or go back up to the bridge. If I went up, I'd have to remake my lee, and if that didn't work, I'd have go to the next port. I didn't want to look like a wimp and be *"carried off,"* especially being a pilot for only ten months, so I took a deep breath and scurried down the ladder. Just as I descended, the ship took another ugly roll toward the pilot boat, and when a ship takes a big roll like that, the ladder swings away from the hull and you go out with it, which is an odd sensation, since you are literally out over the ocean. *California* was having a hell of a time staying next to the hull, slamming into it with every wave that went underneath me. When a ship rolls more than 10 degrees, your feet are not below you, but in front, as if you were on a swing with your back angled to the water. This is very fatiguing because your weight is on your arms, not your legs.

When a ship and our boat crashes together, it sounds as if our boat would break apart, and if you were trying to sleep, you could fly right out of your bunk. Fortunately, our boats are built to take this kind of punishment, but even the boat's immense truck tire fenders can't stop all the violent reverberations. The boat operator can't help it if a ship has a rolling fit. I hated when other pilots made lousy lees, causing these impacts that disturbed everyone's sleep. That night it was my fault, and no one was asleep, because they were all on deck watching me.

If the boat falls away from the hull at the same time, you slide down the manrope, then you can fall directly into the sea between the boat and the ship, especially if the manrope is soaking wet and you have on wet leather gloves.

The rain teaming down reminded me of sailing in the tropics during typhoon season. The big difference was I was usually up on the bridge looking down at the pilot getting off, not being a pilot myself. On stormy nights like that one an incredible amount of water accumulates on the ship's decks and eventually it overwhelms the scuppers, so the excess water cascades over the side onto the pilot boat. It's no fun for anyone standing out on deck, and if they don't wear foul weather gear, they get soaked.

As I waited halfway down the ladder trying to time my jump, the Station Boat rose up on a big swell as I was leaning over backwards, looking over my right shoulder at the boat. As I did, one of the big truck tire fenders went by me, just missing my head. If the boat had come against the hull that instant, the tires would have flattened me. Seeing that big black mass skim by so closely really got my attention and frankly scared the crap out of me. Frantically, I tried climbing up as fast as I could to get out of the boat's way. If the tires came at me again, I'd have no choice but to drop into the ocean and take my chances drifting between the ship and the boat. If the ship's screw didn't hit me, I'd pray our crew could find me in the gale-tossed ocean.

No matter how large a ship is, she is no match for Mother Nature, so the longer I waited for the right moment, the more aggressive the rolls became as the ocean bullied the ship. I wasn't experienced enough then to know how to get off ships in such terrible conditions and with all the rolling, *California* wouldn't stay under my feet making me afraid that when I jumped I'd miss the boat's deck entirely.

The pilots trying to help me were getting frustrated by my inaction, bellowing up at me to make a decision, "Either jump or go back up to the bridge and make a better lee!"

Despite the danger of getting off under these conditions, I dreaded the thought of climbing back up to the bridge, it would have been too embarrassing. There also might be a language problem explaining to the Chinese captain what I wanted. Obviously it was always better to make only one attempt at a good lee. I also didn't want to give Wainwright, a know-it-all, the satisfaction of seeing me climb back up to the bridge.

Suddenly, the pilots yelled in unison, "Jump on the next roll!" That's all I needed, because just then, the pilot boat rose up against the ship's hull under me, her tires screeching as they dug into the hull one last time. Even though the pilot boat's deck was at a bad angle to the ship, I didn't care, so I put all my weight on the manrope, sliding down with my back to the boat. Due to my wet gloves, I slid too far and too fast so I hit the deck really hard, and my knees buckled. At the same time, my right thigh smashed into the steel grab rail. I wasn't sure if I broke anything, I was just thankful, despite the pain, to be on the boat and not in the sea. Wainwright didn't even ask if I was hurt, but I didn't expect him to.

Getting out of the maelstrom, I limped into the saloon through a watertight door and slumped into a chair, sitting there for quite a while in my soaking wet foul–weather gear as I tried catching my breath. I was also sweating profusely even though it was cold outside.

I sat there thinking of what could have been and silently said, *Thank God*. I was truly grateful to be alive. Moments like that made me think that maybe I made the wrong career choice.

I was too weak to move when my thigh began throbbing and the pain set in. Despite the pain, I felt fortunate I hadn't broken anything. I was extremely blessed during my career because that was the worst lick I experienced during my career, a black-and-blue leg.

Piloting is a learned profession, even getting off ships, so after that night, I never put myself or the boat crews in this bad position again. I taught myself to freefall as much as ten feet rather than have the Station Boat's deck go over my head again. Once was enough! I learned to get off the ships quickly, knowing the pilot boat captains hated pilots who took too long to jump. The faster you got off, the safer it was.

In 1983, Paul and Sue Rantanan, friends from Florida, stayed with me while I was working. Paul was a tough Miami Beach Police captain who didn't take any crap from anyone and was also a Coast Guard vet. He referred to his old outfit as "The Draft Dodgers Navy," and, considering our relationship with the Coast Guard, I thought that was funny. I grew up on Long Island next door to his wife, Sue, who was also a policewoman, but with Miami-Dade.

I was assigned to take the empty VLCC *Brooklyn* from Anchorage #9 out to sea, so I asked Paul if he wanted to go along. I also asked him if he was afraid of heights, to which he laughed, "No!"

In 1977, when the Trans-Alaska Pipeline opened, American needed larger tankers to transport crude oil from Alaska to the lower forty-eight. I became a pilot the same year the *Brooklyn* was christened at the old Brooklyn Navy Yard, which been converted to civilian use under The Merchant Marine Act of 1970. She was a very large ship weighing 103,900 GRT and extremely long for that era at 1,100 feet—the longest ship I had piloted up until then. The Brooklyn Navy Yard's dry-dock was only 105 feet wide so they could build long ships, only no wide ones, which made her narrow for her length.

I never took anyone along if the weather wasn't ideal, so I asked the dispatcher before I left the house about it. He said there was little wind and a glassy sea with low swells, something almost unheard of on the Pilot Station, so if there was a day for a rider, this was it.

We rode the *Drake* as far south in Anchorage #9, as it was possible to anchor a ship off Hunters Point. I wondered why whoever anchored her thought it was necessary to be so deep into the anchorage. As we approached the ship's stern, I checked the ship's after draft marks, as I always did. As I did, it dawned on me that maybe it wasn't such a good idea bringing Paul along because the *Brooklyn* was immense. I didn't think a macho guy like Paul would back out and ride the *Drake* back to Pier Nine, but I asked him again if he was comfortable with climbing aboard something so mammoth. He nodded yes, but you never knew.

The *Brooklyn* was in ballast, so 50 feet of her was above the water. On a 1,100-foot-long ship, that is a humbling sight: it's like looking at a five-story-high black steel building lining on her side. I hadn't been on her before, but one tanker is more or less like another, except this one was a lot more than less.

To make matters more interesting, they had a pneumatic pilot hoist, not a gangway. Hoists are usually made of aluminum, about 8 to 10 feet tall. The steps and vertical grab rails are completely rigid.

Most ships lying at anchor have gangways lowered to the water so the crew and others, like Customs officials, can get aboard. Instead of walking up, we were going to be lifted 50 feet straight up the ship's hull by a wire hoist. You might think being hoisted would make pilots happy because the hoist does all the work, but we hated using them for several reasons: one was our fate was in the hands of whoever controlled the air supply. If he lowered you too far down, you could wind up lower than the pilot boat, or worse, be dropped in the sea. Judging how far to lower the pilot from far above the sea is tricky. The boat operator usually blew the horn to stop the hoist. They could also break because most rigs only employed one wire. For safety, there should have been two, so in case one broke you weren't screwed. As I rode these hoists, I'd look at the shackles holding the pulleys to the rig and think, *If these pins ever unscrew I'll fall to my death!* Last, ship hoists are prone to twisting because the part you stand on is not very tall, so there weren't many spreaders to help prevent it from spinning around. Spreaders are steps that are wider than the other steps. The longer a pilot ladder is, the more susceptible it is to twisting. I had plenty of ladders twist on me, but none actually turned 180 degrees, as happened to Dan Keon when a wave hit the ladder and spun him all the way around. Dan successfully struggled, eventually turning the ladder back around. If he hadn't, he'd have had to drop into the ocean and hopefully get rescued by our boat after floating past the ship. There were so many problems with hoists, IMPA tried to get them banned as too dangerous, but they still showed up on some ships.

As much as I disliked ship hoists, I liked riding in the "pilot bucket." AAA Shipyard hoisted us aboard ships while they were sitting in their dry-docks. It was exciting swinging up, out, and over the entire shipyard, often higher than the ship's masts looking at the shipyard below and San Francisco up to the north. Their operators were very skillful. They could drop that bucket on a dime without making a sound, so I always felt safe in those buckets, unlike on ships' hoists.

Once a crewman on a Maersk ship accidently hit the hoist's kill-switch, which stopped my trip up the hull midway. I waited motionless, not knowing what to think as the ship increased speed with me dangling over the side like a house painter. If the old man had been looking over the side, as he should have been, he would have seen my predicament. Ships are also required to have a regular ladder next to the hoist as a backup for cases like this, but they never did. Eventually, they figured out the switch problem and I rose up to the main deck.

Tankers only use air–powered equipment to reduce the risk of electrical sparks, so their hoists are always pneumatic. This means they are slower than the electric ones used by companies like Maersk. The *Brooklyn*'s was really slow.

After the hoist lifted me up to the main deck, I told the Mate to drop it back down to get Paul. From 50 feet above the water, Paul looked small for a big guy, but at least I had asked him if he was afraid of heights! Coast Guard veteran Paul didn't say anything about boarding his first big commercial ship as the Mate led us to the wheelhouse, where I introduced Paul and myself to a captain named Peacock. I didn't recognize him, but his odd–sounding name sounded familiar even though I had never been on his ship before.

"Captain," I asked, "Are you related to a Peacock from Maine Maritime Academy?"

"That'd be me," he said.

"Were you the deck cadet on the *Pine Tree State* in July, 1969, in Saigon?"

"Yep, that was me."

"Small world, Cap," I said, "That was my very first job as a Third Mate, and I remember you falling in love with a cute Vietnamese girl who was working with the stevedores." He laughed at my memory.

My ship unloaded fertilizer and jeeps sitting anchored in the middle of the Song Sai Gon River almost in downtown Saigon. It was interesting being in Vietnam as a civilian: you never knew what would happen. For example, one night the Viet Cong launched rockets directly over our ship, hitting a fuel depot about a mile up river and resulting in a big ball of flame. This illuminated the whole river, which had previously been black. Even though it was far away, it scared the hell out of me. Also, the soldiers stationed aboard would occasionally toss a hand grenade into the filthy river, which made a thud as they detonated. When I asked one G.I. what he was doing, he said it was to ward off scuba divers! Wonderful place, Saigon back then. Now Americans want to go there as tourists. I didn't like it when I was paid to be there.

The light went on in Captain Peacock's head as he thought back almost fourteen years. It was like old home week as we shot the breeze about what he had been up to. Obviously, he became a captain, and one of a very big vessel.

I asked Bob to heave up the anchor, which took about thirty minutes. The ship was facing into an ebb flowing out of the South Bay, so she had to be turned around. I ordered Hard Right rudder and Half Ahead. Almost immediately, I had difficulty getting the ship to swing because of the *Brooklyn*'s extreme length–to–width ratio. She wouldn't make a nice tight turn instead, she made a big slow one, but this brought us too close to shoal water off to the west near Pier 96. Each time I went ahead, she got too close for comfort. There was a ship off to my port and I didn't have much swing room, so I had to keep reversing the engines to stop the forward motion. Usually going astern helps a ship turn to starboard because of the propeller's torque. Not her. I kept "backing and filling," as this maneuver is called. I soon came to doubt I could turn her around without ordering tugs, something I never did in an anchorage before.

It was almost embarrassing how long it took to turn the ship around, but I finally pointed her north out of the anchorage towards the "D" and "E" spans of the Bay Bridge. Uneventfully, we sailed under the Bay Bridge and then out the Golden Gate. Because it was such a rare calm day, I wasn't anticipating problems getting off the ship even with the dreaded pilot hoist. I thought it was going to be easy and was sure the ship wouldn't roll much with such ideal conditions. There I went thinking again!

Paul and I said goodbye to Captain Peacock, hurried down to the main deck, and walked a few hundred feet forward to where the pilot hoist machine was hanging over the starboard side. Then I backed over the side of the ship onto the pilot hoist 50 feet above the sea. Looking at the Chief Mate, I said, "Go," yelling as I descended, "When the pilot boat blows the horn, STOP! It's very important! Thanks and have a good trip."

I looked over my shoulder at the Station Boat far below me following the ship some ways off her hull. Gradually, she grew in size as the hoist slowly lowered me foot by foot. The Station Boat never gets directly under a pilot until he is most of the way down; in case the ladder breaks, the pilot won't hit the steel deck.

On normal pilot ladders, the weight is equally distributed along their entire length. This means that if it comes off the hull, it usually does so slowly. With a hoist, all the weight is at the end where you are standing, much like a pendulum. Once a pilot hoist has any momentum, it tends to lift away from the hull easily.

Just when I was about 15 feet above the sea, the ship began a gentle roll to starboard toward the boat, moving the hoist away from the hull. At first I didn't think much of it, but within seconds I was 12 feet off the hull. Soon I was over the centerline of the Station Boat, like I was on a trapeze in the circus! I have never been that far off a hull before or since. Tak, the boat operator, seeing my dilemma, blew the horn. I'm not sure why, but as I was momentarily suspended in midair I thought of Goofy in a Walt Disney cartoon, swinging through the air only to wind up crashing through a wall and leaving behind a black outline of his body, and I certainly didn't want this to happen to me.

I thought, *Holy Crap, I'm going to do a face plant into the hull if I don't get off! Now!* Right then I decided, *Screw it,* letting go of the swinging metal contraption as it reached its apogee out over the boat. I didn't even attempt to use the manrope, I just let go of the grab rails as the pilot hoist dropped from under me, swinging back toward the ship without me. I landed in front of the boat's windows, as my knees buckled underneath me, glad I was safe even if it looked weird landing, the middle of foredeck. Tak stared at me with this odd expression as the hoist went flying in front him hitting the ship with an incredible *thwack*. To my relief, it had cleared all the boat's antennas and radars scanners.

Squatting there, I thought, *That could have been my face slamming into the hull!*

I let out a huge sigh of relief as I pointed up, yelling, "Don't pull away! One more!"

Captain John Winterling, or "Ding-a-ling'" as we called him, was standing on deck watching the show. Acting as if he had just caught someone doing something wrong, he said, "What the hell are you doing bringing a rider along on that big–ass ship?" The funny thing was, he didn't say anything about my aerial act.

Having almost gotten myself killed, there wasn't a lot I could say, but I told him, "Well, they told me it was flat calm out here, so I didn't think it was a big deal. Plus, he's a Coast Guard vet and a police captain in Miami! Did you think a ship would roll like in this kind of weather?" He just grunted something.

Looking up at Paul, I was sweating bullets because if the ship rolled like it did for me, he could get seriously hurt or have to stay on board and go to Alaska for more North Slope crude, and if he did, I'd never hear the end of it.

Paul stood on the hoist facing the hull, never looking down or left or right. I could hear the air winch motor up on deck go *biz . . . biz . . . biz* as 50 feet of cable slowly lowered Paul down to the boat. When Paul was just above the Station Boat's deck, Tak sounded the horn again and the hoist jerked to a stop at deck level. Nervously, I told Paul to step back, which he did, never looking around. He just backed up like he was stepping off a bus backwards as I grabbed his coat, saying, "Let go," and telling him to grab the railing. The ship hadn't rolled 2 degrees the whole time he came down, thank God. We turned and walked inside, where I introduced him to Winterling and Tak. Thank goodness it was me on the ladder when the ship took that big roll, because I know Paul would have had no idea how to get off and might have gotten hurt. It was just luck it was me, not him.

Winterling was a good shipmate, often trading places with me because he wanted summers off to go to his ranch in Montana, and I wanted winters off to go skiing. Sometimes he worked the whole winter to be off all summer. I preferred not working in bad weather, but nothing bothered him.

After I hung up our floatation coats, I told Paul, "Have a seat, the cook will make lunch soon." He didn't look like he was hungry, but then again, many visitors became ill. I felt sorry for seasick victims because they usually wound up outside, something I called "Riding the rails." Sometimes for a long time.

We had a nice lunch, and after we finished it, Paul said something I will never forget: "Man that was unbelievable! That's the scariest thing I ever did!"

I was a little taken aback. First, Paul looked and acted like the tough cop was he was. Second, Paul had been a Detroit cop before joining the Miami Beach Police and was involved in the famous Detroit riots, which erupted in July 1967. There were shootings, especially at the police, so I didn't think anything could be scarier than that, other than fighting in a war.

"You've got to be kidding. Weren't you in the Detroit Riots with people shooting at you?"

As Paul insisted that getting off the ship was scarier than being shot at, it dawned on me that we had to get him onto another ship, but anything would be easier than getting off the *Brooklyn,* at least the way I did it!

That night, he told Sue about his day, and he didn't change his story. Because he was so macho, I was surprised he admitted to being afraid. I knew our job was tough, but I never thought it was scarier than being shot at! Sadly, Paul eventually committed suicide.

In 1962, Exxon christened the SS *Manhattan* at the Fore River Shipyard in Quincy, Massachusetts. She became America's largest tanker at 64,434 GRT and 940 feet long x 132 feet wide, which was good size for any ship in 1962. Exxon wouldn't build bigger ships again until 1986, when they launched the *Exxon Valdez* and *Exxon Long Beach,* each 987 feet × 166 feet and 110,831 GRT.

When the *Manhattan* was built, most people hadn't even heard of Valdez, Alaska; but in 1969, Exxon wanted to test the feasibility of moving oil from the new oil fields in Prudhoe Bay east via the Northwest Passage, so they modified the *Manhattan*, turning her into the world's largest icebreaker at 1005 feet long × 148 feet wide. When she successfully traversed the Northwest Passage, she was only carrying one barrel of Alaskan crude, but Exxon got to say they were the first to transport oil over the top of North America.

On March 9, 1978, I piloted her out to sea for the first time when she was in ballast. It was blowing about 30 knots from the northwest, which was normal for spring, but weather was always a factor disembarking, especially big empty tankers. Empty ships are more of a challenge because they are so high out of the water, and the world's biggest icebreaker-tanker was no exception.

Before I got off, Captain Kachikis, asked if I wanted a "jug," in other words, did I want a bottle of liquor. I always gratefully said, "Yes, sir!" As I was getting ready to leave, I put an imperial quart of Mount Gay Rum inside my "booze" pocket for safekeeping. Right away, I noticed it was heftier than the fifths of Scotch I usually received from masters.

As the Mate and I walked down the main deck in the blustery wind to the pilot ladder, somehow I had forgotten how high the ship's main deck was above the sea, even though I had climbed up the pilot ladder only a few hours before. Leaning over and looking down into the gloom at the incredibly long ladder, I asked the Mate if he was certain the pilot ladder was exactly 10 feet above the water. From fifty feet up, it's hard to judge the exact distance looking straight down at a black sea, especially on a black night. A 50–foot wooden ladder is very heavy, and deck gangs hated readjusting them if the height was wrong. The Mate assured me it was fine, but I had been on too many ladders that turned out to be too short or long, so it was always something I was leery of.

I said good night and started descending fifty feet, hand over hand into the dark. To get a true picture of what this is like, you have to imagine climbing down the side of a five–story steel building on a ladder made of rope and boards only attached at the top end, which means the bottom part is free to move; the wind is blowing 30 knots; it's pitch–black and the building is moving along at seven knots, leaning back and forth. Climbing down is not as strenuous as climbing up, but it's still tiring. The longer the pilot ladder, the more it tends to twist, which uses up even more energy. Imagine climbing up a twisting step ladder. I always grasped the side ropes, never the steps in case a rung broke, so I wouldn't go over backwards.

When I was almost to the bottom, the pilot boat looked small because she wasn't anywhere near where she was supposed to be, just off the bottom of the ladder. Instead, she was off bobbing in the swells. Annoyed, I reached for my radio, which was slung over my shoulder, and held it with one hand while clutching the ladder tightly with the other.

Yelling into the wind, "Fritz, get the hell over here. I'm on the bottom of the ladder!"

He radioed back, "Sorry Cap. I didn't see you on that long-ass ladder." This didn't make me feel any safer hanging twenty feet above the choppy sea.

The Station Boat picked up speed and came towards the hull, at last positioning herself underneath the ladder. The only problem was she was still fifteen feet below me and I was out of ladder rungs! I said to myself, *"Oh, shit!"* as I wrapped both arms all the way around the ladder, interlocking them to rest myself and knowing that fifteen feet between me and the boat was too much to jump. And if I climbed all the way back up to readjust the ladder, I knew I'd be exhausted. Then I'd have to come back down again. If I lost my grip, I'd fall straight into the sea for sure. Also, being practical, I thought I'd have to ditch that expensive bottle of rum that was weighing me down, and I really didn't want to do that.

I tried catching my breath while looking up at all those rungs above my head. Just when I was dreading the climb back up, the ship started slowly rolling toward the boat. Normally, I wouldn't be too happy when a huge ship takes a big roll because the pilot ladder can swing away from the hull, which is very dangerous.

As the *Manhattan* rolled to starboard, like an elevator *San Francisco*'s deck started rising up directly at my feet. When she stopped rising and was about to drop down, she was only eight feet below me. That might not sound like much, but when you are dangling on a 50–foot–long ladder and about to jump onto a heaving boat, it's pause for thought. I knew I only had one chance, so I put all my weight on the manrope and pushed off. As I did, the rope stretched, dropping me onto the pilot boat's deck. As my feet hit the deck, the ship rolled the other way. In an instant, San Francisco dropped down ten feet alongside the hull, with me holding the grab rail, trying not to get bounced off into the sea. That was one lucky roll.

I waved goodbye to the almost–invisible crew high above peering at me in the darkness. Just like any other night, I went inside, except I was more thankful than usual I wasn't in the ocean and I still had my rum! Many times I looked skyward after getting off a hairy ladder, and said, "Thank You!"

When I started piloting, Captain Sever told me, "Don't think about a ship before you get on the pilot ladder and forget about her once you get off." This makes a lot of sense, but it's harder to do than you think, especially when your life is on the line.

CHAPTER 19

"THE SEA IS ... FAST AT SINKING THE UNFIT"

Felix Riesenberg, Jr., mariner, author, and 1897 graduate of my college, wrote, "The sea is slow at recognition of effort and aptitude, but fast at sinking the unfit." As cadets, we had to memorize this. It's as true today as it was when he wrote it.

I always wanted to be involved in a sea rescue, but after I became a pilot, I didn't think that would happen because pilots don't have the capability to rescue large vessels. Our pilot boats have fished many people out of the sea, but to my knowledge, the pilots never saved a ship from destruction during a storm. Like all sea stories, mine starts with, "This is no Bull Shit . . .," but in my case, it's true.

United Nations Convention on the Law of the Sea and the unwritten code of the sea requires mariners, aid fellow seamen in peril. This stems from a belief that if one mariner helps another in distress, then hopefully he will return the favor. Risking your life comes with a caveat: you only have to risk so much. "One hand for the ship and one hand for yourself," derives from this. When you hear *One Hand*, come a running. It comes in handy when the shit hits the fan, which it often does at sea, because you don't have to explain anything.

I became a New York Maritime College fourth classman, or Mug, on September 7, 1965. Indoctrination Week (IDO), our first two weeks of school, were similar to other military academies when cadets learn discipline. My first year was tough, but not as tough as IDO, but I learned the One Hand Rule, something I never forgot. This chapter is about the rescue of the Research Vessel *Peacock*. Everyone that day was in Harm's way, and we came very close to violating the One Hand rule.

A nautical science professor once told us that when the proverbial "crap" hits the fan at sea, like abandoning ship, it's always at night, or in bad weather. In other words, not ideal conditions. The *Titanic* sank in rare flat calm seas, but at night. Two other famous tragedies were the passenger liners *Oceanus* sinking off South Africa in a gale, and the *Costa Concordia*, which stranded at night. My saga started early, but just as Professor Van Wart predicted long ago, it carried on into the night in near–hurricane conditions.

On December 23, 1979, I was supposed to sail *Seatrain Chesapeake* at 0700. I knew it was going to be a really lousy day when I went to bed because the weatherman called for a southwesterly storm. San Francisco's TV weatherman wasn't right often, but he was this time.

I got up early, had a cup of coffee, and gradually woke up. At 1800, I drove my Peugeot from Pacific Heights down through the Broadway Tunnel, then into Chinatown, then down a long hill to Pier Nine at the foot of Broadway. I had the shortest commute of any pilot, but I liked driving in when there was no traffic. The rain during my ride could only be described as torrential, and the storm hadn't even hit yet.

Our offices were above a famous fish joint, The Waterfront, located at Pier 7 on the Embarcadero. We also rented parking spaces from Red Stack Tugs, inside Pier Nine, one pier north. When Red Stack moved, we relocated our office into their old quarters. You can still see "*Welcome Home*" in faded paint on The Bay side of some of these piers, remnants from WWII.

The old finger piers that haven't burned down or fallen apart jut out from the Embarcadero that wraps around San Francisco's waterfront.

No–longer–used shipping piers make wonderful offices, and our shore side Pilot Station is no exception.

When we moved, our new offices were a step up from our cramped quarters at Pier 7 ½. There was plenty of parking with the added bonus of a security fence. San Francisco is famous for many things. One is a surplus of homeless trying to get out of the weather. Our fence was supposed to keep them out, but eventually we had to install concertina wire after a bum tried to scare our female dispatcher working alone by scaling our fence!

When the jet stream slides south in the winter, it brings low pressure systems, which cause the wind to veer around to the southwest. We didn't know in the '70s, but these winter storms are caused by the *El Nino* phenomenon. San Franciscans didn't need a weatherman, all they had to do was look at a flag. If it was pointing northeast out stiff, it wouldn't be a pleasant day, especially out at sea. You could also get a sense of how dirty the weather would be by how much the old rusty corrugated steel shed doors on the south side of Pier Nine were rattling. If they sounded like screaming banshees, I knew it would be ugly.

After parking inside Pier Nine, I ran in the pouring rain up the stairs to the dispatcher's office above the restaurant. I was hoping that Rich Lyons had good news for me, like my ship had cancelled because of the storm, so I could wait for the weather to ease up. He laughed, telling me to get ready, I was still going to sea, weather or not. Standing before him, I had no idea it would be so long before I'd be in the office again.

I never feared taking ships to sea, but only a loon would enjoy piloting a ships out to the open ocean, then climb down a wobbly wooden pilot ladder, and make a leap of faith onto a small boat being tossed about by a storm, but that's what we are paid to do.

The storm clouds were unbelievably gloomy when we got underway at 0730. You can also tell how bad the weather is going to be on the ocean by how rough the South Bay looks. As we left it, it looked like an ocean, not a bay. The Station Boat reported it was blowing a gale, 45 to 55 knots with higher gusts. The swells were already over 12 feet and gaining, so I wondered if I'd be able to disembark. If too rough, I could always stay aboard to the next port, something called, "Being carried away." I never was, but several pilots did, including Howard Idle. He sailed the *Santa*

Mercedes from Pier 30-32, knowing there was no way he could get off in a storm, so he carried an overnight bag with him. I never heard of anyone else taking luggage on a job, but off to Los Angeles he sailed in a raging gale, never even attempting to get off.

Captain Nancy Wagner was in the first class at Kings Point (U.S. Merchant Marine Academy) that admitted females. She followed a family tradition; her father is also a graduate. Following graduation, she was an Exxon deck officer. On February 22, 1990, she became the U.S.'s first female maritime pilot when she was commissioned. Nancy was like the Poncho Barnes of female ship pilots, only better–looking. She is also a friend of mine.

Nancy always carried extra clothes in case she was "Carried away." I never even thought about that; all I knew was I didn't want to get stuck on a ship, especially a small one crossing the Pacific in dirty weather. I dreaded the thought of being cooped up in a tiny cabin, so I always took my chances getting off all my ships and enduring the rolling around on the Station Boats.

Nancy, in addition to being a good pilot, always had a lot of spunk. For instance, one day she sailed a small Korean tanker out of Richmond Inner Harbor. Pan Ocean Shipping, like many other steamship lines for are now out of business. I forget which tanker she was on, but all their ships have classy names like *Bum Dong, Bum Ju, Bong,* and *Long Dong,* and I'm not kidding! When her ship arrived out on Station, I was on deck to assure she got off safely.

As the Station Boat followed Nancy's rolling ship, I noticed the pilot ladder's bottom rungs were already broken, and we hadn't even come alongside! Regrettably, it wasn't uncommon for ships to put out half-assed pilot ladders that didn't meet normal standards. If she had inadvertently stepped on a broken rung, she could have fallen into the sea. I steadied myself, cupping my hands so she could hear me in the howling wind to be careful of the broken rungs. At the top of the ladder, she yelled, but most of her words were lost to the wind. I think she said, "I don't want to lose my f...ing lee and there is no f...ing way I'm going to be carried off on this f...ing piece of s...t ship!" She used some salty language in front of the Korean crews, who, of course, didn't understand a word.

The operator smoothly closed the gap, rubbing the boat's big fenders against the hull, but touched it once and like a flash, Nancy swung off the manrope, landing next to me and smiling. *So much for me worrying about her!!* I used to think I was fast getting off ships, but that must have been a record. Once I thought women couldn't do the physical act of climbing up and down long pilot ladders, some of which are 50 feet high. I got tired plenty of times, but Nancy proved me wrong.

Nancy didn't want anything special, she just wanted to be a pilot, and I respected her for that. She never complained, which is why the pilots liked her, especially me. There are now women pilots all over the country, even on the Columbia River Bar, one of the worst places to board ships, so I think women pilots owe Nancy their thanks for piloting their way.

As *Chesapeake* approached the Golden Gate it was raining so hard, I couldn't make out either 900–foot–tall towers holding up the bridge. The ship's windows were solid sheets of water as the rain cascaded down from the bridge's road deck, as if we were in a gigantic car wash. The visibility was worse than sea fog, and if I wanted to see, I went outside on the downwind wing side and stood under an overhang. I couldn't see with the rain going sideways, but out of habit I looked anyway, praying no vessels were nearby because the ship's radars were useless. If any small boats were out, they needed to have their heads examined because the weather was about to test even professional seamen. At least no ships were moving.

Marine radars send out an electronic beam. If it strikes a hard target, like a ship, an echo returns. Radars measure the time it takes for the beam to go out and back in milliseconds, turning that data into a blip that is shown on a monitor. They work best in calm seas when objects, like buoys, are above sea level. With high seas and heavy rain, radars get what is called a false echo or clutter, so mariners must differentiate between what is water and what is a target.

The radars were useless, so I navigated by using dead reckoning. By timing my passage, I could guesstimate the position of the first two of eight buoys that delineate the Main Ship Channel I was aiming for.

The Main Ship Channel is called a "Bar" channel because silt flowing down from central California creates a huge horseshoe–shaped sandbar that blocks the entrance to San Francisco. So much sediment finds its way out to sea that the Army Corps dredges it every year to 55 feet, so ships can safely cross enter. The channel is 1.1 miles long and 2,000 feet wide and in the middle of the sandbar.

Whenever the Corps seagoing hopper dredges were working the Bar Channel, I had to maneuverer around them because they were "not under command." Those dredges use giant suction pipes that vacuum up tons of mud in the channel, so they couldn't move out of the way. The mud is hauled to a disposal site away from the channel. Whenever I passed one, I thought back to when I spent two and a half years working on them.

Whenever a ship buries her bow into large waves, she immediately slows down, and the whole ship shudders. We weren't making much way, but her speed didn't matter to me; all I was concerned about was could I control her. When the weather turned southerly, ships were often late, so I was in no hurry to get on the Station Boat. Sitting on an 85–foot boat in monstrous seas was tiresome, especially if my arrival showed up hours late, or not at all. So, the less time I spent, the better. *Peacock*'s ETA was 1100. As much as I wanted her to arrive early, to get out of the storm, I wasn't counting on it.

As we approached the Bar Channel, the swells were becoming more formidable the farther west we steamed. Because of the weight of sea water, large ocean swells can easily damage a ship, even a huge one. In extreme cases, waves have broken bridge windows 100 feet above the sea! Green seas were always possible and extremely dangerous, so on snotty days, I always advised ship masters to clear their foredeck long before there could be any problems. Once I advised U.S.S. *Camden*'s captain to clear his forecastle because I was anticipating large swells after passing Point Bonita, but he ignored me. What did I know? I only did this every day of my life! *Camden* was a stem–winder, meaning her bridge was located near the bow, so I was looking right down at the anchor detail who were standing near the anchor windlasses. Typical of the Navy, they had two sailors for every job, so there were plenty of them milling around. Despite her slowing down almost to a crawl, green water kept coming over the bulwarks, flooding the foredeck. Sailors were literally floating around on their butts.

Because there is a lot of equipment on the forecastle, someone could easily have gotten washed over the side.

Chief Mate Dewey Rose, from my college, died securing his anchors for sea when a green wave slammed him into a bulkhead. Securing anchors is not worth a man's life, and this tragedy could have been avoided.

During southwesterly gales, large swells often broke at the Bar Channel corners, especially Buoy # 7 so I moved the ship over to the inbound lane to avoid them. Although it was daylight, I barely made out the ocean-type buoy as we crawled past, but I still heard its distinctive bell, yet only intermittently, as one enormous swell after another broke over it, muffling it. Crossing the Bar like this is very dangerous to all but the largest vessels.

Mammoth waves were also swamping Buoy #2 as we passed it headed for the Pilot Boat *San Francisco,* which was waiting for me three miles ahead, south of the Sea Buoy. The Station Boats usually stayed well south of the Sea Buoy during Sou'westers so they wouldn't get pushed too far off station.

Until 1971, a bright red manned lightship with SAN FRANCISCO painted on her hull in white letters was anchored where the Sea Buoy is today. The lightship was equipped with a big foghorn and, a Fresnel lens light, and continuously transmitted the radio signal "SF," which ships homed in on to find the Pilot Station. Before ships had radar, they couldn't tell how far off they were from the lightship's radio source, and several of them homed right into the lightship and rammed it. The unmanned "Approach Lighted Whistle Buoy SF" replaced the lightship, but I thought it wasn't large enough for a major port's entrance. This proved true in December, 2008, when, despite having radar, a ship ran it over. It was found on the ocean floor still attached to its mooring cable.

On another note: in 1899, the first wireless transmission on the West Coast was sent from the lightship to the Cliff House sitting above Point Lobos.

Chesapeake's crew rigged a ladder for me on the starboard side, ten feet above the sea. It was paramount it didn't hang too low, or our boat's fenders could snatch it, which happened to me once when the boat pulled the ladder to about a 30 degree angle. It popped free of the tires, much to my relief, but it could have broken! Also, if a ladder is too long, waves can push it, which is also dangerous.

We also required a two–inch manila manrope hung parallel to the ladder. We used them to swing away from the ship and to control our descent. When I was ready and the boat was below me, I put all my weight on the manrope, then pushed off using my feet. If I judged my fall correctly, I landed safely on deck without buckling my knees and missing the steel grab rail like I hit once. Making a good lee is a pilot's art. Done well, you are safe and dry. If not, you are in the ocean or worse.

With all the spray and pelting rain, I couldn't see *San Francisco*'s running lights, and she wasn't far ahead of the ship. All our boats were white and they were hard to see on days like this, so now they are painted international orange. Even though I couldn't see her, I could hear her fog- horn coming down the port side. After saying goodbye to the old man, I ordered hard right rudder, giving him a course of 300. I did this so there was no delay. As I turned to leave, I asked for Half Ahead, knowing that even on Half, the ship would still lose a tremendous amount of headway turning through the large swells, and I didn't want her to stall, which would lead to a rolling ship. Ships don't stop when transferring pilots: if they did the pilot boat couldn't stay alongside.

I said, "Merry Christmas," and was off down the inside ladder to the main deck, hoping to get off quickly. The weather was getting worse by the minute. I didn't know it as I walked, but this day would be the wildest one I would ever experience on The Bar.

San Francisco's skipper was Roy Bradshaw. It was always good hearing his deep voice on my radio because he was one of our best. I liked when he was at the wheel, when it seemed to go smoother than with some other boat captains.

The first time I met him, I mistakenly called him Jack, thinking that was his name. This at first pissed him off but he later turned the tables, calling me Jack as if that was my call sign. I never used mine, *Foxtrot*, when I was dealing with Roy. Another reason I liked Roy was he was a huge man. I knew if I fell into the ocean he was strong enough to lift me right out of the water soaking wet with one arm. Luckily I never needed his help in this regard.

As the ship turned through the swells, I could see the bow of the Station Boat plowing around the ship's stern. On rough days, not only does the boat smash into the ship's wake, but also into the ocean swells, which momentarily slows or can even stops the boat. I knew from the black engine exhaust that Roy was giving her "the bullets," or as tug skippers say, Jack was putting her into a "smoke hole." This got her moving to where I was hanging in the middle of the ship.

As she arrived, I pushed off the pilot ladder sliding down the manrope, using it to break my fall until my feet barely hit the deck. When they did, I reached behind, grabbing the boat's hand rail. Once I felt steel firmly in my hand, I let go of the manrope, letting it fall back against the hull. I was glad I got off the ship so easily considering the conditions and wished it went that smoothly all the time. Because lees don't last long, it's important to get off as fast as possible.

I'm not sure if the crew above heard me, but I waved goodbye shouting, "Merry Christmas". into the wind as *Chesapeake* picked up speed. She quickly vanished into the intense seas, and with her went the protective cover she had briefly provided. Now we were all alone to face the full brunt of the winter storm. I didn't envy the ship, even though she was many times larger than we were. Eventually I would go home, whereas they were headed across the expansive Pacific and only God knew how bad the weather was out to the west. Soon enough, we would know for ourselves. I didn't think about it, but sometimes we were the only vessel on the Pacific Ocean for 50 miles.

After I entered the wheelhouse, I closed the watertight door and double *dogged* it to keep out the driving rain. In bad weather, our old Station Boats rolled and pitched so much it was often hard to walk, so I hurried into the saloon to get out of my soaking–wet coat and rain pants before *San Francisco* had a chance to start dancing around. She wouldn't sit still again for a long while.

San Francisco was the first large boat we built to go directly alongside ships to transfer pilots. Formerly, we used small dories to ferry the pilots from a larger pilot boat, like a schooner. She was a fantastic 85-foot all-steel boat constructed in Stockton, California, with built-in flume tanks. These tanks dampen rolling using a water and baffle system. As the boat rolls one way, the water in the tanks goes the other so the opposing moments help diminish the rolling. They weren't perfect, but they made for a more comfortable ride, especially compared to our newer Station Boat, *California*. She was built without them to save money.

Despite the weather, I was hungry, having been up since 0500, so before I sat to get "comfortable," I went into the galley to see if the cook was still making breakfast even though it was after 0830. The galley was spotless. The cook had cleaned it for "Change day" and was asleep. The SF's crew was due for their four days off, so I knew they were happy to be heading in and it was almost Christmas. I was happy for them, but not for me, because at 1000 I would have to leave the relative "security" of San Francisco and transfer over to *California* when she came out On Station. I wasn't looking forward to jumping between the two Station Boats. It was dangerous enough leaping between our 65–foot run boat *Drake* and our 85–foot Station Boats. The difference was that the run boat can't ride up and over the Station Boat because of the size difference.

After I scrounged up breakfast, I went into the wheelhouse asking, "What's on the program?" as I thought my arrival was delayed. Also, Captains Meyer and Mauldin were outbound. After they got off their ships, *California* would relieve *San Francisco*. So the three pilots had to transfer over to her.

A short time later, I was out in the rain again helping Meyer, who was spry for what I considered an old guy, get off his ship. Because I was so young, most pilots looked old to me, which is probably how I looked to the apprentices. Captain Sever was the senior pilot, something I never became. By the end, the only pilot senior to me couldn't retire because he had to pay so much alimony to his ex-wives, which he deserved.

Prior to becoming a pilot, Meyer was the original master of the first, and only, nuclear–powered commercial ship, *Savannah*. Unfortunately she was a commercial failure. Maybe that's why Bill was usually grumpy, except when he had two cocktails.

Bill wasn't looking forward to jumping between two boats in 60 knots of wind any more than I was. When he thought about it, he came up with an idea how to do it more safely. Instead of Mauldin getting off onto *San Francisco* and then the three of us jumping over to *California,* Billy and I would climb onto Mauldin's ship after he made his lee. So we boarded Mauldin's ship, then waited for him. When he showed up, we climbed down onto *California.* Meyer's idea worked like a charm except for getting soaking wet again. I never transferred like this before or after, indicating how ruthless the weather was.

California, built in 1977, was never a great sea boat like *PVSF.* Typical of pilots, they put a pilot in charge of her building who was set to retire within a year of taking delivery. This meant he only suffered for one year while the rest of us endured a poorly designed, uncomfortable boat for the next twenty-five years until we bought bigger, more stable ones the last few years I piloted.

The boat committee didn't do the smart thing and re-use *San Francisco*'s architect's plans and build her twin. Why change a good thing? Instead, they made *California* narrower and didn't install flume tanks. We saved money, but we got a lousy boat in return. The first year we owned her, we had nothing but problems and seasick pilots because she hobby-horsed like crazy and wouldn't settle down no matter what the sea conditions were. We spent almost as much money putting bilge keels on her as the flume tanks would have cost, so we didn't save anything. Our engineering staff also wasted a lot of time experimenting by putting sandbags in different locations and trying to get the weight distribution correct so she wouldn't pitch and roll so much. Until *California* was better balanced, she even rolled at the dock. I felt sorry for whomever we donated her to when we replace her.

Getting a relief cook from the Sailors Union of the Pacific can be difficult anytime, especially at Christmas. Besides the fact that it is a holiday, our boats were small and our cooks didn't even have their own room, like on regular ships. Getting a seagoing job at the last minute is called a "Pier Head Jump," which a new cook named Tom Madrid got when he hired on two days before Christmas. Previously, Tom worked on a private railroad dining car and had never been to sea, so I wondered, *Why the hell did he want to work at Christmas on an 85–foot boat out on the ocean instead of a nice dry homey railcar?* A bad career choice, I thought.

After *California* got the three of us off Tracy's ship, we got to meet Tom the Cook, but by then he was horribly seasick from the rough ride out through the Gate and over the Bar. Tom joined a long, inglorious list of others who became ill on her, except he was almost comatose. He should have gone to his bunk, but he was too weak to move or even get up from the dining table. I swear, you couldn't tell the difference between his face and the dark–green table mat his head was resting on! When lunch time approached, he lifted up his green head and offered to cook, but all three pilots, sort of stunned, said in unison, "Are you nuts? It's too rough!"

No one else wanted the job, so I ended up making half-assed sandwiches for the three of us, which was a neat trick with the boat shucking and jiving. Getting the reefer door open without food flying was a challenge. I feared that the mayonnaise would fly out and smash into the galley. What a slimy mess that would have been. My sandwich experience gave me even more respect for our cooks.

Tom started his seagoing career on the worst day I ever experienced on the Bar, so I didn't expect to see Tom the Cook return. The storm wasn't as bad as typhoons I lived through, but then again, I wasn't on an 85–foot boat during them.

When the next change-day came around, I saw Tom waiting with his sea bag ready to board *California*. I asked him how he could even think of going back to sea after those four appalling days he spent at Christmas.

"Captain," he said, "I really need this job." Tom had a fan in me after that.

Peacock, a decommissioned Navy mine sweeper, owned by Oskco Edwards & Harry Tompkins, was chartered to Fairfield Industries, Inc., a company specializing in seismographic research. Under the terms of the time charter, *Peacock's* owners furnished the operating crew, and Fairfield provided the scientific crew and personnel to engage in seismic research south of San Francisco. Why she was doing it in the middle of winter and why she was coming back into port after sailing out only the day before was curious to me, but I didn't really care, she was just another ship. Before I boarded her, I thought maybe was she was returning for a Christmas break, or to get out of the way of the storm. Later on, I found out it was because a scientist working on deck the night before, without a life jacket, was swept over the side and lost. Being out on deck at night in bad weather isn't too bright, especially without the proper gear, so it wasn't going to be a very nice Christmas for someone's relatives.

I was the "Number One Pilot," so whatever ship came first was mine. I didn't care which or where she was going, I just wanted to get off our boat.

Two hours late for her ETA, *Peacock* finally made an appearance out of the south. She wasn't much to look at. She was small by our standards, maybe 150 to 170 feet long, but anything would have looked ugly in that much rain. She was be the smallest ship I ever piloted except for one private yacht.

As we approached her, we passed starboard to starboard with Mauldin and Meyer sitting in the wheelhouse killing the monotony of waiting around by watching me board her. Unlike them, I was ready to go to work wearing my fire engine red foul weather pants and floatation coat with its big hood pulled on extra tight.

As we passed, I could see, by her size, that I didn't need a pilot ladder. Her main deck was low enough to be able to jump directly across onto her, as we did with seagoing tugs.

After we cleared her stern and motored up parallel to a spot where I thought I might be able to jump over, Billy opined, "You'll never get on her. It's too dangerous!"

Being thirty and cocky, I ignored him and leaned over towards Gunnar, the boat operator, telling him to keep going because I wanted a better look. It was my call, at least I wanted to give it a shot. Anything would be better than sitting around.

When both vessels were wheelhouse to wheelhouse, I knew it was hopeless, as *California* rose and fell over the waves that had grown to almost twenty feet. *Peacock* was too small to make a decent lee, and there was no way to bring the boats safely together. I was let down to say the least because I wasn't going home, but I had no idea it would be another eight hours from that moment.

Gunnar picked up the radio mic, "Skipper, it's too dangerous to board you with these big swells. Go back out to sea and wait for the next arrival due in a few hours. When she shows up, we'll try to use her to make a better lee. Sorry, it's too rough. Will call you on 13 when we confirm, over."

Her captain radioed back he understood. As *Peacock* turned away from us toward the Southwest Traffic Lanes, she disappeared into the gray as I grudgingly took off my rain gear for the third time. I'd already been On Station for three hours, and begrudgingly I thought I had at least two more hours to wait for the next ship.

California had five swivel captain's chairs bolted to the deck around a round dining table. There were also two stuffed chairs against the opposite bulkhead under thick seaproof windows. Bummed out, I slumped into the one next to the scuttlebutt so I could put my foot up against it and brace myself into the chair as I tried to relax.

Billy was sitting next to me wearing his usual nondescript expression, while Tracy did a crossword puzzle sitting at the dining table. Out of the blue, Meyer said, "She seems to be calming down a bit."

I looked at him in disbelief, for just about then the bow took another incredibly steep dive sideways over the crest of a big wave, the kind that made me think that maybe we could roll over in the huge swells. The boat rode up on one swell, then slid down the backside of another. When she hit the trough's bottom, the boat would shake and shudder like a wet dog. After she bottomed out, she'd fight her way back up into the next steep wave, then slowly recover. She did this over, then over as I painfully waited for the next ship to show up. If I hadn't gripped my chair's armrests tightly, I'd have slid right out of my seat. We should have had seat belts.

I tried to zone out and not think about how lousy it felt being aboard, but just as I closed my eyes to relax, the boat fell off the backside of an immense wave like a toboggan. As *California* dropped, almost out of control, the back of my chair rose off the deck, forcing me to grip the armrests even harder. When I was sure the bow would punch a hole into a wave, my foot slipped off the scuttlebutt. I didn't realize it, but the stuffed chairs were not secured to the deck like the captain's chairs, so over went the chair with me in it!

From underneath the upside-down chair, with my cheek firmly planted against the deck, I stared at Bill and said, "She's calming down all right, Bill!" He actually laughed at my predicament, something unusual for him. Replacing it, I tried getting comfortable, wedging myself in even tighter. Whenever the boat is unsettled, it's impossible to read. Even watching TV gave me a headache. At least I wasn't sick. Yet.

Then Ole Olsen, who had taken over the watch, flipped open the wheel-house door like he was in hurry, shouting, "Someone's calling *Mayday*!"

At that, the three of us rushed into the wheelhouse. Anything to kill the boredom of waiting. I thought, *Finally, my chance to rescue someone!*

Ole changed channels. "Group San Fran, this is *California*. We have a bad situation out here. *Peacock* is calling Mayday somewhere to the west of us and has no propulsion and needs assistance. We don't know if we can get a line over to her because it's blowing sixty knots here with higher gusts and we have twenty–foot seas, which are getting worse. We will standby her, over."

"Roger, *California*, please provide assistance. We will get a cutter under way as soon as possible. Stay on channel 16."

"Roger, we're leaving the pilot grounds heading west to find her. We will be on channels 10, 13, and 16. Over." Ole then radioed, telling our office we were headed west and wouldn't be on Station for a while. A very long while.

Luckily for *Peacock,* she hadn't traveled very far west from the Pilot Station because if she had, she would have been directly south of the Farallon Islands. This rocky island outcropping is a marine sanctuary eleven miles almost due west of the Pilot Station, where vast colonies of seals and even great white sharks, who feed on them, live and breed. If *Peacock* had, she would have quickly drifted onto the rocks and been smashed to smithereens. Nothing we could have done would have saved her.

We didn't know it, but the cavalry was never going to show up wrongly, assuming the world's sea rescue experts would send help out right away. For whatever reason, they didn't. As the day wore on, in desperation, we radioed several times asking when help was coming, getting several answers. One lame one was that they were busy rescuing someone in the South Bay, which was ridiculous because they owned many rescue boats stationed, including ones right inside the Golden Gate at the Presidio. I never found out why they never showed up. What was baffling was their boats are specifically built for high sea conditions, even designed to roll over and right themselves. Ours were built for heavy weather, but not for rescuing other vessels.

Once *San Francisco* was outbound and punched a hole into a gigantic wave near Buoy #1. While she was completely submerged, her crew lay on the deck waiting for the windows to break. Instead, she popped out the other side, not even losing her engines. This shows how tough our boats are, but they're not rescue boats and we really needed help. With the seas building and the Bar breaking, we didn't know how long it would be before they would come out to assess the situation, but we hadn't heard any other "Maydays," so we all thought the Coast Guard would attempt a rescue regardless of how bad the weather was. This is what they get paid for and are the best at. If we didn't get a line over to *Peacock* soon, we would both drift, and eventually she would go ashore on the Marin County headlands with her crew inevitably perishing in the surf.

Ole Olsen was driving. Because it was Christmas, the "A" team was ashore so we didn't have our best men, they were all reliefs, including the seasick cook. They were good, just not as good as Bob Porteous, our skipper captain. He started with the pilots during WWII when he was a kid. Because the relief crew didn't work at sea on a regular basis, they didn't have the same *feel* as the men who did it daily. It was unusual for four crewmen to be off at the same time, so there was no senior captain. Also, the conditions were extreme, making it tough for anyone to handle the boat effectively.

Porteous was the smoothest boat driver I ever saw. I always felt safe when he was on the wheel. I sorely missed him because getting a tow line across to another ship without power, from our hobbyhorsing boat, soon turned into a nightmare.

As we chased her, it dawned on me to thank God I hadn't boarded the crippled *Peacock*. Pardon the pun, but I'd have been up ship's creek without a paddle, asking for aid and not getting it. Many times I thanked Him for looking out for me.

Both boats advanced farther and faster north than any of us could have anticipated. At least we didn't have to worry about running into any ships. There weren't any.

Meyer, in addition to being a pilot, also was the "Pilot captain" of *California,* in charge of her maintenance. So he decided to assume command. We decided Tracy would be in charge of the tow line and I would handle communication and navigation. Because I was the #1 Pilot, accordingly, I should have been in charge, but being a rookie I was willing to do whatever Meyer asked of me. Having Bill steering seemed like the right thing to do, but this almost turned into a disaster because pilots are not used to handling boats like *California* in such huge seas. It would have been more prudent to let an operator run her. Even Ole, an older guy, was more used to handling our boats than any of the pilots. Although we were trained to move ships, there was a difference, but I think Meyer was concerned that if the two vessels smashed together, which we almost did a few times, it would be better if the pilots took the blame, not the crew.

First we had to find *Peacock* before we could save her. This was no small feat because we could barely detect her on radar. Seeing her visually through the spray and dark was even harder. If we were on top of a wave and she was in the trough of another, picking her out of the gloom wasn't easy. We also didn't know what kind of line we had on board, if it was strong enough, or long enough to tow something much bigger than us. In order to be effective, tow lines have to be long enough so they have *catenary*, or give in them, or they can part, even if they are strong and new. The one Tracy found in the lazarette was neither strong nor long. It was more of a mooring line.

Luckily, about five miles west of the Sea Buoy we spied *Peacock* in the trough of a huge swell and caught up to her. Thus began hours of fruitless attempts as Billy endeavored, over and over, to close the gap between the two vessels, one of which was totally at the mercy of the waves and winds. If you have ever heard the expression "pissing into the wind," this was sure it because the wind had increased to 70 knots. Even standing in the deckhouse's lee was difficult. It began to look like we'd never get a heaving line over. Maybe if we'd had a line throwing gun, as required on ships, we might have stood a chance.

After following *Peacock* for a while, we lost all communication with her and her running lights failed, making her appear even more pitiful than before. No running lights also made it harder to find her whenever we were blown apart.

As hard as Bill tried to stay parallel, *Peacock* did whatever the weather wanted her to. One minute we would almost collide with her, the next minute a massive wave would sweep between, shoving us far apart. We didn't have a choice, we followed her whichever way she drifted. Repeatedly we were tossed around by the breaking seas, placing us both in danger. What we were trying to do was highly precarious, something none of our boats had never attempted before.

After an agonizingly long time, I decided to tie a life jacket onto a heaving line and drag it in front of *Peacock*. I radioed Bill from the stern to cross *Peacock's* bow, but to leave enough room so we weren't blown down on her. After dragging the line back and forth a few times, a crewman finally snatched it with a boathook, pulling it aboard, much to our relief. We wasted an awful lot of valuable time and sea room until then. Tracy then sent our old mooring across, and once secured at their end, we tied our end to our cruciform bitt. We were towing them at last!

It was then I noticed that their crew were wearing shorts! I think that was the nuttiest thing I ever saw at sea because it was mid-winter and we were in a hurricane! I'm not sure if they were poor, stupid, or oblivious to the icy rain, because even with my float coat I was chilled.

When we started, we thought we had plenty of sea room to drift, but in all the confusion we didn't pay enough attention to our position. We were too busy trying not to collide with *Peacock*, and no one thought it would take us so GD long to pass over one crumby line.

Now that we were tied together, we had to figure out what to do with *Peacock*. As we started slogging into the swells together, I felt like Lois Lane must have when Superman caught her falling off a building and said, "I've got you Miss," and she replied, "You've got me! Who's got *you*?" That was us. We really had no business towing them. They were too big, we were too small, our line wasn't suitable for towing, and the wind was howling at almost hurricane force right into our faces.

As Bill carefully started towing *Peacock* south, it dawned on me how really crappy the tow line was. As I looked aft through wheelhouse windows, it looked old and frayed and was covered with Irish pennants. After we spent so much time getting the tow line over to them, we feared it would part, so I decided to go aft to ask Tracy's opinion, and to see if he wanted to be relieved or wanted some hot coffee. Despite being soaking wet, he said, "Pablo, I'm good with the coffee, thanks. Why don't you re-plot our position and radio the Coast Guard again! They'd better be out here someplace. If this line parts, we're gonna lose these sons-of-bitches!" I told Bill the line was shittier than we thought. He just nodded.

We were towing south in the general direction of the Pilot Station, but we were barely making any headway. I ascertained a fix using radar, then plotted it on the Gulf of the Farallones's chart, which put us far closer to Point Reyes than any of us realized. What was more unnerving was see-ing waves breaking on the edge of the radar screen. They were only a few miles astern of us! The breakers were as clear as if I were watching them on a Hi-Def TV. There were parallel rows of surf, something I had never seen before on a radar, and never wanted to again. If there ever was a "lee shore," this was it, so I didn't waste any time radioing the Coast Guard *again*! I gave them our highly precarious position, saying *Peacock* was under tow, but we weren't out of the woods. I reiterated how bad our excuse for a tow line was and if it parted, we would witness a catastrophe.

I calmly told Billy we needed to get a move on or we'd all go ashore judging from the radar. He nodded, saying he couldn't add much power because *Peacock* was too heavy and he was doing his best against the huge swells. If we had communications with her, maybe they could have passed a better line to us.

I told Bill, "We aren't making much headway, so just to be on the safe side, why don't we head southwest instead of south? Maybe we can drift around Point Reyes." He nodded.

During the entire escapade, we were waiting for a white surf boat to come help. They never did, failing to do what they get paid for. We never thought we'd be left holding the bag, so in my opinion what they *didn't* do was remiss. We were all in mortal danger, so I lost a lot of respect for them that day, and their status as heroes went down a peg.

Almost six hours after the first "Mayday," the C.G. radioed that a commercial tug was outbound. "Roger that," I replied, along with our plan to go west and not south. They replied it would take another hour or more for the tug to reach us. This made us more anxious for *Peacock*'s crew, but at least someone who knew something about towing was coming.

As Meyer headed the boat in a more southwesterly direction, ever–so–slowly we started making westing, pointing southwest, but actually drifting northwest. We never made any progress south, but I breathed a sigh of relief when radar finally showed us drifting safely past Point Reyes, which was to our east. At least we were no longer in any danger of going ashore. If we hadn't traveled west, both boats might have floated ashore into the heavy surf, or *Peacock* would have broken the line and gone in on her own.

The first good thing to happen was the wind easing down to a full gale. The difference is substantial. As it did, out of the gloom came the first lights we saw all day coming from a mammoth seagoing tug plowing through the angry waves as if they were meaningless. I can't describe the sense of relief seeing floodlights illuminating the horizontal rain against the night sky. Her red and green running lights made her look like a Christmas tree, which was appropriate because it was almost Christmas.

As she neared, she spun around and backed up toward *Peacock* as green seas crashed over her towing deck. Crewmen casually stood by as if it were normal to have sea water sloshing around their feet. At least they had on life vests. After a short time, the tug passed a proper towline over and *Peacock* dropped ours as we moved out of the way. That crappy line had done a yeoman's duty and wouldn't be used again, so we deep-sixed it. What took us hours only took them minutes and soon both of them were underway towards San Francisco, leaving us alone in the dark again.

As the tug disappeared, I hoped that was the last time I would see or hear anything about *Peacock* because that was more of a rescue than I had bargained for. Being so close to the breakers at Point Reyes made me realize how close we came to violating the "One Hand Rule." Again I looked skyward, saying "Thanks!"

As Tony Peterson took the wheel, it dawned on us that we had to beat our way back twenty miles to the Pilot Station. All day we had been bouncing around in the huge swells; now we had to steam directly into them as fast as we could to board a ship that was hove-to waiting for us. Due to the bad weather, all ship arrivals were delayed and some didn't even show up.

Tony gave her more throttle to gain speed, but we also began pitching heavily into the steep seas, which on that boat was no fun. As the ride worsened, Tracy and I raced back outside, becoming seasick at the exact same time. It was bizarre because no one was sick all day, except the cook, and I was only sick a few times. This was one of them. Maybe it was the relief of not worrying about *Peacock*, or maybe it was the thought of having to pound squarely into the seas, which were still huge, for the next twenty miles, I don't know. As expected, the motion didn't bother Meyer at all.

After I cleaned up as best I could, I ditched my foul weather gear and plopped into a chair trying to relax. I wanted to get off *California* as soon as possible, go home, get into bed, and not worry about the damn *Peacock* anymore.

CHAPTER 20

THE CALM AFTER
THE STORM?

For several hours the French containership *Lafayette* laid hove–to waiting for us. Once we started making headway, we radioed that we were coming but were not making much speed. Swells from big Southwesters last a long time even after the wind eases up. Knowing our situation, she started steaming to rendezvous. About the same time, the dispatcher radioed that I was relieved of duty. Obviously, *Peacock* didn't require my services and other ships were delayed due to the storm, so I was to ride with Meyer. I had come out early in the morning, been in the storm all day, and wasn't needed after all! But if I had gone in earlier, I would have missed the rescue, something I always wanted to be involved in and was proud we accomplished. If I had been relieved earlier, it was doubtful if *Drake* could have crossed to get me, it was too dangerous to cross. Either way, I was happy to be getting off a bucking bronco named *California*.

Two hours later, I followed Bill up *Lafayette*'s pilot ladder five miles north of the Sea Buoy. Even though she was rolling a lot, her motion was much calmer than *California*'s. As soon as I grabbed the ladder, I felt better. When we entered the bridge, we met a French captain who was glad to see us. Not all captains appreciate pilots, but we come in handy, especially when weather conditions are at their worst. Bill resumed his role as a Bar Pilot. Being the stoic guy he was, except for when he had those two drinks, he hadn't even untied his necktie all day!

Bill started piloting south toward the Sea Buoy, and I couldn't have been happier. We rescued a ship under terrible conditions, but the most important thing was that no one on either vessel was injured. The only casualties were Tracy and I getting sick. No big deal.

Bill checked in with Traffic and replied that the COPT ordered *Lafayette* to anchor due to the high winds. No vessels moved all day after Tracy's. The severe weather had shut down the port. VTS reported nothing was moving on the Bay except for the tug towing *Peacock* near the Golden Gate. This really surprised us because we thought the tug would have been much farther along into the Bay. They had taken over from us hours ago, and seagoing tugs can plow through the seas better than any other kind of boat.

Bill asked for Half Ahead and off we sailed. Once he settled in, even though it was late, the captain graciously asked us if we wanted dinner. I politely declined, still being a little queasy. Being a professional bachelor, for me to turn down a free meal, especially a French one, was unheard of, but it was out of the question. Meyer didn't seem like the type of guy who thought much about meals, unlike me, who plans dinner at breakfast. Not Bill, he perked right up, "That would be fine captain." The captain motioned to the Mate to have dinner brought up for Bill. Soon a steward placed a large tray with a towel over it where Bill could eat and still pilot. I was surprised by the nice spread they brought up considering we were still in the tail end of a huge storm. You never knew what to expect with ship meals; some were mediocre, but on occasion they could be something really special.

Seeing such a fine dinner, I said, "I'm not hungry Cap. Why don't I pilot so you can eat in peace?" He quickly agreed and went over to the tray and starting eating.

Because I had nothing to do but sit and watch Bill, piloting would kill some time. I would much rather pilot than observe anytime. It was his license on the line, not mine, and I was helping him out so he could eat. I knew he was thinking about what I was doing, just not saying anything.

I took the Conn and headed into swells, which were still steep despite the wind abating the ship down to 35 knots, which is still a moderate gale. I had never approached the Bar Channel with such big seas before, so I was interested to see how the ship would handle. That was one of the great things about piloting: I got to experience different conditions on different ships. I wasn't worried about hitting the bottom, even with the big swells. I was more concerned about getting her safely into the Bar Channel and keeping her inside the buoys with the wind blowing the beam so strongly.

The captain asked me, "Mr. Pilot, may I put out my stabilizers? We took them in while boarding you." Even though I had the Conn, I deferred to Bill, who was obviously the senior pilot by age and looks.

Bill said, "No, no, captain, we're going to be close to the bottom with these big swells!"

I thought, *Why wouldn't Bill put the stabilizers out? They would help slow our rolling.* Rolling increases the draft and a 20–foot swell reduces the channel depth by 20 feet, so a ship drawing 33 feet would be near the ocean floor. Bill was the senior guy, so I didn't say anything. I had only piloted 775 ships, so I was still considered a rookie.

We were coming down from the north while fighting the southwesterly wind with swells coming from both the northwest and the southwest, which creates tough conditions crossing the Bar. Because of the confused sea state, I delayed my approach into the channel, which course is 070 degrees. The big swells and strong wind were shoving the ship toward the north, so my plan was to steer 090 and see what happened. The ship was yawing wildly, so I only gave rudder commands until she was safely in the channel. The ship was gaining speed, but it was still making a lot of leeway, so I did my best to hug the red side of the channel.

I thought, *Everything is going just fine considering the storm. I'm off that bouncing pilot boat, headed in, and I'm technically off duty, even though I'm bringing the Lafayette in. And I'm feeling better.*

I loved piloting, especially in extreme conditions. Nothing compares to being on the ocean under terrible conditions with a giant ship rolling and pitching like hell. It was always breathtaking seeing Mother

Nature in action. My highs of piloting often came on terrible days like this one.

The water depth at the Pilot Station is about 90 feet, but once a ship is within one mile of the Bar Channel it decreases rapidly, rises to 60 feet, then levels off at 55 feet through most the channel. This compresses the waves, forcing them up so that they are taller and steeper than a mile west. The swells travel a long way from the Northern Pacific to reach us. The Bar Channel is the shallowest water they were in since they were created. This night was no exception, except there were additional huge cross swells from the southwest caused by low pressure that had roared through.

As we neared Red Buoy #2, I altered course to 078 while the *Lafayette* continued rolling moderately from side to side, but the rolls weren't too intense, so I wasn't worried about them. Swells affect ships almost up until the Gate, so was looking forward to getting there and being in calmer waters, where I knew my mal de mer would go away.

About the time I was confident everything was fine, the ship started another roll to port, but this time it was stronger and the starboard bridge wing kept rising. The wing rising is perfectly normal with big seas, and I wasn't apprehensive about it until it didn't stop! I watched in wonder as it slowly rose and rose, then rose some more until I could no longer see the storm–tossed ocean through the starboard door. Instead, I was looking up at what should have been the sky—except I couldn't see it because it was still pouring. If it had been clear, I would have been able to see the stars through the door from where I was standing next to the steering compass.

As the wing continued its rise, I thought, *Oh, no! The bloody stabilizers aren't out!* And I was certain a ship built with stabilizers doesn't have bilge keels. *So what's going to stop the roll?* I had been going to sea since 1966, and no bridge wing had ever risen like this before. With it so did my anxiety.

You have to understand when a ship rolls only 10 degrees, it feels like a big deal and you must hold on to steady yourself. At 20 degrees, it's time to have a "Come-to-Jesus meeting." Anything more is very, very uncomfortable, so when the ship reached a list of 40 degrees, I was grasping a grab rail and putting all my weight on my left leg. I was seriously afraid I'd start sliding downhill or even fall over. Unflappable Bill, who had a hell of a lot more sea experience than I did, never said a word. Maybe this was old hat to him, but I was thinking: *She's going to roll over!*

Then it happened; anything and everything that wasn't secured started shifting toward the port side. As friction gave way, the increasing list, papers, pencils, nautical instruments, cups, plates, you name it, all started to move, slowly at first, then faster as the incline increased. Like the 1893 Oklahoma Land Rush, the whole shebang went downhill. Then, when I thought there wasn't anything else left, the file cabinets began to slam open. All ships' cabinets have mechanical stops to prevent them from opening during rolling, but the power of the immense roll stressed them past their breaking points, snapping them one after another. Clatter like gunshots sounded as the drawers started flying, forcing the crew to jump out of the way as the debris field of steel drawers headed north.

I thought, *What if this thing rolls over? What happens to me?*

As I did, she abruptly hesitated, then ever–so–slowly rolled back to starboard, reducing the list by about 20 degrees. She rolled to port again, but not even half as much as the first roll. Finally, her energy spent, she leveled off as the ship shot out of the Bar Channel into deeper water to the east, with me still holding on tightly, as if I were on an amusement ride.

As we neared Mile Rock Light, Bill drolly said, "Okay, Cap, that was enough fun for one night, I got her."

I told him, "You can have her!"

I looked around at the mess, except where Bill had eaten his dinner. He had eaten everything, including bottled water and a glass of red wine. Nothing had slid off his tray and there was no food on his blazer.

I looked at him with admiration, "Cap, how the hell did you eat dinner and not have it go all over the place?"

The master of the understatement said, "I just leaned into it."

As the ship approached the Golden Gate, the seas had calmed down, further easing my stomach, so I was much happier. As we went under it, the air was as clear, as if it had been scrubbed. It was a beautiful San Francisco moment. No one in the city probably knew or cared what transpired on the ocean. She was dressed up in her finest colors, waiting for Christmas. Coit Tower, to starboard, was floodlit in red and green, while the Embarcadero Center was outlined in white lights like every

Christmas, giving The City a festive look. The lights were particularly striking after being in weather all day that can only be described as black.

The only good thing about seasickness is that it goes away immediately once the rocking stops; at least it did for me the few times I experienced it. Since I felt better, I asked the captain if it was possible to have dinner because there was still another hour before we would be anchored. I was quite hungry, having eaten nothing since throwing together those so-called sandwiches.

The captain said, "Mais oui, Capitain, but of course!" telling a crewman to escort me to the dining room. I thought, *This is great. I'm safe and I'm going to have a fine French meal after a day from hell.* I asked Bill to get me when he finished anchoring.

The dining staff were gracious, showing me to an empty table. No one was eating except me, which wouldn't happen on an American ship, where there are regular meal hours. At 1831, you don't eat, union rules. Those French guys didn't mind, setting a place for me.

As I was waiting for my meal, I noticed stains all over the white tablecloths. I thought, *Oh my God. That big roll threw condiments all over the place. What a mess!* Obviously, putting the stabilizers out would have been the right call, but knowing Meyer, he couldn't have cared less. Me, I was a little embarrassed by the whole thing. However, as they say, it was an Act of God: *Peacock* and the mustard on the overhead!

Bill anchored the ship, then *Drake* came for us and we stumbled into the pilot office exhausted after 2200. It had been a trying fifteen–hour day and I only moved one ship. Due to the weather, shipping slowed down to a crawl, so I didn't pilot until 0400 Christmas morning, when I piloted *Arco Fairbanks*. By then, the worst weather of my career was long gone, off to the east. I saw many bad days, but this took the cake. Thank God, I never experienced weather that ruthless again because I had 5,678 more ships to pilot until I swallowed the hook.

As the years passed, European ships like *The Lafayette*—which I piloted four more times—became a rarity. I came to miss the different foods, coffees, and the culture of those ships as they were slowly replaced.

The odd thing about this whole escapade was, we never heard one word: not from the *Peacock*'s crew, not the owners, no one. If it had been my sorry butt on that derelict, I know I would have made inquiries and found out who had saved my ass. I thought they might have been just a little more grateful. Who knows what they were thinking? Maybe because they had no radar, they never knew waves were breaking right astern of them. If they had, they might have had a better idea what goners they were without us and our crappy tow line. And there wasn't another boat for miles, including the Coast Guard, that could have saved them. Perhaps their lawyers didn't want them to admit how far up shit's creek they were without us. Maybe if they had done the proper thing, "Crazy Horse" might not have gone on the war path. Then again, that was Tracy's style.

CHAPTER 21

CRAZY HORSE ON THE WAR PATH

I was glad to be done with *Peacock*, but I had no idea the saga would go on long after we cast off the tow line. We survived a terrible day, but we returned to moving ships 24/7 as if it never happened.

Captain Tracy Mauldin, a former Delta Lines master, was a Bar Pilot long before I showed up when we became friends. It was always good to hear, "What's up, Pablo?" whenever I landed on the Station Boat. Tracy was aboard doing his crossword puzzles, something I later became addicted to, as well. Pablo was all he ever called me. I never knew why, but my best friend Luis, a Cuban-American, and my Peruvian friends also called me that, so it fit. It was always fun shooting the breeze with him.

Tracy could be intense, sometimes too much so. Once he was so wound up, he admitted himself into hospital because he thought he might be having a heart attack. He eventually did have one, climbing up a high ladder on an empty Arco tanker. The Coast Guard medivaced him off. He should have retired, but he was too ornery, coming back to his love of piloting. A stroke made his decision for him to swallow the hook.

Tracy wasn't only smart, he was cagey. Because of this and his personality, some pilots didn't care for him, which didn't bother him at all. When he didn't like the way the pilots ran our business, he stood up and told them about it, so some pilots called him "Crazy Horse," as a put down. Not me,

I always made it a point to call him that, which he liked coming from me. Tracy was crazy all right, like a fox, and you will see why.

When Tracy crossed the Bar for the final time, his wake was held aboard FDR's classic presidential yacht, *Potomac,* moored at Oakland's Jack London Square. When I got aboard, I noticed Tracy's widow, Millie, and his daughter greeting other mourners, so I wandered over to introduce myself. I told them how sincerely sorry I was losing Tracey, what a fantastic shipmate he was, and how much I missed him as a shipmate. Mrs. Mauldin said she knew who I was, then looked at me with this funny expression as if they didn't believe me. "Thanks Paul," she said sadly, "but I didn't think some pilots cared for Tracy that well."

I told her I couldn't speak for them, but I said how much I enjoyed, and respected Tracy as a man, and pilot. I mentioned the great sea stories Tracy told, then retold one, trying to cheer up that sad day. I emphasized Tracy's seamanship during the *Peacock* rescue, and why, from my point of view, he was one of our most pleasant and skilled pilots.

Unfortunately, I visited the *Potomac* several more times as the turns of other pilots, such as Captains Meyer and Filipaw, came to cross the Bar.

I didn't think much about *Peacock* other than it was another adventure I survived and how we could have done a better job of passing the tow line over. After the rescue, we put better lines aboard the Station Boats.

Tracy, being Tracy, kept tabs on *Peacock* while the rest of us forgot about her. He learned that after the tug took over from us, somehow their tow line parted near the Golden Gate. Her captain didn't monitor his tow very well, because without realizing it, *Peacock* floated back out to sea on her own! Frantically the tug turned around, found her, and towed her into AAA Shipyard. It was strange indeed that our ratty tow line didn't part and a commercial seagoing tug's did.

Luckily for both the tug and especially *Peacock,* she hadn't drifted onto Potato Patch Shoal, where she would have foundered for sure. I can't imagine what those poor bastards thought about those two horrific days: losing the plant, spending hours worrying if they would be rescued, almost going ashore in the surf. Then when they were almost safely under the Golden Gate, their tow line parted, leaving them helplessly drifting again. I wondered how many of them swallowed the hook after what they experienced. The real tragedy was the overboard scientist.

Weeks after the rescue, Tracy told me the tow boat company had filed a salvage claim against *Peacock*! Typical of him, he always seemed to know these sorts of things, but I was flabbergasted. I'm not sure why Tracy was so interested. Maybe it was because he had been involved in another salvage case, but if not for him, the pilots would be less rich, so to speak. I didn't know much about salvage, except for what I studied in admiralty law classes in college, where our professor didn't go into it very much.

"Salvage rights!" I laughed, "They didn't perform salvage, we did! We risked our necks. Not only that, those bozos almost lost her!" Thinking back on that long, trying day, it made me angry they considered claiming salvage.

Legally and by tradition, pilots can't claim salvage because, theoretically, a pilot could handle a ship, put her in distress, have his brother pilots rescue the ship, and then claim salvage. We had no choice. Under the United Nations Convention on the Law of the Sea, we had to respond and provide assistance. Because the Coast Guard never showed up and the tug hadn't arrived in time to prevent her from floating ashore onto the Marin County headlands, we saved her from complete annihilation. The tug was never in the danger—we were.

In contract salvage, the owner of the property and the salvor enter into a contract provided by Lloyd's of London called Lloyd's Open Form. It must be signed prior to the commencement of salvage operations. What the salvor is paid is determined by contract. It can be fixed or based on "time and materials." If the salvage is unsuccessful—No Cure, No Pay—then the salvor wouldn't be paid. Roughly, a vessel owner bids out a job and after agreeing, they say, "Go get our vessel. She's drifting around someplace in the Pacific." The tug finds the vessel, then brings her back for repairs.

Pure salvage, on the other hand, is when mariners expose themselves to risk or damage to their equipment to save someone else's property. No contract exists between the vessel in peril and the salvors; it's implied by law. The salvor must bring his claim in a court, which awards money based upon the merit and value of the property. We brought our suit to Northern California's U.S. District Court. Several factors are considered in establishing the salvors' award, including the difficulty of the operation, risk involved, value of the property saved, degree of danger to which the property was exposed, and the potential environmental impact. We obviously fulfilled the definition. Other requirements must be met: the services are rendered voluntarily, and the salvage must be successful in whole or in part. Examples of pure salvage are boarding a sinking ship in heavy weather or on fire, raising a ship or sunken property, or towing a ship that is in the surf away from the shore. The premise of salvage is that mariners will take extra risk to help vessels in peril. With an economic incentive, plus the "One Hand" rule, mariners might be more willing to help vessels in distress. There was no doubt we were at risk, and we came too damn close to going on the rocks ourselves. Thinking back, we only owned two Station Boats, and if one of them had foundered, half our equipment would have been lost along with Mrs. Lobo's son. This would have been catastrophic to the pilots and to my mother.

If the tug hadn't claimed salvage, Crazy Horse wouldn't have gone on the war path. Or, as mariners say, "Tracey went up California Street," meaning we retained Hall, Henry, Oliver & McReavy, San Francisco, California, admiralty law firm to defend our rights.

Legal disputes arise from salvage claims, and they did in our case. One key thing we demanded, in addition to *Peacock*'s value and the lives saved, was the value of survey data collected and seismic equipment not owned by *Peacock*. It obviously would have been lost if we hadn't rescued her two days before Christmas 1979. The court's decision to compensate us didn't occur until May 17, 1984, four and a half years later.

Crazy Horse, Tony Pederson, Gunnar Larsen, Ole Olsen, Bill Meyer, myself, and the Bar Pilots Association all shared in the award. Even Tom Madrid, the seasick cook, received a share. I received $2000, which was a lot of money in 1984. I was pleased, thanks to Tracy's effort.

Yeah, Crazy Horse was crazy all right, like a fox, and I still miss seeing him and hearing his sea stories that always started with "Pablo, did I tell you about the time. . . ?"

CHAPTER 22

ANCHORS AWEIGH: PILOTING FOR THE U.S. NAVY

I was proud to be commissioned Ensign in the U.S. Naval Reserves in 1969, and I was active until honorably discharged as Lieutenant-Commander in 1985.

If a Navy ship floated, I probably piloted it, because I piloted over 123 different foreign and domestic naval vessels. From submarines, to supply ships, to research ships, to aircraft carriers, I moved them all, including a "spy" ship.

Piloting naval craft was always "interesting" because naval ships are built by class, and their classes are so different from one another, especially compared to merchants. Merchant bridges, while not always the same, feel familiar to pilots, but each class of naval ships is completely different. With the exception of aircraft carriers, most naval ships are far smaller than merchant ones. When I began, carriers seemed immense, but after a while they were just another big ship. They were much beamier than any merchant ship I ever piloted, which included huge crude oil carriers, the widest of which was 180 feet. A carrier's flight deck is 267.

When I walked onto a commercial ship's bridge, I expected to take operational control almost immediately, while on Navy ships I never knew what to expect. While I never assumed command, I technically was in control of a ship, and no one issued speed or course commands except me. On naval ships, I never knew if I would receive the Conn, and if I did, whether I would keep it.

President Lincoln once told this anecdote in regards to politics, but it can be applied to going aboard naval ships as a civilian pilot. One day a man was riding a horse when it started bucking so violently that he could hardly control it. His horse finally leapt so high, it put one hoof into a stirrup. The startled rider, seeing his dilemma, indignantly said, "If you want to get on, I'd better get off!" This relates to piloting because only one person should be in control of the ship. Piloting by committee doesn't work.

Here is an example of Lincoln's anecdote: Once I boarded the U.S.S. *Shasta*, a Kilauea class underway replenishment ship going into Oakland Middle Harbor. As mentioned, San Francisco has extremely swift current. Depending on the state of the tide off Oakland Middle or Outer Harbor, it's not only strong, but runs at a 90–degree angle across their entrances. Every time I piloted, I calculated the exact amount of water flow and estimated how it would affect my ship. Then as the passage progressed, I reacted to what was really happening or the ship could quickly get out of control. If that happened, the ship could easily hit the corner of the container docks or quickly run hard aground. There is virtually no water outside those harbors, so there is no bailout room. Once a ship was committed, she had to make the entrance. Also, as soon as a ship entered Middle Harbor, I had to slam on the brakes because it was a dead end.

On my first voyage as a ship's officer, my ship docked at Middle Harbor after we returned from Saigon. That was a very busy place during the Vietnam War, but it was eventually filled in with dredge spoils from the Port of Oakland channel widening project. This created Oakland's Port View Park.

Captain Pottenger asked me if it was okay for his OOD (Officer of the Deck) to pilot the ship into the dock. Occasionally, Navy officers wanted to pilot their own ships. On those, I didn't have the Conn. This was a bad one, because I never liked being put in this position. Watching them was actually more difficult than piloting the ship myself. When I didn't have the Conn, I wasn't supposed to interfere, and the crew is only supposed to obey the person who has it. Observing them was a fine line between letting them get in trouble or risking interfering. In either case, I could have been found remiss if something went wrong. It was stressful enough watching our apprentices train. The difference was that they were handling ships 24/7 under a senior pilot's supervision, and all of them had masters' tickets prior to becoming a trainee. This was completely opposite of someone who might have just graduated from officers' candidate school or been at sea for weeks on end. The Navy has many fine ship handlers, but too many of them aren't accustomed to maneuvering large ships in confined places, especially when dealing with strong currents. Maneuvering at sea is one thing' doing it around docks is quite another. Teaching a rookie how to maneuver ships in strong currents is like teaching someone in driver's ed how to drive on an icy road. Extremely tricky. After a short time, the captain realized the OOD was out of his depth and asked me to take the Conn, which I gladly did.

Here is another example of "Who has the Conn," and why captains should let the pilots do the piloting. On April 28, 1983, The U.S.S. *Enterprise,* the *"Big E,"* one of the Navy's largest vessels, ran hard aground entering Alameda Naval Air Station. Her CO, Captain Robert Kelly, after six months at sea, thought he had the "feel" to pilot his huge warship into Alameda NAS' Channel with a huge crosscurrent. Unfortunately, when a ship passes a certain point it's beyond hope, which is what happened when Kelly misjudged the current. The *Enterprise* was swept out of the 42-foot–deep channel coming to an ugly halt in 29 feet of water on the channel's south side. *Enterprise* had safely sailed across the Pacific to wind up 1,750 yards short of her home berth as the Navy band, standing on the end of the pier, played on. Thousands of dependents, who waited six months to see their men, waited hours longer. She was finally freed by eleven tug boats when the current changed. Also, the entire crew stood on one side of the ship to help refloat her. Oddly enough, *Star Trek's* George Takei was aboard. Maybe he should have been steering.

This wasn't only embarrassing, but unnecessary, because there were three expert ship handlers aboard. A Bar Pilot, a civilian Navy docking pilot, and an observing pilot drank coffee as the ship grounded. Unfortunately, being captain of a colossal warship doesn't necessarily mean you are a skillful ship handler in confined waters. Captains with any nautical savvy should let the pros do it. The pilots knew, as always, that whoever had the Conn was in charge and not to interfere, as it should be. Unlike the horse, the three pilots didn't try to get into the saddle.

My whole life, I have been awed by the ability of our Navy to launch big jet fighters day or night from a ship steaming along at 30 knots. I was also surprised how confusing it can be to pilot Navy ships compared to merchant ones. Naval vessels' bridges, in addition to being smaller than those on a merchant ship, are also way too noisy because there are too many people on them. One day, I counted forty people milling around a carrier's bridge while I was moving her! Some were civilians on a "ride-along," but that is far too many. Even being in the Naval Reserves didn't change my view.

The major difference between merchant and naval ships is how they are manned and operated. A typical Navy bridge entering port has: the CO, XO, OOD, JOOD (Junior Officer of the Deck), a navigator, a backup navigator, a helmsman, a lee helmsman (the backup guy), and a navigation team plotting the ship's position. In addition, there are sailors on each wing using bearing compasses relaying bearings to the "Nav" team. In addition, there can be all sorts of other non-essential personnel around, which is confusing if you are used to being on a merchant bridge, which has a tremendous amount of space for a few people. On them there is a helmsman, a watch officer, and the captain. Modern merchant containerships are 150 feet wide. As a comparison, a Navy-guided missile frigate (FFG) is only about 60 feet wide but has over 200 personnel.

Some merchants have enclosed wings. Ships with enclosed bridges were my least favorite type of ships next to stem-winders. No matter how awful the weather, I preferred being out in it during dockings, because I had a better feel for how it affected a ship. I also disliked looking through windows during dockings, especially if they became steamed up or it was raining.

One big difference between naval line officers and merchant marine officers is we feel comfortable on either bridge, but I'm not sure naval officers would be comfortable standing a sea watch by themselves as merchant officers do, often without a lookout. Unlike the Navy, whose manning levels have not changed much over the years, the crew levels on merchant ships has never been lower.

We knew we weren't always the Navy's most welcome guests because, naturally, they want to be in control. I didn't blame their attitude, but San Francisco is a tricky place to pilot ships. They may not have always liked having us aboard, but we came in handy, as I will show with a few examples. One Navy captain told me a pilot saved his bacon, so he never entered port without one.

I think what pilots disliked most about the Navy was the way they boarded their ships, which seemed like an afterthought. Their ships are strictly oriented to their function, like shooting missiles, blowing stuff up and going fast. Unlike commercial ships, many naval ships don't have vertical sides or are flared so pilot ladders don't always rest flat against the hull, as required by IMO. On ships without vertical sides, the bottom rungs of the pilot ladder, can move in and out, making it hazardous for pilots. I'm sure the Navy's are exempt from these requirements, but they shouldn't be because they board sea pilots all over the world, and getting them safely aboard should be a priority. We also never knew where they were going to put the pilot ladder as every Navy ship was different. The ideal place is in the middle of the vessel, but I saw Navy ladders too close to the bow and way too far aft. I even saw ones made out of metal, which are the most dangerous kind and something never seen on any other type of ship. Also we could never get them to stop attaching "pullup" or "tag lines" on the bottom of their ladders. Tag lines are used to haul the ladders back up on deck, but they can get wrapped around the station boats' big truck tire fenders and lead to broken ladders and injured pilots. So boarding Navy ships, except aircraft carriers where they used their helicopters to fly us out to them, could be a chore.

Navy ship hulls often have half round metal covers over their overboard discharge ports (we called them "pier destroyers"), so they're not flush with the hull, which makes sliding a ship along a dock impossible. If you slide those ships, they will tear a dock to pieces.

I'm not sure if every Navy ship has a sky pilot on board, but once (and only once) I was greeted by an officer whose insignia told me he wasn't a line officer, but a padre. I was glad he met me because you need a pilot of a sort, even a sky pilot, to get to the bridge of naval vessels. They have some strange passageways, hatches, and ladders leading in every direction, unlike on a merchant ship, where once you find the door on the main deck marked "Up," you follow it to the bridge.

While we were walking up to the bridge, I noticed quite a few women aboard his ship. This was a far cry from when I was in the reserves, when no women went to sea, so I sarcastically asked him, "What percentage of the women get pregnant during Westpac?" I thought that question might make a padre a little nervous, but he didn't even hesitate. "About 30 percent," he replied, like it was no big deal. I assumed a lot of hanky-panky was going on aboard Navy ships even though it's forbidden to fraternize in the military. When the fleet sails they are gone for up to six months, so I'm sure it's lonely for everyone, but getting pregnant? I'm still amazed the Navy lets women crew their ships, because the berthing areas are very tight.

Every fall, San Francisco hosts Navy Fleet Week. We supplied all the pilots for Saturday's grand parade of ships, which had as many as twelve Navy ships of all types and sometimes two carriers. Because some of the pilots didn't like moving Navy ships, the association had to ask for "Volunteers." I always did, because I like any kind of parade, especially one with aircraft carriers!

I didn't mind piloting their ships as long as they did what I asked, but as you will see, that wasn't always the case. Once I piloted the Canadian oiler HMCS *Edmonton,* invited by our Navy to join the parade. After I boarded her and received the Conn, I positioned her directly ahead of the carrier, U.S.S. *Carl Vinson,* the last ship in a long line. She followed us in from the Pilot Station.

Coming in was uneventful, but once the *Vinson*'s bow passed under the Golden Gate, she started launching F-18s', two at a time, right over the top of the *Edmonton*'s masts as the fighters started a steep climb! I thought, *How many people in the world have ever been directly in front of an aircraft carrier with fighter jets flying over their heads as they went under the Golden Gate Bridge?* One reason I loved piloting, you never knew what would happen next!

As ships ahead of us passed Alcatraz, they started scattering toward their assigned berths around the waterfront. Ours was quite a ways farther south at Pier 94 near Hunters Point, south of the Bay Bridge. As ships started moving toward Piers 27, 35, and 45, the *Edmonton*'s captain thought we were going too fast and stopped the engines without consulting me. I had the "Conn," yet he bypassed me, something he is not supposed to do. I emphatically told him we had plenty of sea room to go around all the other ships, and the flood current would turn his ship in a circle in a heartbeat if we didn't maintain minimum headway. Also, the *Carl Vinson* was still directly astern of us moving towards us with the current, so if we had turned broadside in the current, she could have rammed us! The ship began to get out of control, so the captain realized I was correct. As the anecdote goes, he tried getting into the saddle when he didn't know enough about our tidal conditions to ask my advice or let me do my job. After almost getting his ship into irons, he let me handle her without further interference.

Except for putting two tankers alongside each—so they could transfer cargo—we didn't berth too many ships together, but I did when I docked her alongside an American destroyer at Pier 94.

The Blue Angels air show was the spectacular highlight of Fleet Week when they performed incredible stunts over San Francisco, which was always a great show of our naval might. They flew so low over our home in the Cow Hollow area of San Francisco's famous hills, we could almost see the pilots' faces. We could also see thousands of our neighbors on their roofs watching like us. Commander Kevin Mannix, the "Boss," or the #1 Blue Angel, at one time, graduated from Fort Schuyler ('86). Not a bad career for going to a state merchant marine college. Who knew? Captain Scott Kelly, space shuttle pilot, is also an alumnus ('87).

I always enjoyed Fleet Week, except when I was piloting a commercial ship around the time the air show ended because we never stopped commercial ship traffic, we stayed out of the Coast Guard's safety zone. When it ended, all the yachts, once stationary, moved in unison toward their marinas, so I had to be particularly vigilant not to run them over. Many yachts didn't know the Rules of the Road, and carelessly crossed in front of moving ships. During Fleet Week, it was a nightmare. Time after time during events such as this, the Coast Guard denied requests to clear paths for ships, except when I was moving ammo ships when it was required.

My very first piloting experience with the Navy happened during my ACDUTRA (Navy Active Duty for Training). During my two weeks I trained with Navy docking pilots on Treasure Island Naval Base, a man-made island in the middle of The Bay, T.I., as it's called, was named for the novel *Treasure Island* because Robert Louis Stevenson lived in San Francisco in the 1870s.

T.I. was created when the Government filled in The Bay to make a seaplane base for Pan American Airlines' flying boats in the 1930s. *Indiana Jones* portrays a Sikorsky S-42 clipper taking off from T.I., but unlike in the movie, no commercial flights took place because the plan was scrapped to make the 1939 Golden Gate International Exposition. When Japan attacked Pearl Harbor, the Navy wanted the property for a naval base, so San Francisco agreed to swap T.I. for a much larger piece of property on the Peninsula (later becoming San Francisco International Airport).

During my tour, Navy docking pilot Captain James Pringle said we were flying out to bring in the U.S.S. *Coral Sea*. The Bar Pilot would pilot her in from sea, then he would pilot her after the Bay Bridge into Alameda Naval Air Station. I was trying to become a docking pilot. so seeing such a big ship maneuvered was going to be a great experience, and there is no substitute for watching pilots work.

I'll never forget the morning when an immense, dull, steely gray Chinook helicopter, with its distinctive twin rotors, came roaring out of nowhere over the top of the old Navy seaplane hangars situated next to the base's marina. After hovering a short time, it landed on a big red "H" near the Navy docking pilots' office next to a smoking orange flare an MP had ignited a few minutes before. As the big helo gently bounced, her stern ramp hit the pavement at the same time. In a flash, the Chinook's crew chief jumped down the ramp and walked toward us wearing a helmet equipped with oversized tinted goggles, making me think he looked like a human insect. He handed each of us a Mae West life vest, motioning to put them over our heads and buckle them around our waists. Because we couldn't hear a thing over the din of the two spinning rotors above our heads, he motioned like a traffic cop. First he pointed at Captain Pringle, then at the bar pilot, and finally at me to follow him up the waiting ramp.

I was excited in general, but there was no way I could have imagined someday a crew chief would point at me to get aboard a helo, and not as an observer. It came sooner than I ever thought possible.

When I got into the cavernous body of the helo, I strapped myself into the last web seat running along the fuselage next to the ramp. I nervously cinched my seat belt extra tight because I'd never been in a helo before, especially one with the stern ramp partially open, allowing me to see everything below!

The helo pilots didn't waste any time revving up those two turbo shaft engines because as soon as the ramp was up, the helo rapidly ascended. In a thundering racket of exhaust gases and dust, we rose straight up into the air and then quickly banked out and over Treasure Island.

The chopper flew right over the top of infamous Alcatraz Federal Prison, then leveled off at about 1,500 feet over the middle of the Golden Gate Bridge, flying between the two huge orange-colored bridge towers. I'd been under the Golden Gate untold times. That was a first, flying over the top of it!

My first helicopter ride was exhilarating, but with the stern ramp partially open, it was electrifying. Nothing blocked my view, not even a window. I could see the entire Bay, including tide rips where currents moving in different directions caused big seams across The Bay. I got a greater appreciation of how currents moved in different directions in different parts of The Bay.

I wasn't sure if I would ever become a ship pilot, but flying to the *Coral Sea* was special. As we flew west, I kept thinking, *What a cool way to go to work!* I couldn't fathom getting paid to pilot ships, but I sure wanted to.

We flew twenty miles southwest before I finally got my first glimpse of a carrier under way. From our altitude her flight deck looked small for such a giant ship. She didn't slow down, she kept steaming north toward the Pilot Station. As the helo pilot slowed down, we began losing elevation as the chopper banked sharply off to starboard making a big round turn, then headed toward the carrier. That dot in the ocean quickly became an airport runway.

As we flew over the carrier's stern, I watched the ocean quickly disappear until all I could see was the battleship gray deck. The pilot matched the forward speed of the carrier and hovered us a few feet off the flight deck, then set her down with a small *whump* as the wheels hit. I was surprised by how long it took to set us down. I assumed the ship was pitching as heading north into the everyday Pacific six-foot swells. The pilot had to be careful not to set down when the deck rose up. Taking so long to land really gave me an appreciation for how hard it must be to land anything on a carrier, much less a fighter jet going 150 knots.

Once I was invited to go on a Dependents Day Cruise (Busman's Holiday?) on the carrier *Carl Vincent*. This is when the sailors' families go out to sea and observe firsthand what their relatives really do. The Navy pilots put on an awesome mini-airshow for us, launching jets off the side catapults and performing "touch and goes" right in front of a huge crowd of cheering relatives. They even broke the sound barrier in a fly-by. It's stunning what our Navy is capable of, even if they have trouble getting us sea pilots aboard.

On September 21, 1977, I was eager to be flying out again by helicopter to a carrier just as I had as a Lieutenant on active duty, but this time I was flying out to pilot in my first Navy ship, the U.S.S. *Enterprise (CVN 65)*, America's first nuclear-powered aircraft carrier. Why not start piloting Navy ships with something really humongous? The world famous *Big "E,"* built in 1960, was home ported in Alameda and had a long and distinguished career until 2012.

Flying in helicopters of any kind was always adrenaline-charged, but taking the Conn of a nuclear powered ship that was 1,123 feet long by 257 feet wide and displaced 94,781 tons was beyond words, especially so early in my career. She was my 115th ship. When the helo landed on the flight deck, a young Lieutenant-JG escorted me up to the "Island," where I met her skipper, Captain J. W. Austin.

After discussing the ship's particulars, Captain Austin asked me if the OOD could pilot her in. I had never actually piloted a carrier before, so I tried not to show how extremely disappointed and surprised I was by his request. But it was his ship and he could do what he liked, so I reluctantly agreed, then settled back in a chair with a mug of black Navy coffee someone handed me. Off we sailed with a junior officer doing my job! Regretfully, I watched, but was ready to help if needed. You never knew with the Navy. As I sat there thinking I should be piloting her, it dawned on me I was looking down on 4.5 acres of floating airport, which, not matter how many carriers I was on, never failed to amaze me.

The OOD was doing an okay job bringing the ship through the Bar Channel, and everything was fine until we approached Mile Rocks Light. There, we ran smack into zero visibility as sea fog swallowed the ship. Since I couldn't see anything past the flight deck, I wondered how the OOD was going to handle such a big ship in fog. Well, I didn't get to observe very long because Captain Austin didn't waste any time coming over to where I was standing and asked me to Conn the ship. I was standing because it didn't feel right sitting while the ship was in fog. Captain Austin took me by my arm over to a radar with the coffee mug still in my hand. When I first looked into the radar hood, I was surprised that the screen wasn't of a better quality, because I was accustomed to commercial ships' radars. Most ship radars had good pictures and easily identifiable controls, except maybe the Russian-manufactured ones that still used mechanical range ring controllers when all other manufacturers had changed to electronic ones. The Navy's highest-tech radars are located in the Combat Information Center, called CIC, located several decks below the bridge. In any case, the carrier's radar wasn't that great, but I dealt with it.

As we entered the fog bank, the OOD had put the ship's four propellers on Ahead 1/3, slowing her down before I took the Conn. Ahead 1/3 equals about Dead Slow Ahead on a merchant ship, which was much too slow for the strong ebb that we were experiencing. Sometimes going too slowly can be worse than going too fast despite what the NTSB thinks!

As we steamed along, I could hear CIC in the background over the bridge's intercom reporting several unidentified contacts with zero CPAs ahead of us, meaning we were a collision course. The Navy calls unknown vessels "skunks" or "bandits," but they were probably fishing boats heading out to sea as they usually did. I didn't think fishing boats were much danger to us; however, years later, the fishing boat *St. Francis* rammed the side of containership *NYK Surfwind*, which had the right of way, in clear visibility, outside the Gate. The pilot tried to move around the fishing boat that never changed course until she hit the ship at almost a 90–degree angle. She disintegrated on impact, killing two of her crew and sending her captain to the hospital. No one knows why the boat didn't slow down or take evasive action in this needless tragedy. Luckily, our pilot, who took evasive action, was exonerated. So collisions were always possible.

Anyway, I told Captain Austin, "Captain, we may or may not run over all these "skunks" CIC is reporting, but if we go any slower and don't steer toward the bridge, we damn well *will hit* Mile Rocks Light, which is immediately off to starboard!" He agreed, so I ordered Half Ahead, as I pointed at the middle of the Golden Gate. This immediately stopped the *Coral Sea*'s set toward the south. There wasn't any outbound traffic, so I headed her right for the center of the bridge: I wasn't taking any chances with this floating airport. In another mile and a half, the *Big E* slid under the center lights of the bridge as I turned her east entering The Bay. Three miles later when we were south of Alcatraz Island, the ship popped out of the wet fog, which is what I was hoping for. Once we were past the "C-D" span of the Oakland Bay Bridge, I gave Captain Tobin, the civilian Navy docking pilot, the Conn, and he piloted her the rest of the way into Alameda. So I got to pilot my first aircraft carrier, and I felt damn good about it.

One of the more interesting (for lack of a better word) experiences I ever had piloting for the Navy was when I piloted the U.S.S. *Boxer* (LHD-4), a Wasp class amphibious assault ship that was launched in 1993 at Ingalls Shipbuilding, Pascagoula, Mississippi. She was named for a British ship captured by the United States during the War of 1812.

Boxer is a vertical assault ship, small by carrier standards (844 feet long x 106 feet wide, 40,700 GRT) but carries a big punch acting as a forward air base. Marine Sea Stallion helicopters and Osprey vertical takeoff aircraft use her deck, while landing craft are floated out her after well deck ,allowing marines to attack a shore side target. *Boxer* and U.S.S. *Bainbridge* recused the *Maersk Alabama*'s captain from Somali pirates in the Indian Ocean, made famous in *Captain Phillips*.

I boarded the *Boxer* near the Sea Buoy, but unfortunately I didn't fly out by Navy helo. I used our station boat. Our boat operators always had to be extra vigilant when coming alongside certain types of ships like the *Boxer* because they had overhanging projections that could hit our mast. My orders were to take her to Pier 30-32, Delta Steamship Lines' former pier, south of The Bay Bridge. Delta, like many other shipping lines, especially American ones, either went broke during my career or were absorbed by other companies.

Quite a few of San Francisco's aged piers burned down when I lived there, including Pier 7, where our offices were once located, but the Port's biggest fire occurred during the night of May 9–10, 1984, when Pier 30-32 went up in smoke. The wooden cargo sheds burned right down to the pier's surface in a lengthy five–alarm battle, causing over $2.5 million in damages. All night long, San Francisco's firemen gallantly fought to save the pier, but, most important, they saved Red's Java House, a gastronomical emporium to the hot dog, from certain destruction. Engine 35's firehouse and the fireboat *Phoenix* berth are only about a block away at Pier 22 ½. Both of them engaged the fire.

Red's was a reasonably priced greasy spoon, so it was always jammed with longshoremen, cops, business types, tourists, firemen, and the occasional pilot. Even Anthony Bourdain, the TV food guy, has eaten there.

Because of a big flood current, I had to turn the *Boxer* around and point her into it to land portside-to. Only when I was stemming the current could I even think of safely docking her. It's always more difficult and dangerous to control a ship when the current is pushing it from astern, especially a big ship like a carrier.

Aircraft carriers and LPH's superstructures are called "Islands," which are built on their starboard side. This creates more room for helicopters and aircraft to maneuver. In most cases, a docking pilot can see the wharf he is approaching, but it's far more difficult to dock a carrier port side alongside, because you aren't looking straight down at the dock as you get near it. Carriers are normally berthed where there is no current, so they are always docked starboard side alongside. I had no choice with the flood: she had to be port side alongside.

The *Boxer*'s captain was the only African-American I piloted for, and he was also the only one who didn't have *any* communications with his officers during a very delicate docking maneuver. As we were approaching the berth, I needed as much information as I could get, since I couldn't see the dock. At first I was shocked when the captain of this multi-million-dollar modern warship couldn't get me any information what-so-ever from his First Officer down below supervising the tie-up. To safely land all 844 feet of the *Boxer*, I needed to know exactly how far off the pier we were, if we were parallel to it, and if we were where the wharfinger wanted her. If a ship doesn't land flush, this can lead to a lot of damage, because its weight isn't equally distributed along the dock. The entire time I moved closer, and closer I never received one report of distance off from anyone. It's hard enough keeping a ship parallel to a dock when working in strong currents when you can see it.

As she moved slowly toward the dock, I waited in vain for someone, anyone, to tell me the distances as thousands of people waved at us to get alongside so they could come aboard for a visit. Finally, somewhat frustrated by this clinch, I thought, *Well, if they won't tell me what I need to know, I'll keep pushing her sideways until she stops and hope she is parallel to the dock. This big-ass ship can't stay out in The Bay all day!*

On merchant ships you never look across the ship's width when docking, so there is no optical illusion that the ship is too close to the dock. Looking across *Boxer*'s flight deck made it seem as if she were going to hit the pier at any second, even though she was several ship widths off the pier when I started shoving her in sideways.

One good thing about the Navy was they always ordered big assist tugs, so I had three working with me. Once I made my decision to move toward the dock, I ordered all of them to push on her hull at Dead Slow as I tried gingerly to keep her parallel to the dock face while I played the flood current. As she got closer, the flight deck started going over the pier, making it appear as if we were about to touch it at any second. First the dock disappeared, then the waving people, then Red's Java House, and finally the Embarcadero, which was about a quarter of a mile away. Just when it felt as if the battleship gray flight deck would touch downtown San Francisco, the ship gently nudged the dock and stopped moving laterally. Incredibly, she landed exactly where she was supposed to, much to my relief. I didn't even have to move her fore or aft. Thank the Lord, because that was the first and only time I didn't receive any help from a captain during a docking.

At least the crew threw out their mooring lines to the pier and tied us up in short order. The old man, completely oblivious to what just happened, thanked me and gave me a souvenir baseball cap with *Boxer's* name embroidered on it as I went down "brow," which is Navy speak for gangway. I jumped on one of the tugs and headed back to Pier 9, happy that everything went so well.

I was always pleased when it was my turn to pilot the baddest warships in the sea, U.S. submarines. They were so different from other seagoing vessels, so I always wanted to handle these boats. I say boats because subs are called that, while all other vessels are "targets." I piloted quite a few subs, such as the U.S.S. *Russell, George Washington,* and *Parche,* several of which I took to Mare Island Naval Shipyard when it was a sub refueling base.

Anytime I was aboard a sub, I was always in awe of the firepower they represented, especially the "Boomers," which are subs loaded with ICBM missiles. You could always tell them by their flat decks, as opposed to the attack subs, which have rounded hulls that are built to destroy shipping and other submarines.

We couldn't risk touching a sub's sensitive hull with our big station boats, so we boarded them using an Avon raft stowed aft on the Station Boats. After launching the Avon, I'd climb over the railing and climb down a ladder on the stern, then jump in. One of our crew would motor me over to, what I can only describe as something terribly evil–looking, as the matt black hull sat waiting in the swells. Riding over sitting only a few inches above the water was always a humbling experience, and looking up, from literally sea level, was strange, to say the least. Also, every time I boarded one, I knew I was about to get wet despite wearing my waterproof float coat. If nothing else, my shoes always got wet.

Subs don't put out a conventional pilot ladder, so they draped a large piece of canvas over the rounded part of the hull, which fell down to the water's edge. To give us something to step onto, wooden battens made out of 2 × 4s were sewn into the canvas, which turned the canvas into a half-ass ladder, but it worked. As we approached the sub, sailors standing on deck would heave a manrope into our boat as my boatman revved up the outboard to full power and then rammed the Avon up the sub's hull as far as it would go next to the canvas. As the boat bounced, I'd leap out of the Avon onto the canvas ladder and pull myself up hand over hand, using the manrope. If I didn't fall into the Pacific, I was fine!

Whenever I boarded a sub, I was usually escorted directly to the conning tower by a junior officer. One day, we went down a hatch into the main body of the sub, which was something I had never done before. It felt awkward walking among sailors milling around as we passed through "Sherwood Forest," where those big missiles are stored, on the way to a vertical ladder leading straight up to the conning tower. Of course, I was the only one wearing a sport coat, so I definitely looked out of place next to those missiles.

One stormy night, an outbound sub couldn't safely disembark one of our pilots, so he stayed aboard as the sub continued west after submerging near the Pilot Station. A few days later, the same pilot took her back in. On another night, a sub made the mistake of crossing the Bar in a raging gale without a Bar Pilot. Unfortunately, her CO was tragically washed overboard and not recovered.

Piloting up in the *sail,* or conning tower, where the periscopes are located and where the crew conns the boat when not submerged, was a unique experience. One reason was that I was completely exposed to the elements the entire trip. Once, trying to stay out of the crew's way, I sat on the edge of the tower because the crew wanted to see the Golden Gate. I couldn't blame them for that after being cooped up in a big can for two months under the sea. While sitting there, I failed to notice a spinning radar mast behind me, which smeared heavy grease on my float coat. That one got thrown away.

On July, 14, 1996, ten pilots were assigned to pilot a small fleet of Japanese warships on a courtesy call to Alameda Naval Air Station. We took the run boat out, then boarded all the neatly lined up ships waiting for us according to our place on the board. One by one, the small flotilla of the identical ships headed in looking like a long gray conga line. My ship was *Hamana.* Immediately, I was surprised no one, including the skipper, understood English. Because of my experience piloting Japanese commercial vessels, I assumed Japanese Naval Officers learned English at Etajima, the Japanese Naval Academy. On most Japanese ships I ever piloted, the captain spoke English, the crew made a tasty cup of coffee, and their ships were always spotless. For example, they put white gauze around the rubber radar hood, so when I looked into it, was clean, and for some reason their helmsmen also wore white cotton gloves.

Since I couldn't speak Japanese, I wasn't sure how I was going to bring their ship into port, but I was thankful I wasn't on the lead ship. Maybe her captain spoke English because my ship just followed astern of the others. As far as my ship was concerned, they didn't understand or take any orders from me, except when I made wild hand gestures or waved my arms trying to make them understand something was going to affect their ship. This was nerve-racking, because as a pilot, I wanted and needed to be in control. The trip went on like this without them doing anything I suggested all the way to Alameda, which I had pointed out to the captain on the chart when I boarded.

By some miracle, we safely arrived outside the entrance to the Air Station, but I wasn't done having fun with the Japanese Navy yet, because I was still in for a wild ride. Because the current in the air station channel sets at a 90- degree angle to it and you don't compensate for it, the ship will slide right out of the channel, as the USS *Enterprise* did in 1983. I didn't want a repeat disaster because these jokers didn't speak any English. As she entered the channel, as I knew it would, the current quickly grabbed the small ship, shoving her south, so I had to act quickly. To get the helmsman's attention, I stood directly in front of his steering station frantically waving my arms in his face like the flag man on an aircraft carrier that controls approaching planes. I did my best to get them to turn her to port because we were drifting dangerously toward the red buoys and were about to run them over.

Miraculously, she didn't run aground, and somehow we wound up stopped in the turning basin. By then, I'd had enough fun and knew the safest thing to do was to not deal with the crew any longer, so I indicated to the captain (in sign language) to take the tugs' lines. I then proceeded into the berth as if she were a "dead tow." Without any help from the crew,

I turned her around, backing her alongside one of the other already-parked ships. Maybe the captain thought I was good at waving because he gave me a beautiful set of cuff links I still wear.

When I first moved to San Francisco, California had many naval installations. Over the years, most of these formidable bases were closed, including: Mare Island Naval Shipyard, Alameda Naval Air Station, Treasure Island Naval Base, Oakland Naval Hospital, and Port Chicago Naval Weapons Station. After San Francisco turned down the chance to home-port a decommissioned battleship, I think the military had had enough.

≈≈≈ • ≈≈≈

CHAPTER 23

SOME PILOTS OF NOTE

Pilots can be real individuals. I know I wasn't like anyone else in the Bar Pilots, so my book is a cast of characters that made up the story of my piloting career. Several are worth mentioning, a few for their piloting skills and some for their personalities. Some were even known for their poor piloting skills, or I should say, not all pilots have the same expertise.

Captain John Egga was a tall, fit guy who possessed a shock of thick curly silver-grey hair. When he was bored, he did chin-ups on Station Boats. He was also affable unless you came between him and a plate of food. He owned the reputation of big eater and astounded everyone with how much he could stow away, so I never wanted to arrive on Station after him, especially before meals. This might have had something to do with his wife, who was always saying things like "she and Johnny" should go on a diet. I don't think John got much to eat at home, so he made up for it at the pilot office or on the Station Boats. Once I watched in disbelief as he ate three servings of prime rib, including the ribs. There was nothing he wouldn't eat. For example, one afternoon I was scrounging around in the reefer when I noticed a note on a pan with uncooked chickens: "Don't eat RAW!" This note was obviously for Egga, since he was outbound. When Jim, the cook, showed up to start dinner, I asked, "What's with the note?" Apparently a pan of uncooked pork chops disappeared when Egga was aboard, forcing Jim to come up with another dinner entrée. Yuk! Cold pork chop sushi? Egga was like Blimpy.

On another occasion, John and I arrived on Station at 0630, an hour before breakfast. If I had enough time I would take a nap; if not. I read my paper or waited to get something to eat. John couldn't wait because when he spotted half of a leftover cherry pie from last night sitting in the galley, his face lit up. I called this "putting in a little dunnage." That is, eating before eating. Half of a pie wasn't enough. To make it tastier, he sliced avocados on it. The sight of green avocados on a red cherry pie at 0630 was enough to make professional eaters like Joey "Jaws" Chestnut wince. Anyone prone to seasickness would have fed the fishes!

John polished it off about the time the cook, Andy Andersen, asked if we wanted breakfast. Having been awake for almost four hours, I hungrily said yes. I ordered pancakes while John ordered bacon and eggs, and I don't mean two: he wanted half a dozen with bacon, plus toast.

After this exhibition of gluttony, John leaned back with a toothpick in his mouth, smiling. "Maybe I overdid it, that pie made me a little full." *A little full?* Half a pie and enough breakfast for three men? He was too much.

In addition to out-eating all the other pilots he had a bad habit of trying to finish my *New York Times* crossword puzzles if I left them lying around. Even if I wasn't done. Sometimes if I slipped below, leaving mine behind, when I came back John would be working on it as if it were his paper. John never bought a paper, as I did. I gave mine to inbound captains who appreciated them because they probably hadn't seen a paper in a while.

Whenever I caught John doing my crosswords, I'd say, "Hey, that's my puzzle!" He would always chortle and say he thought I was done with it, knowing I wasn't. Once he tried finishing my crossword and was stumped. "What's this letter? I can't read your writing. Your penmanship is terrible."

I told him, "Buy your own newspaper and you won't have a problem with my handwriting!"

The British luxury liner *Queen Elizabeth 2* (*QE2*) visited San Francisco for her second time when John and I were on the Station Boat. Many years before, thousands lined the shoreline watching her sail into San Francisco on her inaugural voyage, as if Queen Elizabeth had arrived.

The real Queen wouldn't come here for several more years, when she sailed in aboard HMY *Britannia*. Unfortunately I didn't get to pilot her "yacht," which was really a small cruise ship

I wanted to pilot her in the worst way because she didn't visit often and during my last year at college, McAllister Towing invited several First Classmen to watch the *QE2* make her maiden voyage into New York Harbor aboard their tugs. On that beautiful May morning in 1969, there were so many other tugs, airplanes, helicopters, tour boats, yachts, and people cheering, it looked as though a war had just ended. Even the Staten Island ferries were listing because so many people were trying to get a look at the magnificent new liner. Not only was she beautiful, she was also really big for that era. At 963 feet, she was a little shorter than the SS *United States*'s 990 feet, but she was heavier at 70,327 vs. 53,330 tons. She was big then, but today's passenger ships are getting so large that San Francisco regularly receives liners over 90,000 tons. In 2006, the 148,528 ton *Queen Mary 2* at 1132 feet—as long as a carrier—visited San Francisco.

John was ahead of me in rotation, so the *QE2* was his arrival. I tried not showing how much I wanted to pilot her, but, being the good guy he was, he traded places. I received great satisfaction piloting her so many years after first seeing her in N.Y. On January 25, 2006 at 2200, I was the last Bar Pilot to ever to handle her because she never returned and is now permanently retired to Dubai.

The Bay Area has five huge refineries processing over 652,400 barrels of crude oil per day, so we piloted hundreds of tankers coming from all over the world. After 1977, more and bigger American tankers started moving Prudhoe Bay oil south. Coastal tankers like the *Austin*, the *Keystoner* and the *Texaco Rhode Island,* tiny by today's standards, were the norm in 1977. For example, the *Keystoner*—the first tanker I ever piloted—weighed less than 12,000 tons. The biggest tankers I piloted then were Chevron's foreign flagged tankers such as the 50,000 ton *R. G. Follis*. Soon I was piloting 110,000 tonners on a regular basis.

The *Exxon Valdez* spill was ten years away when oil companies became the bad guys with a PR smear is still going on today. No one wants spills, they are too costly, and the bad PR is horrific, but occasionally protesters demonstrated against Exxon by doing silly things like chaining themselves to the rudder stock of empty tankers sitting at anchor so they can't move. The only problem with these hypocrites was that they used Avon-type boats that are 100 percent rubber, which is made from oil. They also used two-stroke engines that burn oil, which is discharged directly into the Bay, so I thought if they hated big oil so much, they shouldn't use their products! Unlike them, I liked big oil: it helped pay my bills.

In the late 1970s, Miller Beer had an ad campaign called "It's Miller Time!" which featured working people drinking a Miller after a tough day. Miller Beer wanted to incorporate the new Alaskan oil trade, along with the pilots who moved the tankers, into a new ad campaign, so they hired us and our boats to use as filming platforms. Captains John Winterling and Woody Johnson were chosen to be in the ad. I was hoping they'd pick me, but I was too young-looking at the time. Damn.

Their producer asked us to arrange for an American oil tanker to pass under the Golden Gate at sunset, which they thought would make for a nice backdrop. The Port Agent informed them we had no control over when ships sailed, we just piloted them. Nor could we guarantee a ship would be exactly under the bridge at sunset, or if fog would screw up the filming. This didn't faze them at all. They told Port Agent Billy Meyer to just go rent a ship!

"Rent a ship? Do you have any idea what it costs to charter a tanker?" he said. It might have cost $100,000 per day to charter a ship, and no one was even sure you could charter one by the hour or day. They wouldn't be put off. "Go ahead," they insisted, but obviously nothing came of this.

No tanker companies, despite the good PR they might have garnered, were interested in having film crews running around their ships. The risk from sparks from camera lights was too great. They couldn't chance an explosion.

In the end, the commercial was filmed on a containership's bridge going under the Golden Gate at sunset, as they wanted. John looked very nautical peering through a pair of binoculars and using the ship's radar, while Woody was shown drinking a Miller Beer in a local pub after a "hard day" of piloting. The *Evening News with Walter Cronkite* ran it for several months. Today, it wouldn't be made because alcohol and ships are strictly taboo together, especially after the *Exxon Valdez's* captain was accused of drinking.

When I set out to be a pilot, no one promised me, or any of the other wannabe pilots, a piloting job, but I kept riding along with them and hoping. Over four years, I rode on countless ships observing different pilots work ships to gain experience. One encouraging pilot I especially liked was Perry Stiltz, a terrific man. I learned something every time I rode with him. He was easy to be with, unlike pilots like Davies who only begrudgingly took riders along.

Late one night, Perry and I took the *Inland Pilot* out to a ship waiting for him in Anchorage 7, ready to go to Stockton, seventy-two miles upriver. I usually stayed out of the way when pilots were working a ship, but Perry liked it if I asked him questions. That night, I stood next to him waiting to see what his first order would be. Instead of giving one, he took me aside and whispered, "Paul, how do you feel about taking the ship up tonight? I'm dead tired. I know you can handle it. I'll just be resting. Call me if you need me."

Without another word, Perry handed me his radio, disappeared into the chart room, and quickly fell asleep on a settee as if he didn't have a care in the world. He also didn't tell the captain I was going to pilot his ship. Incredulous, I didn't know what to say as he disappeared.

I already had my pilot's licenses, so what I was doing wasn't technically illegal. But no one had authorized me, including the captain, to pilot the ship. I wasn't worried because I had been up and down our bays and rivers too many times to count, especially when I captained *Komoku,* the last freighter on San Francisco Bay. However, I'd never piloted a large ship past the Union Pacific Bridge before, especially with the pilot asleep in the middle of the night! Only a few river pilots let me handle their ships because there was no formal apprentice program back then. They were under no obligation to train the wannabes the way our apprentices train today.

Not only did I want to do it, but I was flattered Perry had so much confidence in my ability, especially with him snoring away. Third World bulker captains often disappeared down to their cabins during night trips to get some shut-eye, but never the pilot! No American captain ever left the bridge with me, except for short periods of time.

Years later when I was a pilot, bulker captains seldom bothered informing me when they slipped below. How they slept for fifty miles leaving their ships in the hands of a total stranger was beyond me. Even though our accident rate is as low as any port, things go wrong all the time, so having the old man nearby is important, especially if the Mate didn't speak English very well. In fact, it was dangerous if he didn't understand me because it could make a bad situation worse. For example, if I needed to drop the anchors in an emergency, I was never sure if these junior officers would understand my commands, never mind if the anchors were even ready to let go. To make matters worse, sometimes when I asked for coffee, the Mate would take over the wheel from the AB, then he would disappear below to make my coffee. No other ships did this coffee run except Third World ones, because almost all ships have coffee pots or kettles on the bridge, so there is no need for the Mate to be steering. Besides, officers are supposed to be in charge of their watch, not steering.

That night, the captain never knew or cared that I was an apprentice. For the first time in my life, I was piloting a large commercial ship, giving all the directions without anyone observing or helping me. It was a strange feeling indeed to actually be in charge. But, I have to admit I did a damn fine job maneuvering Perry's ship all the way through the UPB, then up to New York Point, while Perry quietly slept. By the time the ship was moving through Middle Ground approaching New York Point, in inky blackness, I thought, *Maybe I better wake Perry up. I think I'm passed out of my comfort zone.* I felt complete confidence until then, but I didn't want to risk going through New York Slough, a very crooked narrow slip of water, to say the least. Perry got up without fanfare, thanked me, and took the Conn back just as if he had been awake.

That was an incredible learning experience because watching pilots work, as opposed to making all the decisions yourself, is a steep learning curve. I wasn't cocky, but I knew I had what it took to pilot, and I hoped my chance would come someday.

I never let any apprentice Conn my ship if I wasn't watching over his shoulder like a hawk, because my licenses and career were on the line while they were with me. As much as I appreciated Perry's faith, I seldom had that much in any apprentice.

Captain Nick Ernser was a hell of a pilot and another pilot I learned many piloting tricks from, especially in regard to handling tugs and barges because I'd never worked on them, as he had.

Nick also had a keen sense of humor, which helped when you piloted. For example, when President Carter cancelled American participation in the 1980 Olympics after Russia invaded Afghanistan, a Russian captain asked if the U.S. was going to attend.

Nick said, "Sure, Cap, how else can we beat you?"

One of the more infamous ship accidents, unfortunately, involved Nick when he piloted the 626-foot tanker *Gulf Knight* when she crashed into the Ozol on the night of May 27, 1975. Ozol was a T-shaped pier situated in a bight on the south side of the Carquinez Strait, where the Navy stored and pumped aviation gas up to Travis Air Force Base in Fairfield, about twenty-five miles east of there. Ships could only dock there on flood current because the ebb current was too unpredictable.

The night of the accident, SS *Exxon New Jersey* was bound for the Phillips Amorco Dock, which abuts the UP Bridge, closely followed by the tanker SS *Houston,* bound for the Shell Oil Martinez, where Nick had just departed from. The three tankers were going to converge near Buoy #25, so Nick made passing arrangements and successfully passed the *New Jersey* between #25 and Shell. Then he noticed that the *Houston* had stopped, blocking the channel. There wasn't enough room to go around the *Houston.* Nick knew what was about to happen and ordered Full Speed Astern, immediately followed by a "Double Jingle." Even when a ship goes to Emergency Full Astern, it takes a long time to get a loaded tanker to stop, especially a steamship, because steam used to turn the propeller shaft has to be diverted from the main stages of the turbine to a smaller reverse turbine to make the propeller spin in the opposite direction. The *Houston*'s pilot had put Nick's ship in extremis, and he needed to act quickly to avoid hitting her, so Nick aimed the *Gulf Knight* at Ozol. If he hadn't, the two ships would have crashed into each other, resulting in an even worse calamity. The damage to the Ozol pier was bad enough, but if the two loaded tankers had collided, there would have been an immense oil spill, maybe even an explosion. The two ships might have drifted in the swift current into one of the oil refineries that line both sides or smashed into the 680 highway bridge, causing catastrophic damage.

The *Gulf Knight* plowed into Ozol going Full Speed astern, but still ruptured oil transfer lines running under the dock, igniting residual oil in them. As she hit the dock, she immediately backed out of the hole she had just created, but was surrounded in flames.

What made this story personal for me was that in October of 1983, I piloted the *Gulf Knight* out of the same berth Nick had. As the ship passed Ozol, I asked the crew about the explosion at the dock off to our port eight years earlier. The captain said he wasn't aboard and he had no knowledge of it.

As the helmsman, an older African-American man with the whitest hair I have ever seen, steered the tanker down the Carquinez Strait, he piped into the conversation, "Cap'n, I was aboard. Matter of fact, I was on the fo'c'sle head when we hit the pier and she exploded in a big ball of flames all round us."

I looked at him, kidding him, "Did you have all that white hair before the explosion?" He turned toward me, "No, Sah, I surely did not!"

The *Houston*'s pilot never admitted being aground, but shortly after the accident, the Coast Guard relocated Buoy #25 into deeper water, making the turn there too tight to pass another ship. I foolishly passed another one there once, but it was far too dangerous.

Nick joined the Million Dollar Club, but the accident didn't end his career like John Cota's did.

When Don Hughes passed away in 2011, he left an incredible void in the pilot character department, because there are more stories involving him than any other pilot I can think of, so he was definitely our most interesting pilot.

Don was a solid man, well over six feet, with a reddish-gray bird's nest of a beard and a mass of matching curly hair. Don had a deep booming voice that could be heard across the waterfront, especially if he was mad at you.

All the longshoremen called him "Red," and he addressed them by their first names like long-lost buddies. No other pilot did this. I sure didn't know any longshoremen personally.

Don was probably not our best pilot, because he certainly visited the Commission more than any other pilot I knew about, and for the state to lift your license you really had to screw up, which he managed to do several times. Hughes had an air of invincibility about him, acting as if he could get away with anything, and sometimes it bit him right in the ass.

Here is one of many Don sagas: On November 8, 1991, Don piloted the empty Russian bulker *Kapitan Dublinsky* up to Stockton to load grain. With his usual bravado, he insisted on docking the ship speaking Russian of all things. This was totally against regs requiring ships to speak English so everyone is on the same page. Apparently, Don did a lousy job *govorya russkim* (speaking Russian) because Don's ship swiped a grain elevator, knocking it over on its side.

A week later, I piloted the same ship, now full of grain, from NYP down to anchor. Sailing through San Pablo Bay, her captain cried on my shoulder, telling me his tale of woe about Hughes's most recent accident. In broken English, he related how, as his ship approached the grain elevator, he begged Don, "Please Mr. Pilot. No more Russian! Your Russian is terrible!" I can see Don in my mind's eye going right ahead with the performance until its tragic end.

When we still had docking pilots, I was sitting in the dispatch office waiting for Don to undock a German ship in Oakland so I could take her out to sea. We didn't go over with the docking pilot as a waste of time, so a docking pilot would undock the ship and a Bar Pilot would meet it with our run boat somewhere near The Bay Bridge, then took it out to sea. When I was on the bridge, I always wanted to do the piloting, not watch someone else. Don didn't get the ship underway at sailing time; in fact, he never showed up. Don was piloting another ship, so this delayed the German one. As I have written, the docking pilots tried keeping as much work for themselves as they could.

Finally, the agent called, requesting I come over and take the ship to sea before it got any later. I was just killing time, so I was glad to get going. The *Drake* rushed me over to Oakland, and I climbed up to the bridge and introduced myself to a pacing, red-faced German captain who had been waiting for over two hours. I did my best to calm him so I could safely take him to sea.

He and I walked out onto the bridge wing just as the crew was heaving up the gangway. Suddenly, Hughes appeared out of a beaten-up blue Dodge with *Martinez Taxi* painted on the doors sitting at the foot of the gangway. In those days, pilots were allowed to drive directly to the ships. Now, a terminal security guard drives everyone to the ships. I preferred arriving by boat, it was just so much faster.

Don had a loud deep voice. He was using it, bellowing and pointing at the deck gang to stop heaving up the gangway and let him aboard. He also had a bad temper, acting as if the ship was late and he was the one being inconvenienced.

The crew obeyed Don as if he were the captain, dropping the gangway back down onto the pavement. Meanwhile, the seething captain and I stood out on the bridge wing waiting for Don to appear. Unlike the captain, I thought it was funny and couldn't wait to hear Don's alibi. Don finally trotted out onto the wing as if nothing was wrong and greeted the captain, then me, and made some lame excuse why he was two hours late. I heard that Don was an ordained minister, but fibs obviously didn't apply to him. The captain, totally exasperated, wasn't amused by Don's calm demeanor. He scolded him, pointing his finger at Don's chest and saying in a stern, heavily accented voice, "Herr Hughes, *dies ist das zecont time you av been late por meinem schiff by more den einer hour!*"

Nonchalantly, and without blinking an eye, Don, always the gentleman, replied, "Well, Cap, that's my style. Now kindly single up all lines, if you don't mind." The flabbergasted, flush-faced captain, not knowing what to think, screamed into his radio, telling the crew to get the lines in. After Don turned the ship around, I took her out to sea without much fanfare. Only Don could get away with such tomfoolery and keep getting docking jobs from the agents.

I think Don invented that phrase and used it often. When Don started out to be a river pilot, naturally he had a hard time getting jobs because the Inland Pilots didn't want any more members or competition than necessary. Before the pilot merger, anyone with a Federal pilot's license could dock ships if a ship agent gave them the job. Only state-licensed Bar Pilots, like me, could bring ships in from sea and take them to their docks. Over the years, several pilots managed to get their foot in the door by convincing a ship agent to throw them a bone, and Don was one of them. This slack system had no standards or training for pilots, which we corrected when the pilot groups merged.

I was still riding observer trips for my upriver licenses and needed more night trips. When I heard that Don had a Stockton job, I called him to ask if I could ride along. Even though he didn't really know me, he said he would be glad to have me along. He was such a rookie, I was surprised he did it because I'm sure that was his first Stockton job, and as you will see, it showed.

That evening, we took a launch out to Don's ship waiting in anchorage and quickly got underway, heading north towards the San Rafael Bridge, where the infamous San Quentin Prison sits at its west end.

That night turned out to be a completely different learning experience from the hundreds of other observer trips I made. The first strange thing I noticed was that Don had a big olive green army surplus duffle bag with him when we boarded. All of the other pilots I rode with only carried their walkie-talkies or a small shoulder bag. I never saw any other river pilots even look at a chart, or anything else for that matter, except maybe a tide table.

When I started piloting, I only brought along my tide book, a penlight, and a small loose-leaf containing my personal chart with notations. Later on, I used a shoulder bag when the Commission required us to carry two radios, one as a backup, because someone had hit a pier when his radio battery crapped out.

I didn't want any captain thinking I didn't know what I was doing, so I never flaunted my little chart book and seldom referred to anything because most of the information I needed was already in my head. To pass my pilot exams, I had to know where every beacon, bell buoy, gong, foghorn, power line, underwater cable, and shoal spot was for 200 miles, as well as the width and vertical clearance at all stages of the tide of all nine bridges we went under. When people asked me how I could remember so much information I told them I know The Bay like they know their bedrooms in the dark because I studied it so much. And I never stopped studying it until I dropped anchor for the last time.

Part of the mystique of piloting, besides being a good ship handler, is having all the charts, tides, and currents in your head. Not Don. That wouldn't have been his style. He brought along *all* the un-cut charts, which are 3 × 4 feet rolled up, needed to get a ship to Stockton, and that's a lot of charts. The problem with rolled-up charts is, once rolled up, they have to be weighed down or they keep rolling up like a window shade. In fact, charts are always folded in the ship's chart desk so they don't roll up. Also, the C. G. requires all ships to have corrected charts on board before they can enter San Francisco, so theoretically, a pilot doesn't really need to bring charts, he can use the ship's.

Don, not the least bit fazed about rolling out his charts, asked the Mate for paperweights to hold down what appeared to be unused charts. If I had been the captain witnessing this display, I might have had some serious reservations because we still had seventy-two miles to travel through three bays, a strait, and a winding river, plus six bridges to pass under. All during the passage, he kept referring to his charts as if he didn't know where he was going. Never having watched him pilot before, I started wondering about Don's piloting ability.

A mile past the San Rafael Bridge, Hughes turned the ship east into San Pablo Bay near the Brothers Lighthouse on the starboard hand I described previously. There is plenty of deep water on the Brothers's north side, but I was about to learn just how deep it really is and how close a ship could get to it without running aground or hitting it!

To my surprise, Don turned the ship east much earlier than I had ever seen it done before. I had passed by the Brothers hundreds of times, and I knew the ebb sets directly onto the northeast side so a prudent mariner would never want to get anywhere near that big rock. There is plenty of sea room and deep water north and west of it, so you don't save much time by turning early.

As the ship neared the island, the Brothers's intense white rotating light slowly receded under the starboard bridge wing, something else I had never seen before. I thought, We *are going to run over this solid granite island when we don't have to be anywhere near it!* As the ship got closer and closer I thought, *I don't want to witness an accident,* so I walked out onto the port wing, the side away from the island, and had a smoke. Just when I was sure the ship would grind to a sickening halt, the light started to recede behind the ship and somehow we kept moving. Never having been so close to the Brothers before, I was surprised we made it. At least I learned you could get right on top of the Brothers and not run aground. I was glad we didn't because I needed more observer trip tickets to get my license upgraded, plus I didn't want to be on the first ship to hit The Brothers. We were just beginning our trip and I thought, *How is he going to top this stunt?* Several hours later, by the skin of Don's teeth, we slipped it into New York Slough. I was about to find out how.

At night, navigation bridges are kept completely black or you can't see outside, so any interior lights are always red ones so they don't interfere with night vision.

Most pilots use penlights for the same reason. Not Don, he used a big three cell Maglite. Every time he changed course, his flashlight flooded the pitch-black bridge with its offensive white beam blinding everyone as he looked at a chart. This is not only annoying, it's dangerous, especially if the helmsman can't see the steering compass.

As we started through New York Slough, Don pointed his torch at his chart without first looking at the steering compass. If you look at the compass before changing course, there is less chance of giving the wrong order, as Don was about to do.

Speaking in a forceful, deep bass voice, Don gave the order, "Ah, Helmsman, please come to 'er 280 degrees."

The helmsman, doing what he was just ordered to do, spun the steering wheel hard over trying to turn the ship around, because Don had inadvertently given him the reciprocal of the course he really wanted! In about one second, as Don watched the bow lunge toward the port side bank, he realized he'd made a huge pilot error. Confused, he looked at the chart one more time, then in this calm voice, as if he didn't realize the danger he had just put the ship in, said, "Belay that last order helmsman, hard-a-starboard, now kindly come to one zero zero degrees!" If he hadn't corrected his mistake immediately, we would have been hard aground in about ten seconds, as the river is very narrow in New York Slough.

Ships try to be docked just prior to 0800 so they can start cargo operations with the cheapest longshoremen rate. The ILWU charges overtime before 0800 and after 1700. Arriving at 0800 may be nice for the ship owners, but it's tough on pilots and the crew, who travel ninety miles upriver in the dark. These all-night river trips are tiring because you are on your feet for eight hours, but it's also tough on captains coming in from sea. They have probably been on the bridge for an hour before arriving at the Sea Buoy, and if the ship had been in fog or bad weather, the captain could be doubly fatigued. This is why they often disappeared below to their cabins to get some rest.

Meals aren't served on foreign ships at night. The cooks are asleep, so it can be quite a while before you might get something to eat. When I worked all-nighters, I never expected anything, unless a particularly kind captain woke up the cook, unlike Jean, a St. Lawrence River pilot friend of mine, who said if they didn't serve him "sandwiches" during the night, he'd anchor the ship until they did! Try doing that in San Francisco! American ships serve "Night lunch," because half of a ship's crew is awake at some point during the night. It wasn't always appetizing, but I ate it anyway because I was usually hungry when I worked all night.

About midnight, Don asked if I was hungry. I assumed Don was going to ask the old man to wake up a cook. Even though I never heard other pilots make this request, nothing was beyond Don. Always hungry and a confirmed a bachelor, I was usually looking for a free meal, day or night, so I said, "Sure, Don." Unbeknownst to me, Don's duffle bag of tricks contained not only his charts, but a virtual deli. Inquiring like a counterman, "What would you like? I've got ham and cheese, tuna, and maybe turkey." I kept thinking, *He's got to be kidding!* I had ridden with dozens of pilots, and none of them ever brought food along or a duffle bag, for that matter. Typical of Don, he wasn't kidding. Then he asked, "How do you like your coffee?" Now I was sure he was pulling my leg because there is a coffee pot on every ship bridge in the world. Some even have espresso machines. Out of his bag came a big thermos full of steaming hot coffee. I thought, *This is all right: fresh coffee and sandwiches and I'm getting one trip out of the way.* I was also learning what not to do, which helped me be a better pilot.

By the grace of God, Don made it to Stockton without hitting anything or running aground. Having an empty ship helped, but once again luck overcame skill.

About an hour before sunrise after finishing a job at Berth 55, I stood waiting by the ship's stern for our run boat. Whenever I worked all-nighters, I was always in a hurry to get home to get in bed before the sun came up.

The *Golden Gate* roared up, then stopped at my feet as I jumped aboard. Inside I plopped into one of the pilot chairs. I didn't even take off my coat because we normally made a beeline toward Pier Nine, but after we left the Estuary, Steve Ross, the boat captain, turned the boat hard right into Oakland Outer Harbor. Surprised and not wanting to run all over The Bay, I asked him, "What's up? I thought we were going home."

Steve replied, "Sorry Cap, we have to get Hughes, he just whacked Berth 23 and the office wants him back to get drug tested."

I thought, *Not again!* He hit a grain elevator speaking Russian, ran a ship aground in San Pablo Bay, was late for sailings, and left an apprentice in the lurch. Now what?

In the dim morning light, as the boat slowed down approaching Hughes's berth, we started looking to pick him up. I was also curious how much damage the dock had sustained. All I saw was the silhouette of a big, aqua blue-colored Maersk containership docked portside-to, but everything else seemed normal, with no cargo operations going on. At least all the dock's cranes were still standing. I was surprised to see both ship's anchors in their hawsepipes, not in the water, and I didn't see any damage. Then I noticed the ship's bow, which looked as if someone had used a giant laser to cut out a 20–foot–deep, perfectly shaped parallelogram. Looking through that gigantic hole, I noticed shed lights on the other side of the ship! That was the most damage I ever saw happen to a ship.

Dock surfaces are held up by wooden piles driven into The Bay by floating pile drivers. The dock is concrete with wooden fendering on the waterside that ships rest against. Pilings cost a fortune to repair; I know because I broke a few.

Finally, Don appeared near the bow of the ship, then stepped aboard as the boat nosed into the dock. As he entered the wheelhouse, I muttered hello to him, which he acknowledged.

I said, "Bad day, eh?"
He replied, "Not my best moment."
I'm sure he didn't want to talk about it, but I couldn't help myself.
"Hey Don, why didn't you drop an anchor? It might have saved your butt."

As he sat down, he replied, as if he didn't care, "But she was gonna stop!" Well, she didn't, and now Hughes had another multimillion-dollar mess on his hands.

Don made several cardinal errors: going too fast for the situation, not tying up his assist tugs to help him turn the ship around, and not letting go an anchor when all else failed. Those were rookie mistakes. I dropped an anchor three times in emergencies, and they saved my ass every time. My assist boats always put up their tow lines even if I was going to reposition them after turning a ship, because I wanted all the help I could get if the shit hit the fan, which happened to me. Because Don's tugs didn't have their lines secured to the ship, they could only push on it, not pull or help stop it, which gives stability in a docking job.

San Francisco always had cheap tug rates because of the stiff competition. Because of this and unionized crews, which they hated, Crowley Maritime, one of the world's principal tug companies, moved their entire operation to Jacksonville, Florida. Crowley was a maritime fixture on San Francisco Bay since 1892, when Thomas Crowley, Sr., bought a Whitehall rowboat to service ships on The Bay. Eventually, his company grew to include tugs, barges, launches, and even the tourist ferries that serviced Alcatraz National Park. It didn't matter, Crowley moved. Two Red Stack tugs (Crowley's signature color) eventually returned to work ships, but their presence was never as great as when old man Crowley ran the company here.

I was never anywhere in the world except San Francisco where only one small tug was used to dock a ship. So our port had a bad reputation, as far as tug boats were concerned. Stingy ship owners got away with this nonsense because of the competition among docking; in addition, many of those tugs were underpowered. Ships calling here sarcastically used the expression, "We got to use the poor man's tug boat," meaning San Francisco pilots dropped anchors a lot during dockings. For pilots using only one, or two small tugs, it's always safer to drop an anchor while docking. This greatly increases control, especially when mooring in a current. These small, single screw tugs were the kind I learned to dock ships with, so I didn't know the difference. But using small tugs and dropping anchors made me a better pilot, but only a fool wouldn't love tractor tugs.

Tractor tugs are tow boats that don't have conventional fixed screw propellers and traditional rudders like twin screw boats. Instead, they have two rotating propellers in nozzles that can turn 360 degrees or use a system made by Voith Schneider that uses blades that turn like egg beaters. The spinning blades or the two nozzles can propel and turn the tug at the same time. Because of this, tractors can *spin* in a circle, whereas conventional twin screw tugs can only *turn* in a circle. Many years ago, a new tractor tug company started operations on The Bay about the time tractors tugs were becoming commonplace worldwide, everywhere, that is, except San Francisco. Unfortunately, this new tug company didn't last long because they got into a pissing contest with the docking pilots, which they lost. The docking pilots didn't know, or want to know, how to utilize this new technology to their best advantage. Docking pilots were stuck in their old ways or maybe they thought the new technology would make them obsolete, so some of them didn't want to use the new tugs, or the ships didn't want to pay for them. Old habits die hard. The tractor company also had the wrong attitude toward the pilots, acting as if they were going to teach the old-timers how to pilot the modern way. Eventually, the tractor company went belly up and their tugs left the Bay. As a result, San Francisco didn't have these terrific tugs for many years. I think the old-timers made a colossal mistake because tractor tugs are far superior to any conventional tug, and today's ships being so huge, pilots are more essential than ever.

The most bizarre event I can recall regarding Don happened shortly after his license was lifted for the flu incident. I knew he'd be bummed out, so I called him to give him moral support. I'm not sure how many other pilots felt pity for Don, but as a pilot, I did.

When I asked him how he was feeling, he replied, "Well Paul, you know bad things come in threes."

"Why is that, Don? Did something else happen?" I thought, *What could be worse than losing your license and being humiliated?*

"Well, my mom died this week and now the cops have gone and killed my son!" That statement hit me like a sucker punch and has been with me all these years later.

"Don, what do you mean the cops killed your son?"

Very dispassionately Don went on, "Dale took a shot at a Santa Rosa cop and they killed him at a bus stop."

Silence.

What can you say to someone who has just lost his mother, and his son was shot to death during the same week? That was Don's life. Dale, like his dad, worked on tugs on the Bay.

As Captain Tony Chadwick, one of my partners and another golfing buddy, said to me the other day, "Life was more fun having guys like Don around." I always enjoyed Don, a real character.

Before the pilot merger, most ships used docking pilots even though the Bar Pilots never charged extra to dock them. To save money, some companies, like U.S. Lines, used us to dock their ships until the time they went belly-up. Like many other American steamship lines including Delta, American Export-Isbrandsten, States Lines, and Pacific Far East Lines, U.S. Lines declared bankruptcy and, like most of them, left us holding the proverbial bag after they went under.

U.S. Lines was a powerhouse since the 1920s, owning two of the world's greatest passenger ships during the 1950s and '60s, the S.S. *America* and *United States*. I'm proud to say the only captains to ever command America's greatest liner were alumni of my college! Captains Harry Manning, John Anderson, and Leroy Alexanderson. The *Big U* still holds *The Blue Riband* signifying she is the fastest passenger ship to ever cross the Atlantic, in three days, ten hours, and forty minutes. It's a shame that these once great American steamship lines are no longer. U.S. Lines's demise occurred on November 24, 1986, when they still owned forty-three ships. I piloted over ninety-two U.S. Lines ships myself, so they were a good customer.

In the end, U.S. Lines owed us so much money, the Port Agent instructed pilots not to bring their ships in unless paid in cash. My turn to collect was Thanksgiving morning 1981. When I asked the old man for the money, he didn't seem to mind as much as I did. He was actually quite cheerful, considering his company was sinking below the financial seas, as it were. When I was done tying up the *American Lark,* I said, "Happy Thanksgiving" to the crew and walked down the gangway with a paper bag full of hundred-dollar bills, making me feel like a bag man. This wasn't a very pleasant way for either of us to spend a holiday.

I don't want to brag, but I think I hold an interesting pilot record. I was given the most bottles of liquor from one ship in one day, and this is no BS.

On August 17, 1984, I boarded the German ship, *Lloyd California*, at Pier 80. Immediately, I noticed how heavily laden she was. Also, her gangway was almost parallel to her main deck with almost no rise to it. When I walked aboard I wasn't walking uphill. Instead, I bent over to pass under the steel frame, called a gallows, which lifts the gangway up. I brushed my hat against it as I walked aboard. Looking at the situation, I thought the ship might be aground, which gave me pause for thought.

When I entered the bridge, I met the captain, who seemed a little tipsy, but no matter how inebriated captains were, I never made any trouble. The Coast Guard wanted us to report them, but I didn't get involved if it didn't interfere with my piloting. On August 12, 1983, as I piloted the Spanish ship *Pontecosa,* her captain keeled over right in front of me after passing out. I didn't know what to make of it. His unsympathetic crew just left him lying there, walking around him like it was no big deal. So I asked the Mate, in Spanish, "Infirma?" He looked at me and just shrugged. He wasn't sick, he was gassed. I still didn't tell the Coast Guard because it would have caused untold problems.

Before 9/11, it was fairly common for captains to have shore visitors in their offices enjoying libations before sailing, and occasionally the captain had one too many, especially the Russians. Once, after Captain Clarke finished docking a Russian, we were invited to have a "small" drink in the captain's cabin. "Small drink," in Russian, means once the vodka was opened, you finished it. Their bottles didn't even have caps, just aluminum foil. Afterwards, we happily strolled down the gangway, something I don't recommend. I never drank when I worked; booze and ships don't mix.

If we reported a drunk captain and he hadn't been drinking, he could sue us, so I never got involved. As an example, one of our pilots thought an American helmsman was drunk, so he called the Coast Guard on his cell phone without consulting her captain. VTS ordered the pilot to anchor the ship, then had the sailor drug tested. The sailor wasn't drunk, which caused all sorts of problems for the pilots because the ship owner was understandably irate. That call cost the ship a lot of time and money for nothing. I had more trouble with poor steering than drunks.

While I was waiting on the bridge drinking coffee, the German captain said something into his radio, then disappeared, seeming frazzled about sailing on time. A short while later, I walked out onto the wing to speak to my tugs, when I noticed him yelling at someone on the dock. When he was through, he came back up the gangway in a huff and didn't duck low enough, hitting his head on the gallows. Soon blood started dripping down his face. By the time he arrived on the bridge, he was holding a red towel to his head and his formerly white shirt was pinkish with blood. He acted like it was normal for the skipper to hold a towel to his head leaving port.

After the crew stowed the gangway, I got the ship underway and we proceeded out to sea. Nothing more was said about his wound other than that he was okay. As we approached the Pilot Station, he asked me if I wanted to take a "few bottles" of "Viskey" with me. I told him, "That would be terrific," thinking he meant one. Little did I know that when I arrived at the top of the pilot ladder ready to get off, the crew was carrying several buckets of liquor toward me. Usually the captain gave me a bottle on the bridge when I said goodbye, never a bucket.

California was on station with Bob Porteous driving. Bob liked having a drink on off because he hung out in a bar I knew about in Petaluma. I radioed him not to pull the boat away when I landed on deck because after I did, the booze literally started flowing off the ship in buckets. I wasn't sure if the captain's injury made him give up drinking or he wanted to rid the ship of booze, but I received every kind of liquor imaginable. After I put the bottles inside the boat, I casually asked Bob if he'd like a bottle, pretending he hadn't seen all the bottles coming over the side. I gave him and everyone else who was aboard a bottle.

I asked Bob, "When did a pilot give you a choice of booze?"

He said, "Are you kidding Cap? Nobody has ever scored like this, not even Sever." I saw Captain Sever talk a captain into giving him three cartons of cigarettes, and John didn't smoke.

CHAPTER 24

RIDE-ALONGS, OR WANT TO SEE SOMETHING REALLY DIFFERENT?

Over the years, I brought along pilots from other ports, ship captains, and a few friends of mine with me on piloting assignments. I was proud of what we did, and I liked showing how we worked. I took many people on the pilot run boat around The Bay and occasionally I got them on tug boats, but being on the bridge of a large ship underway watching the operation is a rare experience. Passenger ships give bridge tours, but people only see the ship underway and not how it's handled. I always thought it was important that non-pilots see the kind of work we did, along with the risks when we moved ships in tight places.

Five buddies and I took a guys' trip to Venezuela and wound up in a small village near the Orinoco River, home of blind white dolphins. Jeff changed some traveler's checks into local currency so he could buy more Polar, the local brew, which we drank a lot of on our Venezuelan safari. The bank teller misspelled Jeff, writing "Jett" on his receipt, which really cracked us up. He has been Jett ever since.

In any case, he wanted to go, so we met after his work day was over and mine had just begun at 1700. The *Drake* took us out to relieve another pilot already underway. It was winter, so it was already dark. As the boat pulled alongside the ship, Jett asked, as if he was worried, "Aren't they going to stop the boat first?" I laughed, "No, the ship has to keep moving or the boat won't stay alongside." He thought it was strange that ships don't stop for us.

We went up to the bridge, I piloted the ship out to sea, and we arrived on Station at dinner time. The ocean was calm, so I just assumed Jett wouldn't get sick. After this trip, I never took anyone along unless the weather was fair, and they took Dramamine before we left the dock!

The cook prepared a delicious lamb dinner. I thought Jett, who is Armenian-American, would enjoy that. Dinner looked great until Jett suddenly jumped up frantically trying to open a heavy steel watertight weather deck door. He wasn't used to the "dogs" that open the doors, so I went over to help him escape. Once outside, he started "feeding the fish." He never ate a thing, he just stayed outside until we got on my inbound ship and headed into San Francisco.

When I finished, it wasn't late and we were both bachelors, so I asked him if he wanted to get a "heave ahead." He looked at me like I was crazy. "Are you kidding? After all I have been through today, you want to have a drink?! Jett didn't think riding along was much fun.

My niece, Meredith, visited me one summer and wanted to go on a ship, so I took her on the American tanker *Philadelphia Sun*. It was the ideal job. The *Philly* was fairly small and not going very far, shifting from Richmond Long Wharf down to Anchorage #9. This was before 9/11, when there were fewer restrictions. Today, permission guests entering a refinery or commercial wharfs is taboo. No one can enter them without being on a special list and having the proper ID.

She was all excited about going on a big ship with her uncle, as she had never even been on a cruise ship then.

When we got on the bridge, I introduced Meri to Captain Sparacino, whom I knew well because I moved his ship over twenty-three times. George was just the way I liked captains to be, friendly and not uptight like some tanker captains. She asked him where the ship was going on that striking summer day. George answered, "We're going to anchorage." Meredith, not getting his drift, said, "We're going to Alaska today?" That cracked up the crew.

Meredith is the only woman I ever took on a ship with me, other than Captain Nancy when she was training.

Bobby LaBianca, my golfing buddy, was certainly my most memorable ride-along. He asked me many times to come along. As we were playing golf at my club, Lake Merced C.C., the dispatcher called, telling me an auto carrier at Benicia Industrial Dock wanted to sail at 1700 and I had an inbounder going into anchorage. The time between jobs was short, so I thought it would work for Bob to come along. I never took anyone if there was a long wait between ships, because they invariably became seasick.

I also knew the two ships would be easy to climb on and off of. Bobby was the former New Jersey State Wrestling Champion, my age, and in better shape, so I wasn't worried about him. We quit playing golf, went into the clubhouse, and I changed from clothes to my everyday pilot attire, which was a sport coat and tie. I always wanted to look like a professional, not like I was going to paint my house, like some pilots who wore jeans, which was too casual for me. When I started, all the old-timers wore suits, so I followed their lead.

We drove to the pilot office, saw the dispatcher, then took a cab to Benicia, where the *Eminent Ace* was waiting after discharging her cargo of hundreds of Japanese Toyotas.

Never having been on a ship, Bobby was fascinated by all the navigation instruments, so I explained what they did. I also described each crewman's function. Soon the tugs were backing the ship off the pier, and we were underway. The weather was sunny and windy. In Benicia, the wind blows so often and forcefully that sometimes you didn't need a tug to undock.

Bob asked the captain if he could look around the ship. He said to have at it. Auto carriers Roll-on/Roll-Off ships, or Ro-Ro's, are high sided giants. Basically a big void built with decks just high enough for cars to fit in. Unlike containerships, which have hundreds of boxes stacked on deck, all the cargo is inside. Some decks are adjustable, allowing high-profile vehicles like trucks and yachts to be driven on and off using a huge stern ramp. Up to 4,000 cars come off the ship, as seen above at the Port of Richmond.

The living spaces, consisting of the crews' quarters, offices, dining rooms, and the galley, are on the top deck with the wheel house above that, which is always forward, unlike most ships, where the bridge is aft.

I didn't think Bobby's self-guided tour would take long. In fact, I thought he would return after a short time because there wasn't much to see below except empty car decks. It wasn't a big deal if he was wandering around, but after an hour, I wondered where he was. When I called him on my cell phone with no answer, I thought that he might be lost in one of the cavernous car decks. I knew he wouldn't run into anyone because only a few crewmen are working at a time.

A half hour later, I started a big swing off Angel Island State Park turning toward the Golden Gate, but still no Bobby. I wanted him to see the bridge from underneath, but more important, I needed him with me in time to get off at the Pilot Station, or he was going to Japan for more new Toyotas! Just when I was getting frustrated, I looked aft and saw Bob casually strolling toward the bridge in his cleat-less golf shoes with a golf glove hanging out of his back pocket like he was about to putt! I had forgotten about our golf game and that Bobby hadn't changed, so he looked as if he were going on the links.

Most car carriers have sideports that open off one of the lower car decks near the water, so the pilot ladder is short, making them easier and safer to get off because short ladders don't twist.

The ocean behaved and was calm by our standards when we arrived on station at supper time. When the Station Boat came alongside, Bobby went down the ladder without any trouble.

We didn't have to wait long for the American tanker *Seabulk Pride*. I was glad it was *Seabulk* because they had copacetic crews unlike some American tankers that were extremely uptight. I piloted over 218 Exxon ships, and on some I didn't always feel welcome because of the second-guessing by their captains of how they thought a ship should be piloted. On the hundreds of other tankers I moved, I didn't feel as though they were looking over my shoulder all the time. As an example, I could pilot a foreign-flagged Chevron VLCC from Anchorage #9 to the Long Wharf in far less time than when I was a similar size Exxon ship. It was the same job with the same result, but Chevron saved an hour to two every time, which on a large ship is a lot of money. During my last two years, I didn't move a single Exxon ship, because Exxon had sold their huge Benicia refinery to Valero, so I was happy not to.

The *Pride* was in ballast with thirty feet of freeboard, so climbing up was the equivalent of going up the outside of a three-story building, except it was moving. I instructed Bobby how to grab the pilot ladder so he didn't go into the drink, but I was confident that the former New Jersey State Wrestling Champion would be okay because he had gotten off the car carrier with no trouble.

I climbed up first, then waited for Bobby on the main deck. He got on the ladder fine, but as I looked down thirty feet, it was as if he were in slow motion. He climbed hand over hand as instructed, but he was extremely sluggish. I wondered what the hell was going on. He never looked left or right, he just stared straight ahead at the ladder rungs, pressing his chest against them every time he came up one rung. The ship was slowly increasing speed, but she was moving without me up on the bridge where I belonged. Finally, Bobby stepped off the ladder and the crew steadied him so he wouldn't fall over the side.

I took Bob aside as we walked toward the deck house. "What took so long? These guys are waiting for us to get going!"

He self-consciously looked at me and said, "I'm afraid of heights!"

Holy crap! I'd never have brought him if I'd known that, especially because he was the one who asked me to come. If I was afraid of heights, I wouldn't want to climb onto a moving ship out on the ocean. Bobby wasn't the least bit fazed as we hurried up to the bridge, where we met Captain Potter, who seemed happy to have Bobby along.

Just as it got dark, everything in front of the ship disappeared as we entered a fog bank, so I asked for the horn to be blown every two minutes as we headed in. Because I knew the fog was going to last until we were deep inside The Bay, I was afraid Bobby might get bored looking at nothing but dark grayness. I was also hoping Bob would see the city all lit up from sixty feet above the water, which is a fantastic sight. Fog or not, I proceeded to do what pilots do and guided the *Pride* in.

As we approached the Golden Gate, all three of her massive foghorns ahead of us were bellowing out their three distinct warnings. These horns are very loud if you are under or near them, but the only one I really cared about was the one on the South Tower off on our starboard hand. When I glimpsed the base of it in the mist, as long as it wasn't in front of the ship, I could start my turn into The Bay.

I took Bobby on the starboard wing, telling him to keep a sharp lookout for the bridge. I wanted to see how long it took him to see it. We could hear the horns, but not yet see the bridge because of the impenetrable fog. We never did. If I couldn't see the South Tower visually, I would use the radar to keep the ship a half mile off of Fort Point. When she reached it, I would turn the ship into The Bay and head toward Alcatraz.

As the *Pride* slipped under a dripping Golden Gate, I asked Bobby if he could see the road above us. We clearly heard tires humming, but we could barely make out a few diffused yellow lights far above us as the ship moved along.

I pointed the ship south of Alcatraz three miles ahead, which we also passed but didn't see. I kept the ship a quarter mile off The City front, making a slow right turn off of famous Fisherman's Wharf. At that point, the fog dissipated as I headed for The Bay Bridge. Three more miles and we dropped the anchor. When I finished up, I asked the crew to rig a gangway instead of a pilot ladder, thinking it would expedite Bobby's departure since he was afraid of heights!

Whenever I want an ego boost, I ask Bobby to retell his version of going to sea. It's fantastic the way he embellishes our day, getting more mature by the year. By the time he's done with his sea story (which he insists is true), I was piloting the *Titanic*, the fog was never denser, and he had to duck to let the cars go over our heads under the Golden Gate. Bobby is an Italian-American and a fellow New Yorker, so the hand gestures really get wild as he lays it on thick and I sit back and laugh like hell. It feels good that someone thought my job was so hard. It was worth taking him, just to hear his version of what happened. The ending always is, "I'd never do that again. It scared the crap out of me!"

CHAPTER 25

═══•═══

THE GOLDEN GATE BRIDGE

No book about piloting on San Francisco Bay would be complete without mentioning the biggest, most majestic sight in the whole Bay Area, the Golden Gate Bridge, one of the most recognized symbols of San Francisco and the United States. *Frommer's* wrote, "Possibly the most beautiful, certainly the most photographed bridge in the world." The American Society of Civil Engineers called her a modern Wonder of the World.

It was a marvel when built and still retains its iconic appeal. It was something I loved steaming under for over forty years because I got to watch her odd rusty color change as the sun struck from different angles and at different times of the year. On fogless days as you look west through her 4,028 foot span, the sunsets are stunning. I have been all over the world and few cities have such a spectacular and welcoming entrance. Sydney, Australia, might be the exception.

The Golden Gate has a vertical clearance of 225 feet, so no ships have ever had a problem getting under. The Bay Bridge's four main spans are lower, so whenever I moved aircraft carriers, I used the two middle spans for extra clearance. Not too many ships did this. The new mega-ships have higher navigational bridges, so now you can see the rivets holding the Bay Bridge together, something I hadn't seen before then.

San Francisco–Oakland Bay Bridge is much larger and six months older, but it's more of a working man's bridge. The Golden Gate Bridge is both functional and beautiful, something no one ever says when referring to The Bay Bridge. It's too plain and too gray. It serves a hell of a purpose, as hundreds of thousands of cars cross it daily, but there is no comparison between these two great spans.

The Golden Gate is famous for three things: being the world's longest and tallest suspension bridge from 1937 until 1964, when New York's Verrazano-Narrows Bridge opened; its famous Art Deco design; and suicides. Many attention-grabbing events occurred in regard to the Golden Gate Bridge during my career, and here is one Captain Sever described many years ago: John was on an inbound freighter when the captain's wife entered the navigation bridge to watch her husband's ship go under the Golden Gate on a rare fog-free morning. As it approached the bridge from the west, she asked Captain Sever whether anyone had ever jumped off the bridge. Captain Sever, who had probably seen everything that related to the bridge, replied, "Yes, ma'am." As The City came into view from behind the south tower, Captain Sever said, "I believe the Coast Guard reported that 498 . . . no, no, better make that 499 . . .," and just at that moment a jumper leapt off the roadway high above the ship. As the latest lost soul tumbled into The Bay, John moved the ship to miss hitting the floating body. As the ship turned, John heard a *thwump*. When he turned around, he saw the captain's wife passed out in a heap on the deck.

It was odd that someone jumped facing west, because almost all known jumpers faced the city, which is to the east. I'm not sure why, maybe it's because the west side walkway is often closed to pedestrians or maybe they just wanted one last look at one of the world's most beautiful cities.

The very first jumper ever recorded was a WWI vet who supposedly said, "This is as far as I go," before he ended his life. Two people even jumped together!

It sounds a little uncivilized, but the bridge was a magnet for jumpers because it was so easy. First, the bridge has no suicide barriers. A Coast Guard life boat station that was located in the Presidio just east of the bridge recovered the bodies, and nearby Letterman Hospital produced the death certificates, so the whole death cycle was very convenient in a macabre sense.

Prior to its closing, the Coast Guard allowed us to use their pier. If we were busy shuttling pilots, using their pier saved us about thirty minutes each way. To get out of the weather, we waited inside their boathouse. The first time inside, I was a little startled to see neatly stenciled hash marks that looked like "卌" covering all four walls, so I asked another pilot what they meant. Each one indicated five bodies recovered by the CG! There was a hell of a lot of hash tags, with more added the longer I piloted. The last time I visited they were whitewashed over, but still visible under new paint. Apparently, the Admiral didn't think it was funny that his crews kept count of the "Floaters," as the cops called bodies found in The Bay. I think the lousy paint job meant the boatmen still wanted to keep track.

California Highway Patrol is responsible for bridge security, so if someone jumps they know because of the call boxes and surveillance cameras on the bridge. They knew when the total was approaching 1,000, so they halted the official count at 997. The newspapers also stopped publishing this macabre information to avoid a stampede to be the 1000th jumper. This may sound irrational, but San Francisco is a crazy town!

The San Francisco Chronicle wrote that 1,200 people had jumped up until 2005. This seemed too low, as known jumpers averaged nineteen a year, with 1977 holding the sad distinction of being the highest year on record.

I also believe their number was too low was because in 2004, documentary filmmaker Eric Steel's *The Bridge* caused a controversy when it revealed the CHP hadn't reported twenty-three suicides that Steel's clandestinely hidden cameras had observed filming day and night.

Even before this revelation, there were calls to build a barrier to stop suicides, but unfortunately some people are determined to jump no matter what. It would be a good thing to stop them, but what if they don't jump from the bridge? Would they do it from a building and hurt someone else? As an example, the Highway Patrol once convinced a man not to jump and took him to Letterman for psychiatric evaluation. Regretfully, as soon as he was released, he went right back and finished what he started.

A second sad example was Sarah Birnbaum, who survived her first jump, but sadly succeeded in her second attempt.

One of the stranger deaths involved a professional high diver like those seen at carnivals, the ones who plunge into small pools. He thought with his expertise he could beat the odds and survive a free fall of over 245 feet, which are long odds indeed because jumpers have a fatality rate of 98 percent. Jumpers hit the water in about four seconds, reaching speeds up to 75 mph so their chances are slim.

The stuntman must have thought about the twenty-six people who lived. One said he did it for "fun." Another was nineteen-year-old Kevin Hines, who battled bipolar disorder and decided to end his misery by walking out on the bridge, where he cried alone for forty minutes. A tourist approached him, not to comfort him, but rather to take her photo. Hines thought that proved no one cared. After taking her picture, he leapt, plunging forty feet into The Bay, but miraculously survived!

The stuntman had a bridge film crew and another waiting in a boat to photograph his feat. No one knows why, but he hurried, maybe to avoid the Highway Patrol because he didn't have permission. In any case, he failed, so his crews threw the film into The Bay.

The only time I personally witnessed anything remotely relating to a suicide was when Traffic advised of a potential jumper. They asked me not to be directly underneath the jumper. I changed course, and the captain and I went out outside. High above us was a Highway Patrolman talking to a man clinging to the superstructure. He reminded me of William Holden in *Network,* when a cab driver thought Holden was going to jump off the George Washington Bridge, pleading with Holden, "Don't do it buddy, you have your whole life ahead of you!" My jumper didn't, but hundreds have since.

One day the *Golden Gate* rammed into the south tower of the Golden Gate when the operator became confused about how to get the boat out of autopilot. The damaged was embarrassing enough, even more so because we had just taken delivery of her from Gladding-Hearn Shipbuilders in Somerset, Massachusetts.

Instead of stopping the engines, the boat drove herself directly into the bridge's fenders going full speed. The impact was so severe that we had to replace the commode knocked off its mounts. We also had to get a new operator, as Bob was fired.

At the end of my career, we built two new Station Boats equipped with computer and satellite systems, which was a technological leap from the old boats. We received the Internet as well as cable TV. Up until then, we only received four TV channels, so life was more pleasant living on the new boats.

Once a pilot, while waiting for his arrival, couldn't figure out how to use the new computer, so he asked the watch captain to show him. The operator put the Station Boat on autopilot, which was normal so the helm was unattended, meaning the boat kept moving eastward. This was a very expensive mistake, because they took so long figuring out how to fix the computer that *San Francisco* glanced off Mile Rocks on her own. Our boat captain failed a mandatory drug test, joining Bob on the unemployment line. I think they were both guilty.

Mile Rocks Light, an unmanned light sitting atop Mile Rock and Little Mile Rock. It's the first lighthouse on the south, or San Francisco entering from sea. Black Head, Lobos, and Pyramid Rocks are a half a mile north of Point Lobos and have always been considered a navigation hazard. In November, 1889, the Lighthouse Board marked the rocks with a bell buoy, which proved inadequate due to San Francisco's incessant fog, strong currents, and huge waves, which often submerged it. There was a fog bell at Fort Point, but it was inaudible at Mile Rocks and was removed in 1890.

NOAA recently found the remains of the SS *City of Rio de Janeiro*, San Francisco's worst maritime disaster, buried outside The Gate. Pacific Mail Line's *Rio* sank near Fort Point on February 22, 1901, with the loss of one hundred and twenty-eight, eighty-two of whom were saved by local fishermen who heard the ship's distress call. Among the dead were Chinese and Japanese immigrants and Hong Kong's U.S. Consul-General.

Outrage over the *City of Rio de Janeiro* led to the establishment of a more powerful fog signal at Fort Point, as well as approval for Mile Rocks Lighthouse. I don't know why it's called Mile Rocks; it's not a mile from anything.

On May 20, 1988, I was outbound on the *Arco Anchorage* when the office radioed to be careful because The Bar was breaking worse than usual. The Bar breaking on the north side wasn't unusual, but I was always careful crossing if I thought The Bar would break. That transmission was the only time the office ever warned me of anything, so it got my attention. The odd thing was as I rounded Point Blunt heading toward the Golden Gate, I saw waves breaking underneath it. Obviously, I had seen waves there before, but never breakers like on a sea shore. At mid-span the water is 330 feet deep, so breaking waves don't usually form in deep water without tremendous winds. The prevailing northwest winds are partially blocked by the Marin Headlands that create a wind shadow, so unless it's blowing a southwesterly gale, there shouldn't have been any breakers.

Waves break constantly on San Francisco side against a sea wall in front of Fort Point. Fort Point—a National Historic Site—is a Civil War, era granite fortress built to protect gold still being mined in the Sierras from Confederate raiders coming from sea. It's a favorite spot for surfers even though it's dangerous due to all the rocks nearby. In any case, I never saw large breakers under the bridge before, so I mentioned to Captain Lawlor how odd it was.

He had a perplexed look when he asked, "Captain Paul, you sure you want to take us out to sea today? Looks nasty to me." Obviously, he was as concerned as I was to suggest aborting our passage. It wasn't the breakers that worried me so much as what crossing The Bar was going to be like because crossing one is nothing to take lightly.

Always looking for an excuse to go home early, I said, "Well, Cap, I haven't seen anything like this before. What do you think?" Once my ship was underway, no matter how awful it was, I always made it out to the Pilot Station. I told him I'd check with the Station Boat to see how bad The Bar was before we aborted going to sea. Interrupting a ship's schedule for any reason costs a great deal of money. Not only do cancelled sails lengthen their trip, but they can also lose their charter or their next berth to another ship, so ship owners always want to keep moving.

Captain Steve Wallace, who had already crossed The Bar, radioed that the waves were particularly nasty, but The Bar was passable on the south side. He advised to disembark well west of the Sea Buoy in deeper water.

Who knew, maybe he just wanted company on heaving Station Boat. We kept going.

I usually disembarked east of the Sea Buoy, but the swells were steep, so I drove the ship two miles west of the Sea Buoy, smashing into one massive swell after another. The aftermath of storms always leaves behind large swells.

These swells roll towards the coast in sets, and if the visibility is fair, you can count them. Usually there is a short lull between each set, so I was relying on that to make a decent lee. I couldn't keep going west indefinitely, I had to off the pot, either climb down the pilot ladder or go to LA. Because Wallace had gotten off, I knew I had to at least try, so I started counting until the correct number of waves passed the ship as she steamed into the teeth of them. Just as the last large wave rolled underneath the bow, I ordered hard left and asked for Full Ahead to start my lee. I knew the tanker was going to roll her guts out, so I hurriedly said goodbye to Captain Lawlor and raced down to the main deck following the Third Mate, whom I encouraged to keep moving. Luckily, I got off swiftly before she started taking some nasty snap rolls. Getting off ships in titanic swells never ceased to amazed me. I didn't fear the sea, but I always respected her power.

Jumpers off the Bay Bridge are rare, but I will tell about the most famous one. Truth was definitely stranger than fiction when a couple headed east on the lower deck of the Bay Bridge and had a fiery argument in the middle of the bridge, or maybe he didn't like the way she was driving. It doesn't matter, because it really became heated, as you will see.

For some reason the gal stopped the car in the right lane and the guy jumped, which is insane because there are no sidewalks on the Golden Gate, so there is very little room to get off the roadway. In other words, he was asking to get hit by cars whizzing by. To make a long story short, she pleaded with him to get back in as she slowly followed him. As would be expected in heavy California traffic, her car was rear-ended almost immediately, splitting open the fuel tank and spilling gas, which ignited and turned the man into a human torch. I have to assume he thought the easiest way to put out the fire was to leap off the bridge, because that's what he did, falling straight down over 220 feet! He was one lucky son-of-a-bitch because he survived, unlike the professional high diver off the Golden Gate. Hitting the water is the equivalent of hitting concrete because water doesn't compress. His second "stroke" of luck, in addition to putting out the fire, was crash-landing near a surprised kayaker, who dragged the fireball's sorry smoldering butt over to the Fireboat *Phoenix* station. Their EMTs took him to City Hospital.

On March 28, 1776, Juan Bautista de Anza sited a property for a fort that became the Presidio. Later that same year, José Joaquin Moraga built a fortification for New Spain, making it the military center for coloniz-ing the area. When Mexico won their independence, California became theirs until the 1848 Mexican-American war, when our military seized it, making it the headquarters of several U.S. Armies. Several famous gener-als, such as William T. Sherman, lived there. The Presidio, and Letterman Army Hospital—named for the Army of the Potomac's medical director, Jonathan Letterman—were involved in all of America's military engage-ments in the Pacific.

I sailed by the Presidio almost every day unless I was upriver or shift-ing a ship in the harbor. We were fortunate enough to live one block away from the base in the lovely Cow Hollow section of San Francisco, which got its name from dairies that once covered the hills. It was a wonderful place to live.

Whenever I passed the Presidio, within a few shiplengths the ship would pass by Baker Street, where we lived. Our street runs down a big hill from the mansions in Pacific Heights all the way to the boats in the Marina. I could easily see our place from The Bay, and whenever my grand-daughter, Sydney, was visiting, I'd blast the ship's horn, letting her know which ship Cappy was moving.

The Presidio's appearance was breathtaking from the water as the sun-light altered its appearance at different times of the day and year. On some days, the identical white marble headstones of our interned heroes at San Francisco *National Cemetery* really stood out in relief from the dense sur-rounding pine and Cypress forests. Among the hundreds of brave men and women buried there is Major General Frederick Funston of the Spanish and Philippine-American Wars and Commander of the Presidio during the 1906 Earthquake that leveled San Francisco when he declared martial law to save it. The Union Army commander at the first major battle of the Civil War called Bull Run, General Irvin McDowell, is also there. "Major" Pauline Cushman is interned there. She is said to be one of the first known female spies, spying for the U.S. She was captured and sentenced to hang by the Confederates, but was rescued by Federal troops. Major was an honorary rank supposedly granted to her by President Lincoln.

From The Bay you can't help notice the tall flagpole with its extra-large American flag fluttering in the wind in the center of what was once the army parade ground. Now it's a parking lot surrounded by vintage red brick buildings.

When the Presidio was still active, you could set your watch when MPs fired a field gun at the base of the flagpole, rendering colors smartly every morning at exactly 0700 and at 1700 every evening. Whenever we had guests and they heard the big cannonade echoing throughout the water-front, they would always ask what it meant. I'd yell, "Cocktails," because, as San Franciscans like to say, "San Francisco is not a city, it's a cocktail party!"

On October 1, 1994, the longest continuously operated military base in the United States became a National Park. The city lost a good neighbor, as both the Army and the hospital were used during the 1989 Loma Prieta Earthquake and San Francisco already has many fine parks. Also, the Presidio was always open to the public who used its beaches, playgrounds, and tennis courts without interference from the Army.

Historian Matthew Brady called sailors' cemeteries the "Fo'c'sle of the dead." The "fo'c'sle" was the unlicensed crews' living quarters on sailing ships because they lived under the forecastle deck near the bow. Sailors today still use "fo'c'sle" to designate their living quarters. The Presidio is home to one of these sailors' cemeteries, but few know about it because it was ingloriously buried under 16 feet of debris from a 1950s Nike mis-sile site. It's the only cemetery remaining in The City besides the National Cemetery and a small pet cemetery in the Presidio.

The sailors' graveyard is located 200 yards away from the abandoned Marine Hospital at 14th and Lake Street, where Captain Sever went to see the Sky Pilot. Historians think the cemetery was used from 1885 to 1912, but it, like the many sailors buried there, is long forgotten. Graves once had neat wooden headstones enclosed by a fence.

Records show that most of the dead were young men, many in their twenties. Sailors were often considered outcasts, many with no families, who worked long hours under arduous and dangerous conditions. Going to sea rarely attracted people who had better options. Because of the type of individual that went to sea, the government considered them wards of the state, which is why the Federal government built marine hospitals (later re-named Public Health Services) in many U.S. ports

I worked with quite a few tough individuals when I sailed. Many lived from allotment to allotment, staying ashore only until out of money. Then they returned to the sailors' union hall to get another berth.

On a side note, The Presidio also has four creeks named Dragonfly Gulch, El Polin Spring, Coyote, and Lobos that are currently being restored by park stewards and volunteers. Have you noticed how the Lobo name keeps coming up in San Francisco?

CHAPTER 26

ILLEGITIMI NON CARBORUNDUM, OR WHY I AM GLAD I RETIRED

"ILLEGITIMI NON CARBORUNDUM," read a plaque on Captain Sever's desk in his Marina home, not far from where I lived. I never thought much about its meaning until after he passed. It doesn't mean anything, but this is the gist: "Don't let the bastards get you down!" I think I understand why John had it so prominently displayed, because it could be applied to many things that happened during my career: the crucifixion of John Cota by the press, the government, and even by some of our partners; the fact pilots could go to prison for making an error in judgment; dealing with VTS and the Coast Guard and PMSA; and the way our board of directors ran our company.

Piloting was one thing, but dealing with issues out of my control was something I never cared for. Whenever I was on a ship, I was completely in charge of everything that happened in relation to moving it from the time I arrived on the bridge until the time I grabbed the pilot ladder in my hands. No one issued any speed or rudder commands and no one told the tugs what to do except me. No one dropped the anchor or put out lines until I said so. This was an unbelievably satisfying feeling. That kind of power is rare and one of the reasons I loved piloting so much.

Pilots rarely agree on anything, but the one thing I think all retirees will is how nice it is not receiving phone calls from the dispatchers, especially in the wee hours of the night. Because pilots work vampire hours, especially in winter, not getting those calls is heavenly. The other half of that equation was job changes, because job assignments changed like San Francisco's weather, which changed often. Strange as it may sound, I rarely knew if I would actually board the ship I was assigned to. Captain Sever warned me, "Never think about a job before you get on the pilot ladder and forget about it once you let go of it." He was so right.

Because of the weird hours we worked, to get as much sleep as possible I would lay out my clothes like a fireman before I turned in on work nights, ready to put them on in a moment's notice. In this way, I didn't have to think about what to wear when the dispatcher called. I just rolled out of bed and immediately started putting them on. I also didn't want to disturb my wife by turning on the lights. Leaving my bedroom in the dark, I'd be half dressed as I flipped on the coffee pot, walking into the head tying my tie as I woke up.

Captain Diggs's words of advice when I took his place were: "Never make any plans when you are on call." He was also right.

One dispatcher was a pain to work with. When sailing orders changed during the night, he'd wake us up, even if there was only a slight change in a job, say fifteen minutes. He thought if he was miserable, we should be also. I wasn't the least bit sorry when he retired midway through my career.

Another dispatcher, Frank, an older guy, occasionally hit the bottle in the afternoon. As a result, sometimes he screwed up job assignments. Once he relieved me on Station, so I made the two-hour run back in from sea on the *Drake*. I should have gotten in my car, but instead I happily walked upstairs to ask Frank for my next day's assignment. I thought I was going home, but when I said, "Hi," Frank stared at me as if I had two heads.

"What the hell are you doing here?" sounding as if I had sent out the run boat myself.

I replied, "You relieved me!"

He told me to get my sorry butt back out on Station and bring in the ship I was supposedly late for! I went back down the stairs and rode the *Drake* for back out to sea. *Drake* was an extremely seaworthy boat. She could really take a licking, but unfortunately she only made 12 knots, so all our trips out to sea were long.

Unlike many other ports in the world that have only one small area that ships moved in, such as the Savannah River or Port Everglades, Florida, San Francisco has a complicated system of ocean, bays, and rivers covering more than 200 miles of pilotage waters with over one hundred docks, so dispatching sixty egotistical pilots is a challenging job. Frank was a nice man, but that was one for the books.

Some of us thought the dispatchers were out to get us personally. Unfortunately, we must have had a worse effect on them than they did on us, because two of them committed suicide! One of them burned himself to death, which besides being a tragedy was peculiar because he was one of the more pleasant dispatchers.

Many cities use that expression, but I think San Francisco invented it because it was so true, especially out on Station. Whenever I took a nap on the Station Boats, my job, or even the weather, could change in that time I was napping. Once I went below and took a catnap while waiting for the tanker, *Texaco Rhode Island*. When I got into my bunk, the weather was relatively decent, meaning I didn't have to hold on to the bunk's lee boards. When I woke up a few hours later, the wind had veered around to the southwest and cranked up to a full gale. I had no idea the wind had increased to over 40 knots until I started getting dressed, when I had trouble tying my shoes because of the violent motion.

The *Rhode Island* was in ballast, so she was rolling heavily in the steep wind chop. When she slowed down so I could board her, green seas were overwhelming her weather decks. The green water was cascading down over the ship's side even on the lee side, right at us. The crew hung the pilot ladder from the lifeboat deck—one deck above the main deck—so I had more protection. This lifeboat deck is. This was something I had never saw before.

I dislike wasting time, but as a pilot, we seemed to do a lot it. If I piloted six thousand one hundred ships and half of them were departures and twenty minutes were wasted per sailing, I would have used up than forty days of my life! Twenty minutes doesn't seem like much until you do the math. As much as I loved piloting, I was always running around doing things like playing golf or working on one of my small businesses like the commercial embroidery business *Capnco* that Carol and I started. Our little side business did a lot of work, airlines such as America West, and we even made hats and shirts for some of the steamships I piloted like Horizon Lines and Matson.

Whenever I showed up on a dock and saw a conga line of semi-trucks waiting to go under the container cranes, I knew the ship wasn't sailing anytime soon. Countless times I waited around, sometimes for hours, for a ship to finish up loading, cancel the sailing, or for the fog to lift. Over my career I can safely say I witnessed millions of containers swinging over ships' sides from up in the pilot house waiting for the longshoremen to finish up.

All ships are required to have a designated pilot cabin ready for the pilot in case of delays. However, using them wasn't always an option if the crew didn't understand what I wanted, and some ships were too filthy to even consider using it. In any case, I always brought along something to read. On the contrary, if a ship was ready to sail, the linemen didn't have to let the lines go until the posted sailing time due to their work rules. They could show the ships who was really in charge. Many times I waited at 0755 while the linemen sat around until 0800, then let the lines go to make their point. These delays were senseless because linemen received four hours minimum pay to handle lines and left immediately after.

On the other hand, if no linemen showed up to handle the lines, the ship just sat. As foolish as this sounds, once I landed a ship in Oakland when no linemen showed up. This is not only annoying and costly, but it can be dangerous. I pinned the ship using my tugs, hoping someone would show up. After half an hour the captain, who wasn't happy, decided it wasn't safe for his ship to sit indefinitely, so he lowered the gangway. Several crewmen went ashore and handled the lines. When I returned to the office, I got to hear how mad the longshoremen were because the ship's crew tied up the ship! The ship still paid for six linemen!

Before 9/11, the linemen were allowed to drive down to the docks, and some of them showed up in some pretty fancy cars, indicating those were choice jobs. Whenever one particular lineman finished throwing the lines off the bollards, he'd take off his coveralls and gloves and throw them into his baby blue Rolls Royce's trunk. Then he'd put on his Stetson and drive off. We were paid well, but no pilot I knew owned a Rolls. Long-shoremen are well paid. Whenever they had openings, their union held a lottery because so many people wanted those jobs.

Getting up in the middle of the night to go to work was annoying enough, but going out "light" at 0300 was never fun. I definitely don't miss that, especially when the run boat was pounding into heavy seas on the way out to the Pilot Station, as she did all winter and much of the spring. *Light trips* are when more pilots are needed on Station for ship arrivals, so pilots were shuttled out. The ride out took almost two hours on our old run boat, depending on which way the current was flowing, how strong it was, and what the sea conditions were. The worst times to ride out were during a big ebb tide flowing against a strong wind, something called an *ebb chop*, which makes for steeper waves, making the boat pitch a lot.

Formerly, crews, from captain on down, were all citizens from where the ship was registered. This changed when steamship conglomerates forced seafaring nations, such as Denmark, to employ non-nationals to save money. If nations didn't allow this, the conglomerates threatened to re-flag their ships elsewhere, like Panama, Liberia, or the Marshall Islands. This might be good for the shippers, but it's bad for sailors who lost their jobs. Subsequently, crews became a mixture: officers from the flag country and crews from wherever labor was cheapest, like the Philippines. In the end, I saw many ships registered in a country that had no nationals aboard and many with mixed crews. As an example, I might go aboard a Star Line ship registered in Oslo. Once the crew had been all Norwegian. Now the cap-tain might be from Taiwan and the crew from the Philippines. I saw more Filipinos than any other nationalities, and I never met one Panamanian aboard a ship registered in Panama!

In the first half of my career, I'd jump from a Swedish car carrier, to a German tanker, to a Greek bulker, to a French container ship or maybe a Polish fishing boat. I piloted ships registered in fifty-three different countries, including landlocked ones like Switzerland, but in the end it was mostly Third World-crewed ships. As an example, after 1996, I only handled eleven British ships, and four of those were passenger liners. One of the real ironies of my career was that of the two nations that instigated world exploration—Portugal and Spain—I piloted only one Portuguese and only two Spanish ships, which is sad. From a pilot's point of view, and someone who likes to shoot the shit, it was much more stimulating talking to captains from a variety of far-off lands about what was going on in their countries, not just China, Taiwan, or Korea.

When I got out of college, dry cargo ships, called "boom" ships because of their cargo booms, were the ones I wanted to sail on. I didn't want to work on tankers and only did once.

Over time, containerships replaced boom ships. Now, unless a ship is a bulker, it is seldom stowed by hand; it's all done with cranes. Loading techniques are more sophisticated. Ships that once carried a few containers randomly lashed on deck using chains and turnbuckles now have as many as eight containers stacked one on top of another and eighteen wide across the ship. And this doesn't include containers in the holds. During one port call to San Francisco in my youth, it took almost three weeks to load my ship compared to today, when ships are unloaded and loaded in less than a day, resulting in little or no port time for seamen, whom I don't envy. I liked piloting boom ships; unfortunately. they became a rarity.

Along with the change in how ships were loaded also came variations in the way ships were equipped. Ships once had large handmade wooden steering wheels and lots of brass, which the sailors hated polishing. So much so, that they'd paint over it whenever the officers weren't looking. Everything mechanical was eventually replaced with electronics. For example, the beautifully handcrafted brass Engine-Order-Telegraphs were replaced with push-button controls. These new plastic consoles have: "DS," "S," "H," "F," in lieu of "Dead Slow, "Slow," "Half," or "Full," so they're not very classy or even nautical -looking, nor are the plastic yokes used in place of steering wheels.

Today, you just push a button and the massive diesel engine starts right up, using compressed air. On steamships, engineers have to control the steam, which spins the propeller. On diesel ships, the bridge controls the engines, so true steamships are rapidly vanishing off the seas. Despite their utility, diesel engines have one drawback: if you order too many bells, the ship can literally run out of *starting air* and the engines might not be able to be started, or, worse, stop the ships which can lead to bigger problems than the loss of starting air!

Once ships had wooden duck boards on their weather decks. No duck boards, and your feet got wet in a downpour. Blue Star Line, now defunct, had the most beautiful teak decks I ever saw on a cargo ship. Unfortunately, those beautiful and practical wooden boards were eventually replaced with plastic mats or worse. Some cheap ships get away with using cargo pallets that wobbled when you walk on them. So many boom ships were scrapped, it was possible to buy the old duck boards and hatch top covers at marine salvage shops. I made one into a coffee table.

The pride in ship ownership seemed to go away when ships became extensions of trucking companies, so there isn't much glamour in the steamship business anymore. It's all about speed and saving money.

I wouldn't necessarily recommend going to sea for a living. It pays well, but it's a tough, dangerous, and peripatetic life. You are on a ship half the year, most of which is at sea, so half of your adult life you are on the ocean. As W.C. Fields said, "Going to sea is worse than going to jail because you can drown!"

CHAPTER 27

WOULD I DO
IT OVER AGAIN?

You bet! The proudest days of my life were when my mother pinned my Eagle Scout Medal on me in 1962, graduation from the Maritime College in 1969, my wedding in Cabo San Jose in 1994, and when I was sworn in as a San Francisco Bar Pilot in 1977. I loved piloting and I think I was very good at it, but it was definitely my greatest achievement.

I was extremely thankful my career sailed down the channel it did, allowing me to live in one of the most beautiful cities in the world where I could afford a wonderful lifestyle. I miss piloting because being on a ship's bridge was where I was the happiest. I will miss it until I no longer dream. Being in total control and making all the decisions moving the world's largest moveable objects into tight spaces with tricky currents really filled me with pride. Every job was unique, and even the same ship to the same berth was never boring, because I had to take into account weather, tidal conditions, ship traffic, and other factors like air draft. I even miss moving ships in zero visibility.

Ships from around the globe visited San Francisco, so I got a kick out of greeting the world's captains. Because they might have been at sea for as many as three weeks, I was usually the first person a captain talked to who wasn't a member of his crew, since his last port.

Over the years, I learned about the world by conversing with captains from places like Buenos Aires, Botany Bay, Hong Kong, and Vladivostok.

One of the many things I enjoyed about boarding foreign ships was learning how to say hello, goodbye, and a few other phrases in the many languages spoken on the thousands of ships I piloted. I probably wasn't very good at it, but the captains sure smiled when I greeted them in their native tongue. Sometimes they were disappointed after starting a conversation with me, thinking I was fluent, but I warned them my vocabulary was limited; I wasn't about to dock a ship speaking Russian like Don Hughes.

Once I jokingly asked a doctor friend of mine from Lake Merced Golf Club if he was a good hand surgeon. He replied, "No, but I'm a lucky one," so I called Gordon "Lucky" after that. That may sound droll, but you have to have a certain amount of luck piloting ships, just as you do in golf, or life for that matter, because not everything works out the way you planned it. Like Gordon, I'd rather be a lucky pilot than a good one.

Andy Ugarte, a dear Peruvian friend of mine, was very successful. He thought success was achieved by being smart, but you also needed luck. You needed to be in the right place at the right time, which is what happened with Captain Sever.

I was surprised how many pilots agreed on one thing; we all used body English to help move ships out of harm's way. This is the equivalent of golfers talking to their balls. I caught myself moving my hips a few times, hoping to shove a huge ship sideways to avoid trouble. I mumbled a few prayers when ships got too damn close to something. Considering how shallow San Francisco Bay is, it must have helped, because I was only aground three times, and twice it wasn't my fault.

I was lucky I attended the Maritime College because when I was in Malverne High on Long Island, I had no idea what I wanted to do with my life, and I had very little money to do it with. Attending "Maridome or Fort Scupper," as we sarcastically called it, was a life changer. At graduation, I received my Bachelor of Science degree, my Unlimited Third Mate's ticket, and a Naval Reserve commission as Ensign, all on the same day! I also learned a hell of a lot of discipline and a lifelong love of the sea and sailboat racing I wouldn't have learned elsewhere. I could go to sea, enter any branch of the military as an officer, or pursue a business career.

Obviously, I was extremely lucky becoming friends with Captain Sever, and I loved living in San Francisco, especially during her best years before California was called "The Left Coast." I was lucky, I invested in real estate, and lived in some great places. Most important, I wasn't ill often. I was lucky I met my second wife, on a ship no less! I was lucky I only damaged one dock seriously. I'm also convinced that the times I thought I'd knock down the Union Pacific Rail Road Bridge, and didn't, really had something to do with a higher power rather than my piloting skill. Coming so close three times had to be some kind of miracle.

My wife, Carol, and I were lucky to have traveled all over the world. We visited Madrid, Tel Aviv, Rio de Janeiro, Hong Kong, Shanghai, Hamburg, Sydney, and Vancouver, among others great cities, where we met pilots from around the globe at IMPA congresses. We got to stay with many of them, and many stayed with us in San Francisco.

And few people can say they sailed under the magnificent Golden Gate Bridge almost every day for thirty-one years.

My first year at college, like for many other mugs, was extremely challenging. Not only was it academically tough, but Fort Schuyler was also a military academy. Reveille was at 0615 six days a week with formation at 0700. Our Naval ROTC uniforms were inspected twice a day by first class officers before marching into the mess hall by platoon. The regiment marched ever week, and we had a dress pass-in-review every Saturday after attending classes. This left only a day and a half of liberty per week. And there was no gangway during the week except on Wednesday nights, when we were free to visit lovely Tremont Avenue in the Bronx for a quick dinner.

The work load we carried seemed like a lifetime. In addition to all our undergraduate classes, we were required to study celestial navigation, marlin-spike seamanship—called *knot tying*—how to run a ship, and we had to memorized the International Regulations for Preventing Collisions at Sea by heart. To qualify for our Naval Commissions, we also attended ROTC classes taught by U.S. Naval officers.

To make our lives even more enjoyable, instead of partying like other college students every summer, or earning some spending money, we went to sea on our Training Ship *Empire State IV (TSES)*, a converted WWII troop carrier (imagine how luxurious that was in 1966!) to earn sea-time for our licenses. I lived with eight other mugs on my first cruise. Our fore-castle, which we morbidly named the *Thresher* after the nuclear sub that sank around that time, was on the ship's lowest deck back aft. We were actually the lucky ones, because most of my classmates berthed in a con-verted cargo hold with bunks made out of pipes. To say the least, their sanitary facilities left a lot to be desired, even for mugs!

I never enjoyed a long summer college vacation because I was at sea. Not only that, but we had paid to go on these misnamed "cruises," unlike our biggest college rival, Kings Point, whose campus sits directly across Long Island Sound from ours. Their cadets were paid to go to sea on com-mercial vessels.

In June, 1966, I sailed out of New York for the first time. Because mugs don't know whale shit about running a ship, our main function dur-ing our first "cruise" was to clean and maintain the training ship, mean-ing my class did all the chipping, painting, cleaning, etc. During cruises most cadets hung calendars on the bulkhead with big red numbers, called "MFDs," on them. Each one represented how many "More Fucking Days" were left until we made arrival back in New York. *We Gotta Get Out of This Place,* by the Animals, popular in 1966, should have been our school's song instead of *The Bells of St. Mary* because that's how we felt about it. The U.S.S. *St. Mary* was my school's first training (1873-1908).

We trained year round on and off our training ship, but there were two things we especially hated about our first cruise: boats and scrub down. Because we needed physical time in lifeboats for our Lifeboat Cer-tificates, we were lowered away in monomoys. These are similar to whale boats, as in *Moby Dick*. We practiced rowing, launching, and recovering the monomoys and how to command them in the middle of the Atlantic Ocean. We rowed for hours alongside the *TSES* trying to keep up as she slowly steamed along. The second thing, which was even, was being roused out of our warm bunks every third day at 0500 for what was affectionately known as "Scrub Down." The mugs cleaned every inch of the ship from the smoke stack on down. Unless you were sick, or on watch, you were on deck bright and early with a swab and soap bucket. When we weren't doing "boats" or "scrub down" or standing sea watches, we attended classes, such as navigation, for our Coast Guard licenses.

All those things combined made my Fourth Class year unpleasant for me, and I wasn't alone. At a general assembly shortly after we finished IDO week, Captain Spring, the Dean of Students, whom we called *Captain Bong Bong*, told my class, matter-of-factly, "Look to your right. Now look to your left. Whoever is sitting there now won't be here when you graduate!" We thought he was kidding, but at least 30 percent of my class quit before our mug year ended. I was sitting between Bob Groh and Jeff Balou. Balou became part of the 30 percent, while Groh became a ship master, like many of my classmates.

Years later, I piloted Bob's ships, like the *Pioneer Commander,* when he was master with U.S. Lines. It was gratifying that two old schoolmates proved Captain Spring wrong by making it to the top. After docking Bob's ship, we'd go down the gangway together and celebrate, just as we did when we were mugs in Europe on liberty. Visiting different ports was the best part of our summer cruises, but unfortunately, we had *Cinderella Liberty,* so we usually had to be back aboard the training ship by 2300, and there wasn't much late night partying for us.

I considered transferring to another college, but two things kept me in school: reading sea stories and being on the sailing squadron. Being physically on the water almost every day of my cadet life helped keep my head in the game. If it weren't for the sailing team and novels like C.S. Forester's *Captain Hornblower*, I might have quit, and what a colossal mistake that would have been!

I clearly remember the day I made up my mind to stick it out no matter what. Dick Corso, my best friend in college, and I were racing our school's sixty-foot schooner, *Commodore*, in one of the many sailing regattas I crewed in. Dick became a tanker captain, but mysteriously disappeared in the middle of the Atlantic.

I steered, Dick and I sat drinking steaming mugs of coffee, shooting the shit about our futures. As we sailed east with a light breeze, a big yellow melon of a sun rose out of Long Island Sound dead ahead of us. The sun's rays, along with the hot coffee, invigorated us after standing our first two hours of watch in the dark. Watching a beautiful sun rise, drinking coffee, and offshore sailboat racing were special moments for me. I look back on them with great fondness. If I had been on any other varsity sport, I wouldn't have the same connection to the sea as I do. Racing sailboats made me a better sailor. Captain Clarke, a racer himself, thought I had a better feel for ship handling because I had done so much of it.

Until that exact moment, I was unresolved, but on that perfect, clear morning I told myself to man up and complete what I started, or I wouldn't accomplish my goal of seeing the world. As George Bailey said in *It's a Wonderful Life*, "The sweetest sounds in the world are airplane motors, train whistles, and anchor chains," so I couldn't think of anything grander than getting paid to go to sea.

My dream came true because I've been on all seven continents, most countries in Europe, and visited every state in our great country. I've hiked the Great Wall, shed tears seeing the Taj Mahal, went on tiger safaris by elephant-back in Chitwan National Park, Nepal, and celebrated the millennium 1999 overlooking the great pyramids from the Giza plateau. I even climbed inside Khufu's pyramid up to his burial chamber at the very top. I've hiked to Machu Picchu with Peruvian friends, camped in the snow in Antarctica, scuba dove the Great Barrier Reef with shark experts Valerie and Ron Taylor, and had an elephant charge us on one of our African safaris.

Those four long years at the academy helped prepare me for piloting, which was the greatest time of my life. In 1979 when I was only thirty-one, I piloted the new cruise liner, *Pacific Princess,* star in ABC's smash hit, "The Love Boat" for the first time. As I maneuvered her under the Golden Gate, the cruise director played my favorite crooner, Tony Bennett, singing "I left my heart in San Francisco." It just didn't get any better than that, and without bragging, for a kid from Lynbrook, New York, I felt mighty fine about what I had accomplished. Piloting her, the *QE2*, and the U.S.S. *Enterprise* so many years later really made all my hard work at college worthwhile.

Looking back now, what I enjoyed the most about piloting was getting a ship underway just before sunrise, something I did thousands of times. Jumping off the run boat near the stern of a ship I was about to pilot made me feel as if I were performing an essential function and something I loved doing. Waiting in the wheelhouse with a cup of coffee prior to getting underway, looking across the foredeck of something almost as long as the Empire State Building, was very satisfying. When the weather was fair, piloting a ship was the most pleasurable experience you could imagine and a wonderful way to make a nice living. If I arrived at the Pilot Station around breakfast time, our cook would take my order while I read my paper and served me a terrific meal.

If the seas were kind, I might stay up and watch the news or maybe I'd take a siesta while waiting for my arrival. I especially enjoyed those calm times on the ocean. Of course, there are also too many tumultuous days to remember and endless hair-raising nights with huge seas I try never to think about.

The first time I sailed through the Golden Gate was in August of 1969. I was twenty-two and as wet behind the ears as the ink on my original Third Mate's ticket. I joined my first ship, a rather tired tramp steamer, SS *Pine Tree State*, after flying 8,750 miles from Boston to Ton Son Nhut Airport, Saigon, on a PanAm 707. I replaced a very sick Third Mate. It took an entire day, and for someone with little international flying experience, I was in for a big shock when I de-planed out of the First Class cabin and walked into the hell of Vietnam.

After we left Saigon, we sailed to Yokohama for a short stay, then headed out into the Pacific. It took two weeks to cross the 5,133 miles, and we were in constant fog almost the entire voyage. Due to the fog, we didn't get many celestial observations. I only got one accurate fix on my many watches. This meant we had to rely on dead reckoning until we could use our RDF (radio direction finder) when we got close to California. Once our radar detected land, we navigated using that to get to San Francisco Pilot Station.

I never saw a single ship or even one boat during our whole passage across the Pacific Ocean until I spied a white-hulled schooner sitting in the swells with only a staysail set. The old pilot cutter *California* was waiting for us. Seeing her 120-foot-long white hull made everyone, especially me, very happy to see something besides wet gray fog and a colorless ocean.

We approached the pilot grounds from the north, taking extra care as we maneuvered around the lightship using our radar, because in the past several ships without radar had homed right in on the lightship's radio signal and crashed into her. Even though we never saw the light bucket, we could still hear her loud foghorn bellowing in the distance as we slowly moved along in the swells waiting for a Bar Pilot to come over to us. Sadly, all those old lightships were replaced with sea buoys, and the only lightships still floating are in maritime museums, such as South Street Seaport in New York.

After rounding our stern, the pilot cutter stayed on our lee side on a course parallel to ours, mimicking our speed. Soon a small dory was launched over the pilot schooner's side by her crew, and a pilot jumped into the dory's bow and was motored over to us. My job was to greet the Bar Pilot at the top of the pilot ladder and escort him up to the bridge. As if it were yesterday, I can still see him climbing out of the mist up our Jacob,s ladder hand over hand. Then, as he stepped lively over the bulwark landing on the rusty wet deck next to me, I greeted him, "Good Morning, Mr. Pilot," then I led him up to the pilot house.

I couldn't help notice that he was wearing a raincoat and a fedora hat, but underneath he wore a dark suit and a tie, looking more like a business man than a seaman. Since I hadn't greeted too many pilots in my short sea-going career, I thought, *Man, this old guy really looks like he knows what he is doing. A suit and tie in this weather? Incredible!* And he did know what he was doing guiding our ship into San Francisco in the same zero visibility that had haunted us for two weeks, as if it were no big deal.

That pilot coming over in that small dory, then up the pilot ladder out of the fog wearing a coat and tie, made a deep impression on me. I can still see him silhouetted against the bridge windows in the faint dawn light standing next to Captain Waggoner, my first master, like they were old lost friends. He calmly issued course and speed commands. I stood by silently, guarding the engine-order-telegraph. Whenever the pilot ordered speed changes, I rang them up, then wrote them in the Bell Book.

On that cold morning, I couldn't imagine that in only eight years, I would be the one wearing a coat and tie and giving commands to thousands of ship masters from around the globe.

There was another thing I distinctly remember other than the way the pilot came aboard and deftly handled my ship. Just as the *Pine Tree State*'s bow passed out from under the fog-enshrouded Golden Gate Bridge, immediately the fog dissipated, and I could see past the forecastle head for the first time in weeks. As I looked aft toward the sound of the bridge's foghorns all I saw was the tops of the bridge's towers sticking out of what looked like a fortress of fog. That was one of the most spectacular mornings of my life. The City looked like a sparkly dream after I had endured brain-numbing, soggy days at sea. The sun miraculously showing herself was as if God said to me, "Son, this is the place to be!"

For several years, I had that wonderful image on my mind wondering how I could move. I wasn't thinking about piloting, I just wanted to live in the most beautiful city in America. When shipping dried up after 1970, it became almost impossible to get an offshore union job, so I signed on with the Army Corps of Engineers to keep getting sea time on my license. This meant moving to their West Coast headquarters in Portland. I was thankful to have a job, but I visited the Bay Area often. I was miserable living in Oregon with its lousy weather. Working for Uncle Sam helped me get where I am today, but I really disliked it.

When my orange BMW 2002 crossed the Northern California-Oregon border on my way to grad school at UC Berkeley, I didn't even look in the rearview mirror! Moving to San Francisco was one of my happiest days.

The schooners *California* and *Lightship San Francisco* are long gone. So is Captain Johnson, the pilot who guided us in more than forty-four years ago.

My wife and I owned a duplex that sat high on one of San Francisco's famous hills, from which we could see the entire Bay, including Alcatraz. When it was foggy, we could hear the Golden Gate's foghorns. Today I miss hearing them as well as steamships blowing their whistles as they entered The Bay passing by our old home. Now we spend our summers on a different hill. This one is located on beautiful Cape Cod overlooking Martha's Vineyard. Even though I can only hear one lonely foghorn coming from Nobska Light House down Surf Drive, I pretend that the

Martha's Vineyard's ferries passing in front of our windows are cargo ships. Seeing them steam by rekindles fond memories of living and working on San Francisco Bay for such a long time.

Mark Twain, who was considered a "lightning pilot" on the Mississippi before becoming famous, summed up our profession thusly: "The trick to piloting is telling which is the wet part of the river!" I'm not sure if I was a "lightning pilot," but I tried living up to his admonition every day of my long piloting career. I think I was pretty successful at it almost all 6,100 times I handled a ship on San Francisco Bay.

As I sit here typing, I'm still amazed that the Board of Pilot Commission actually let me pilot all those ships!

FINISHED WITH ENGINES!